Howard Frank Mosher
and the Classics

Howard Frank Mosher and the Classics
Echoes in the Vermont Writer's Works

JAMES ROBERT SAUNDERS

McFarland & Company, Inc., Publishers
Jefferson, North Carolina

Also of interest are the following works from McFarland: *Black Winning Jockeys in the Kentucky Derby* (2003), by James Robert Saunders and Monica Renae Saunders; *The Dorothy West Martha's Vineyard: Stories, Essays and Reminiscences by Dorothy West Writing in the Vineyard Gazette* (2001), edited by James Robert Saunders and Renae Nadine Shackelford; *Urban Renewal and the End of Black Culture in Charlottesville, Virginia: An Oral History of Vinegar Hill* (1998; paperback 2005), by James Robert Saunders and Renae Nadine Shackelford; *Tightrope Walk: Identity, Survival and the Corporate World in African American Literature* (1997; paperback 2014), by James Robert Saunders; *The Wayward Preacher in the Literature of African American Women* (1995), by James Robert Saunders

Frontispiece: Howard Frank Mosher (photograph by Renae Shackelford, used by permission).

LIBRARY OF CONGRESS CATALOGUING-IN-PUBLICATION DATA

Saunders, James Robert, 1953– author.
    Howard Frank Mosher and the classics : echoes in the Vermont writer's works / James Robert Saunders.
      p.   cm.
    Includes bibliographical references and index.

    ISBN 978-0-7864-7856-9 (softcover : acid free paper) ∞
    ISBN 978-1-4766-1633-9 (ebook)

    1. Mosher, Howard Frank—Criticism and interpretation. I. Title.
PS3563.O8844Z86 2014
813'.54—dc23
                                                             2014004109

BRITISH LIBRARY CATALOGUING DATA ARE AVAILABLE

© 2014 James Robert Saunders. All rights reserved

No part of this book may be reproduced or transmitted in any form or by any means, electronic or mechanical, including photocopying or recording, or by any information storage and retrieval system, without permission in writing from the publisher.

Cover photograph: Howard Frank Mosher at the St. Louis County Library headquarters on March 29, 2010, in St. Louis, Missouri (Dave Moore)

Manufactured in the United States of America

McFarland & Company, Inc., Publishers
  Box 611, Jefferson, North Carolina 28640
    www.mcfarlandpub.com

For
Renae

Table of Contents

Acknowledgments ix

Preface 1

Introduction 5

    I. First Chancellorsville, Then Gettysburg: Horror, Escape and Restitution in Crane's *The Red Badge of Courage* and Mosher's *Walking to Gatlinburg*   17

    II. Female Vulnerability and Industrialization's Dehumanizing Process in Mosher's *Marie Blythe*, Sinclair's *The Jungle*, Dreiser's *Sister Carrie* and Crane's *Maggie: A Girl of the Streets*   31

    III. The Journey to Salvation in Bunyan's *The Pilgrim's Progress* and Mosher's *Walking to Gatlinburg*   50

    IV. Good, Evil, and the Mystery of Life in Mosher's *Disappearances* and Melville's *Moby-Dick* and *Billy Budd*   69

    V. "The unmitigated temerity to 'feel sorry' for a white woman" in Lee's *To Kill a Mockingbird* and Mosher's *A Stranger in the Kingdom*   91

    VI. The Technique of Humor in Twain's *Huckleberry Finn* and Mosher's *The True Account*   109

    VII. Faulkner's *Go Down, Moses* and Mosher's Mourning the Inevitable Loss of a Kingdom   127

    VIII. Mosher and Shakespeare: On the Immortality of Romantic Love   149

Table of Contents

Conclusion: "Not Gently" in Steinbeck's *Travels with Charley*, Twain's *The Innocents Abroad* and Mosher's *The Great Northern Express* — 167

Notes — 177
Bibliography — 187
Index — 193

Acknowledgments

I owe a debt of gratitude to Purdue University English Department colleagues, including Sandor Goodhart for—at a critical juncture—directing me to take a fresh look at Melville's *Bartleby, the Scrivener*; Robert Paul Lamb for granting me a late-night interview concerning Twain's *Huckleberry Finn*; Charles Ross for his presentation as a participant on the "Sidney and Shakespeare" panel at the 2011 Renaissance Comparative Prose Conference; Renae Shackelford for suggesting that I use Shelley's *Frankenstein* to help in my discussion of Mosher's *A Stranger in the Kingdom* and Lee's *To Kill a Mockingbird*; and Michael Yetman who reminded me to keep thinking of Melville's *Moby-Dick* in metaphysical terms.

In addition, many librarians provided vital assistance. One, Loona Brogan, helped with programming for the first meeting of the Howard Frank Mosher Society, where co-founder and co-director Renae Shackelford delivered one of the plenary lectures. Working out of the Cutler Memorial Library, in Plainfield, Vermont, Ms. Brogan has been a constant source of support in all of our Mosher-related endeavors.

The Leach Public Library, in Irasburg, Vermont, has also been a source of unending support. Laurie Green, in particular, took the time to write me a lengthy informative letter and, along with that communication, forwarded me the results of a governor-appointed board of inquiry's conclusions with regard to the infamous Irasburg Affair. I am also grateful to her for the copy of a 1969 *Life* magazine article that was critical to my understanding of the chain of events that led up to the "Affair."

Robert Freeman, my own librarian at Purdue, was a never-ending stream of support, especially as pertains to getting information with

Acknowledgments

regard to the Civil War. In his quest to uncover sometimes hard-to-attain information, he was not above putting in overtime or turning my question over to his friend, Mark Jaeger, who manages an office outside of the library but, much to my good fortune, is also a history buff who gains special delight in solving certain mysteries. Furthermore, I issue many thanks to everyone at the Purdue Interlibrary Loan Department, for having always gotten whatever I needed, however far away the item was and however difficult it was, though those occasions were rare, to convince the lending facility to go ahead and send it.

Two Faulkner scholars, Joseph Blotner and Douglas Day, were academic advisors of mine when I was a student. Day introduced me to Faulkner's works when I was an undergraduate taking his "20th Century Literature" course. Later, as a graduate student, I took Blotner's "Literature of the South" class where I had the chance to delve further into the intricacies of Faulkner's works. Perhaps more important, I took one Faulkner seminar apiece from each of those professors. It wasn't just that we studied Faulkner in those seminars; it was the respective teaching strategies, the professors used, that enabled me to understand the author in ways that simple lecture or discussion never could have effected. Day had us break into teams of two students each and then, as a team, lead discussion on a particular issue. Blotner's strategy, for his seminar, was to limit the number of texts to four, thus allowing four weeks for us to discuss each book. *Go Down, Moses*, thankfully, was one of the selections, as had been the case in Day's seminar. Needless to say, my own chapter here, where I juxtapose *Go Down, Moses* with Mosher's environmental concerns, could not have been written as effectively if not for the insights that I gained from those professors, one (Blotner) who brought Faulkner to the University of Virginia as a writer-in-residence during the late 1950s, the other (Day) who provided me with details of what Charlottesville was like during those days when Faulkner was around. I am also grateful for having had the benefit of outside-of-the-classroom discussions with Blotner, concerning the novelist's perspectives in general.

When I was nine years old, my mother had me walk to see the movie *To Kill a Mockingbird*. She sent me after having extracted the promise that I would take hold of my six-year-old sister's hand whenever

Acknowledgments

we had to cross a street. I know now, in retrospect, that I grasped very little of the movie's meaning, wondering, as any child that age would have, who I should be trying to identify with at the same time that I was impressed just seeing black people up there on the screen. What that trip did do effectively, however, was lead me to Lee's novel quicker than would have occurred had I not already first seen the movie and yearned to fill in the gaps. I am grateful to my mother for assigning me the task of viewing that movie; and I am grateful for the community that existed at the time, one allowing children to walk by themselves unencumbered by the fear of being harmed.

Of course, my book could not have been written had Mosher not, first, done his extraordinary writing. But beyond that, he has been a generous subject, granting interviews and escorting me to locations that are the settings for his work. During these trips, Renae Shackelford took a number of photographs, including the one that serves as a frontispiece for this book.

One of the things that I noticed, in my interactions with Mosher, was how much we have in common in terms of issues ranging from politics and education to our concerns about the environment and what the future holds for books. Before having gotten a hint of what the concept for my book would be, or even how I viewed his work in general, he made himself available—after he had already given me interviews—to answer my periodic questions. It is his faith that I would do a good job that provided me with the necessary confidence to finish. When I told him that he might not, when I had indeed finished, like what I did, he responded, in private and without having read a word, "I know I'll like it."

Finally, I would like to express my appreciation for Adam Stark, the manager of information technology for the College of Liberal Arts at Purdue. He solved every technical problem that I presented to him and, in the manner that he solved those problems, provided me with additional inspiration that I could overcome any difficulty with regard to this project, computer-related or not.

Preface

It was a warm June evening, in 2010, when I went to hear a presentation by Howard Frank Mosher; the talk was given in conjunction with a book signing for his recently released novel, *Walking to Gatlinburg*. I had already read that particular work as well as the other ten books that he had written up to that point, books that I would see, off and on, when I visited the independent booksellers that are a mainstay of Vermont's literary enterprise. Wanting to learn more about this author, who always seemed to have a little section at those stores reserved for him, I got on my computer and checked with the online MLA Bibliography, but found precious little that had been written about his works, in terms of interpretation. Subsequent to the June talk, the novelist allowed me to interview him whereupon I learned an enormous amount about the historical and personal foundations of his work, interviews that I now regard as having been essential for the undertaking of this book.

One of the things that become evident, upon a close reading of Mosher's novels and memoirs, is the extent to which he is steeped in the classics, older classics, such as Shakespeare's plays and Bunyan's *The Pilgrim's Progress*, as well as more recent classics such as Sinclair's *The Jungle* and Melville's *Moby-Dick*. During my interview with him, during the summer of 2013, I told him that one of the conclusions I had drawn about him is that he is an expert on the classics. His response, to me, was as measured as it was humble, and perhaps more accurate than my own assessment as he specified, "I don't know about expert, but what I would say is that I do have a great *appreciation* for the classics." In many respects, this book of mine is an analysis of that "appreciation."

Interpreting Mosher's works through the classics is but one way of understanding his authorial intent. As we know, it can sometimes take

Preface

centuries to fully understand what a great literary work represents, even as we also know that works, by authors as gifted as Zora Neale Hurston and William Faulkner, were allowed to go out of print during periods of prejudice and general misunderstanding of what a great work is. When I asked Mosher, during the summer of 2010, how he ever avoided being discovered, his simple response was, "I've been hiding out." I reckoned that there was much truth in that statement even as, with a sparkle in his eye, he gave me a mischievous chuckle. By then, though, I was already aware of how much the author values humor, and so I did not bother to question him any further on the matter, sensing that there was indeed some truth to his statement at the same time I knew that, even when some of our greatest literary works are right in front of us in plain sight, we literary critics are often prone to overlook them.

Humor is a topic that I certainly do not fully exhaust in this book. It is a topic, though, for which I do open an important investigation. Other topics that I touch on include timeless issues such as discrimination, good versus evil, the disappearing wilderness, and humankind's capacity for love. These are issues, however, that will need much more analysis, by others, before we, as a critical audience, can come anywhere close to being able to say that the topics have been exhausted. Moreover, additional issues will have to be investigated in order for us to be able to say that we have thoroughly engaged this writer, issues concerning, for example, Ethan Allen's legacy, the meaning of lawyers, the national pastime of baseball, and animals (beyond what I discuss) that have a proclivity to show up in the strangest of places. The investigation of such issues will certainly take a while, perhaps generations; but the undertaking is an important one, beyond what any of us is able to ascertain at the moment.

On September 26, 2013, I went to hear a lecture given by my colleague, Daniel Morris, whose topic was "Pedagogical Personae: On Two Approaches to Literature and Criticism." The talk was part of the "Illuminations Lecture Series," put on by Purdue's Philosophy and Literature Program. In that talk, Morris addressed the issue of literary classics. An obvious question, of course, is what does it take for a work to become classic, and who makes that decision? But Morris delved even deeper into the matter, arguing that the greatest works of literature, as wonderful

Preface

as they are, still do not render us clear-cut depictions. Rather, what the classics—whichever ones we choose—do is, in Morris's words, "draw on the stranger within ourselves." The women and men, who have written the classics, brought with them, to the task, not just their "skill" and insight, but also their "flaws and insecurities," all intertwined, mysteriously, in one big literary effort that forces us, as readers, to acknowledge our own insecurities about who we might actually be. A large part of my own effort, in writing about the connection between Mosher and the classics, has been to grapple with that mystery, to which Morris refers, in the attempt to shed further light on what Faulkner, in his 1950 Nobel Prize acceptance speech, characterized as "the human heart in conflict with itself."

Introduction

Vermont's literary history actually began before it became a state admitted into the Union in 1791. In the succeeding years after the achievement of statehood, it was poetry appearing in numerous local periodicals that spoke most consistently of an incomparable beauty as expressed, for example, by Frances Dearborne in "My Mountain Home," of which the first stanza reads:

> I love my home, my mountain home!
>   Where rude winds gaily blow,
> And flowers of bright and changing hue,
>   In rich profusion grow;
> Where wild birds warble forth their lays
>   Upon the greenwood tree,—
>   Oh! That is the spot
>   By the world forgot,
>   So highly prized by me.[1]

Needless to say, that poem is an examination of the rural features which have always comprised the region, features explored in most of the other poems from Abby Maria Hemenway's 1858 edited collection that included items such as Norman Bridge's "The Thrush," Charles Linsley's "My Mountain Land," and Helen Warner's "Farmers' Boys" with its opening lines:

> Out in every tempest, out in every gale,
> Buffeting the weather, wind and storm and hail,
> In the meadow mowing, in the shadowy wood,
> Letting in the sunlight where the tall oaks stood,
> Every flitting moment each skillful hand employs—
> Bless me! Were there ever idle farmers' boys?[2]

As Dearborne had done in her poem, Warner draws attention to the natural elements—the sun, the woods, and the wind, for instance—but

Introduction

she also pays homage to those who worked in the midst of those elements. In this respect, she is in full accordance with Vermont's first lady of letters, Dorothy Canfield Fisher who, in her all-encompassing *Vermont Tradition: The Biography of an Outlook on Life*, notes the general tendency of Vermonters "to treat people who work with their hands with as much, and as little, and the same kind of pleasantness as anybody else."[3] It makes good sense that such a philosophy would be the case when one considers how important farming communities have always been, not just to the economy but also to the area's cultural history.

I am continuing to call Vermont an "area," at this point, out of deference to Fisher who, even after extensive study on the subject, could only calculate that the *concept* of Vermont "began about 1763," long before it became a state and, interestingly enough, it was never a colony. Instead, it came into being as a consequence of, between 1749 and 1764, the governor of New Hampshire giving grants of land to various groups of people who, for the most part, had their origins in western Connecticut and western Massachusetts. Each grant—there were 135 in all—was approximately six square miles, which would then be subdivided. The grantees only had to pay a modest sum for the land because the governor was more interested in, first, establishing a clearer boundary between his own province and the province of New York and, second, seeing to it that the land was duly cultivated.

One land speculator, who was desirous of taking advantage of the opportunity, was Ethan Allen himself, the future Revolutionary War hero who, prior to the war, was a farmer of the sort that the aforementioned poets and Fisher lauded as being at the core of Vermont tradition. A problem, however, arose as New York began to dispute whether or not New Hampshire's governor, Benning Wentworth, ever had the right to dispense his grants in the first place. What occurred, as a result, were decades-long disagreements over land ownership, disagreements that often found their way into the courts, but sometimes were resolved by violent confrontation. New York had the throne of England on its side and Allen, in a subsequent literary work of his own, would recall the general sentiment against those who sought to take advantage of the new settlers of what would eventually become Vermont. Under the rather laborious title *A Concise Refutation of the Claims of New-*

Introduction

Hampshire and Massachusetts-Bay, to the Territory of Vermont; with Occasional Remarks on the Long Disputed Claim of New York to the Same, Allen expressed what were the concerns of those who had received grants and then were persecuted through a variety of measures by New York authorities aided by England's far-reaching judicial system. Allen maintained that "this royal arbitrary line in the time of the kingly power was in the nature of it incompatible with the rights of a free people as they were thereby deprived of the inevitable privilege of choosing their own form of government, and of electing their chief magistrates; nor were they in such circumstances, in any condition, to know what form or alteration of government might next take place, as the King and his creatures were the sole arbitrators."[4] It was King George III who was intent on keeping control over the colonies and since New York was much more malleable than New Hampshire, he resolved to use that larger province as a proxy for achieving his authoritative goals. The Revolutionary War, with its American victory, is what finally brought the land-grants dispute to an end as English rule itself ceased to exist in the new world.

In 1973, authors Arthur Biddle and Paul Eschholz published their anthology, *The Literature of Vermont: A Sampler*, which with its potpourri of authors running the gamut—from elementary school teacher to lawyer, from magazine editor to the unemployed—was in some ways reminiscent of Hemenway's edition with its eclectic array of poets devoted to portraying the countryside. Appropriately, Biddle and Eschholz begin their volume with "The Capture of Fort Ticonderoga" and "Coming to the Grants," works written by Ethan and Ira Allen, respectively. Also included in the edition are five poems by Robert Frost and a short story and play by Dorothy Canfield Fisher.

Notwithstanding all that, I was nonetheless struck by a statement made by those editors in their introduction, that "Vermont has produced few writers of the first magnitude."[5] It is a statement that I would have quarreled with, even as it was being rendered in 1973. Certainly, Biddle and Eschholz had Robert Frost in mind as belonging to the first tier of American writers. After that, I am not quite sure who else the editors would have included. They use, for an epigraph to the whole anthology, an excerpt from Frances M. Frost's poem "Language," a poem that was included in her 1931 collection entitled *Blue Harvest*, that speaks of a

Introduction

certain serenity even as it offers us the vivid details of a throbbing farm and village life intermingled with breathtaking moments.[6] Biddle and Eschholz knew only too well that if they were going to present a volume on Vermont language or literature, then the most representative short work, on what Vermont literary art was, might best be conveyed through the lines of Frances Frost's poem with its allusions to Mother Nature and those who commune with Her in a most intimate manner. It was also not lost on the editors that, in 1929, Frost had been the recipient of Yale University's "Younger Poets" prize. So, perhaps she was another Vermont writer whom the editors had in mind as belonging to America's first tier.

Though I am not entirely sure, I would like to believe that the editors also contemplated Dorothy Canfield Fisher as being in the first tier. From among the dozens of books that she had published in her lifetime, I would offer *Vermont Tradition* itself. One does not need to read too far into that 500-page treatise to realize that, though the subtitle refers to it as a "biography of an outlook on life," it is, in addition, the work of someone who had a brilliant philosophic and poetic sense of things. For example, in talking about the reluctance of Vermonters to rush into intimate friendships, she explains:

> I insist that you are wrong if you suppose cussedness alone makes the Vermonter hold back from somebody who pretends to pick the beautiful blossom of friendliness when the seed of it has only just been planted. He is acting on a deep conviction that true love and strong lasting friendship are rare events, of slow growth, that they are mysteries to be treated with respect, even with awe and reverence; and that since none of us understands himself or others very well, only after long summering and wintering has given the chance to observe what people do, and so to guess what they are ... only then, occasionally, can a few of us hope to share life intimately with one another.[7]

In that book, Fisher directs us over the entire history of Vermont, drawing from research that she conducted, traveling from village to hamlet, examining the local records and talking to those who had lived the Vermont experience. Beyond the history lesson and the poetic language through which that lesson is conveyed, one also finds a folkloric element in the text, an element that would have been unappreciated in the academic circles of her time, though it is only through the folk culture of

Introduction

a community that one can fully comprehend the essence of a people in terms of their values, beliefs, and flaws.

My uncertainty, about whom Biddle and Eschholz would include in the top tier, also extends to Rowland E. Robinson who, in an introductory note to his 1894 novel *Danvis Folks*, declared that work to have been "written with less purpose of telling any story than of recording the manners, customs, and speech in vogue fifty or sixty years ago in certain parts of New England."[8] Taken a certain way, Robinson could be deemed to have been removing *Danvis Folks* from the realm of art and placing it into a category akin to what an anthropologist, of those times, might have been doing out in the field, collecting crucial data before it vanished into obscurity. Biddle and Eschholz, for their part, actually exploit Robinson's proviso so as to arrive at their own conclusion that Vermont literature, for the most part, is "predominantly regional or local," a conclusion easy to draw as one considers the work of the early Vermont poets as well as Ethan Allen, Dorothy Fisher, Frances Frost and even, for that matter, Robert Frost with his attention to the New England landscape. But I would argue, as others before me have done, that the best way to examine certain universal truths *is* to focus first on the people of a specific locality. Such is what Shirley Jackson did in her 1948 short story "The Lottery" which can be read as a story about Bennington, Vermont while at the same time it is a telling commentary about human nature in general.

Biddle and Eschholz did not include Jackson in their anthology. If they had, they would have had to retreat somewhat from their position with regard to Vermont literature being regional or local. To those editors' credit, however, they did include a story by a fledgling young writer named Howard Frank Mosher. They got his name wrong, in their introduction—calling him Frank Howard Mosher—and they mistakenly say that he was born in Vermont; but nevertheless here he was, little more than a short story writer at the time, working on his first novel, and now tacked onto the end of an anthology as if he had barely made the cut, with no one, perhaps not even Mosher himself, realizing just how transcendent a writer he would become, even as he focused, for his settings, on the uppermost part of Vermont that was known as the Northeast Kingdom.

Introduction

The eight chapters that make up my book trace a process whereby Mosher relies, either directly or indirectly, on the themes and characters of various classic literary works so as to reaffirm the messages of those works while he also speaks to the distinctness of the Northeast Kingdom that Yvonne Daley, in *Vermont Writers: A State of Mind*, describes rather succinctly as "the northeastern corner of Vermont comprising Caledonia, Essex, and Orleans counties. The sparsely populated (roughly 34,000 people) area is rich in natural resources, including 35,575 acres of public lakes and ponds and nearly 4,000 miles of public rivers and streams."[9] Born in 1942, in Chichester, New York, Mosher and his wife Phillis wound up moving, in 1964, to Orleans County, Vermont, making it their home and thus allowing for plenty of time for the author to listen to the old-timers' tales of Vermont as it existed in the early days before cars became the fashion and when farming was a way of life for the nation as a whole.

In my initial chapter, "First Chancellorsville, Then Gettysburg: Horror, Escape and Restitution in Crane's *The Red Badge of Courage* and Mosher's *Walking to Gatlinburg*," I explore the Civil War from the vantage point of young farmers, barely adults, thrust into battle for reasons that are not all that clear to them. Oftentimes, history portrays one side in that war as having been right and the other side wrong, so much so that lost in the discussion are the long-term consequences suffered by those who lived beyond the fighting, how fear registered in their minds and how the hand-to-hand killing of other human beings altered their character forever. In *Red Badge*, Stephen Crane questions how much the Union generals cared about the soldiers who fought under their command; Mosher, in *Gatlinburg*, raises the same issue and presses it even further as he wonders about the motives of the uppermost levels of government, including the office of the presidency. Upon reading each of those novels, we join Crane and Mosher in the questioning, as we are made to think beyond events of just the Civil War and contemplate what it is about our character, over the millennia, that has made war amongst ourselves as inevitable as breathing.

Just as inevitable is that there will be those in positions of authority who are all too willing to take advantage of others who are vulnerable and in no position to protect themselves from such exploitation. In

Introduction

"Female Vulnerability and Industrialization's Dehumanizing Process in Mosher's *Marie Blythe*, Sinclair's *The Jungle*, Dreiser's *Sister Carrie* and Crane's *Maggie: A Girl of the Streets*," I draw attention to the ways in which Mosher's *Marie Blythe* recapitulates the themes of those other novels. For Sinclair, the issue had been what becomes of a Lithuanian family who, in search of a better life, ventures overseas to Chicago. In *Sister Carrie*, it is a matter of what happens when one moves from a small village to a place like Chicago. The setting in that novel eventually makes its way to New York, the city where Crane depicts the consequences of living under the conditions of abject poverty. In *Marie Blythe*, a primary issue is what becomes of French Canadians who venture over the geographical line, into Vermont, in search of a better life. What we learn from all of those novels is that those of us who look different, talk different, or are without financial wherewithal, are likely to fall prey to others of us who hold the most advantageous positions in society. And within those various disadvantaged groups, it is the females who are most vulnerable to exploitation, a consequence that has its basis in sexuality, a consequence that, in and of itself, is quite ironic since all that those females had to do to find themselves in such a situation was go out and look for work.

It seems that such circumstances have been a by-product of human interaction from time immemorial, just as from time immemorial much of humankind has been on a quest for redemption from the flaws that contribute to our imperfect nature. John Bunyan had envisioned such a journey in his seventeenth century work *The Pilgrim's Progress* and, as Mosher's character Pilgrim Kinneson, in *Gatlinburg*, leaves the Northeast Kingdom, venturing towards the pitch of Civil War battle, he is confronting the very demons that Bunyan's own pilgrim confronted on his trek. It is in my third chapter, "The Journey to Salvation in Bunyan's *The Pilgrim's Progress* and Mosher's *Walking to Gatlinburg*," that I seek to draw parallels between *Gatlinburg* and *The Pilgrim's Progress*, although that latter work was written a full 332 years earlier.

The pilgrims of the two aforementioned works are engaged in the quest for salvation, but one wonders whether or not they will ever arrive at an understanding of life's ultimate meaning or, for that matter, an understanding of who created that life. The writer Herman Melville was

Introduction

consumed with those issues as, in *Moby-Dick*, he presents us with the conflict between Captain Ahab and a great white whale. In *Disappearances*, Mosher gives us the very same conflict, his version of Captain Ahab being William Bonhomme whose life is substantially overtaken by a white entity that reminds us of what we had seen in Melville's novel. Mosher's white entity is a phantom-like creature named Carcajou; and my chapter "Good, Evil, and the Mystery of Life in Mosher's *Disappearances* and Melville's *Moby-Dick* and *Billy Budd*" is, in part, an investigation of the whale and Carcajou's whiteness, a whiteness that reaches the level of obsession in the minds of two men (Ahab and Bonhomme) who would otherwise have seemed quite ordinary.

The distinction between good and evil is also a key feature of Melville's *Billy Budd*. As with *Moby-Dick* and *Disappearances*, it is sometimes unclear how the distinction between good and evil is drawn since the protagonist, Budd, seems at first to be an innocent victim, and his antagonist appears to be the epitome of evil. In this novel, as well, the concept of whiteness is a central theme, for a big part of why the antagonist acts as he does has to do with how he might not be pure English, in terms of his racial heritage.

Chapter V, "'The unmitigated temerity to "feel sorry" for a white woman' in Lee's *To Kill a Mockingbird* and Mosher's *A Stranger in the Kingdom*," continues the investigation of whiteness. For the first part of my chapter title, I have quoted directly from Harper Lee's novel where a white lawyer, in 1930s Alabama, is faced with the challenge of defending a black man against charges of having raped a white woman. That female lives in poverty and has indeed been abused; but the perpetrator is her own father. The lawyer, Atticus Finch, actually proves that the black man, Tom Robinson, could not possibly have raped Mayella Ewell; and yet, society dictates that Robinson be punished not just because he is black but, even more inexcusable, he is a black man who dares to consider himself in such a position that a white person is more needy than him and, most egregious of all, that white person is a woman.

Nearly 30 years after *Mockingbird*, Mosher's *A Stranger in the Kingdom* appeared, and in that work we are once again presented with the scenario of a black man helping a white woman who is less fortunate than him. It might be hard to believe that the racism of 1930s Alabama

Introduction

could also have been found in 1950s (the setting of Mosher's novel) and 1960s (the period in which the events of the novel actually took place) Vermont, but such was indeed the case. A black man arrived in Mosher's own hometown of Irasburg and, along with his family, he brought a young white woman who was also anxious to improve her life. They all lived in the same house and so it was not too difficult for some in the community to dredge up the age-old stereotypes, pertaining to blacks and sexuality, and then apply those stereotypes to this situation. As was the case in *Mockingbird*, even Vermont's legal system was, at a point, intent on punishing the black man for his "temerity" rather than giving credence to what was the truth.

The question of truth is also an issue in Mosher's novel *The True Account*. President Thomas Jefferson commissioned the Lewis and Clark expedition to traverse the newly purchased Louisiana territory, and make its way to the Pacific Ocean, in hopes of learning as much as possible about the land and its native inhabitants. Official accounts of an expedition, such as the one undertaken by Meriwether Lewis and William Clark, may be flawed in terms of absolute accuracy. For the sake of posterity, there may have been a desire, on the part of the explorers, to embellish certain events. So, Mosher provides us, in *The True Account*, with his own explorer who recapitulates his version of the exploration story since, as he tells it, he often had to, in an assortment of ways, smooth the path so that Lewis and Clark could stay alive. True Kinneson, Mosher's explorer, in many ways resembles the character Jim in Mark Twain's *Adventures of Huckleberry Finn*. In "The Technique of Humor in Twain's *Huckleberry Finn* and Mosher's *The True Account*," I not only draw a connection between those two characters but I also explain how humor is used by both authors in daring ways that some, in the reading audience, might be inclined to consider offensive.

For William Faulkner, and for Mosher, truth is inextricably linked to the world of nature. The irony is that, for quite some time now, humankind has been bound and determined to deny the link as we strive, more and more, in the direction of technological advancement. One of Faulkner's concerns had been that we would not, as a people, be able to maintain a necessary ethical pace to keep up with the new technological advancements. So, to ward off the inevitable onslaught of the

Introduction

evils accompanying this more urbanized world, there must be people who are willing to hold their ground and give the natural world its due. It is in "Faulkner's *Go Down, Moses* and Mosher's Mourning the Inevitable Loss of a Kingdom" that I consider Faulkner's Sam Fathers and Ike McCaslin as well as Mosher's Noël Lord and Jane Kinneson. It is people such as them, those characters from Faulkner's and Mosher's texts, who provide us with something of a buffer against what has become the movement away from crucial values, values that only an attachment to nature would have been able to sustain.

I had contemplated making that my final chapter, imagining that eventually people would destroy the entire wilderness. Technology would run amuck until it controlled all our lives whereupon there would be nothing left to do but just let the technology consume us and then the Creator would, as He had done in the case before, simply start all over again. But as I thought about it some more, I pondered the relationship that Mosher has with his wife. I pondered it, that is, as much as anyone can ponder, with any certainty, the personal and private world that two lovers have created for themselves against which no outside force can infringe upon, at least not in any permanent way. One or both of the lovers might even die, but the love itself remains long after physical death has occurred.

As we read certain plays by William Shakespeare such as *Romeo and Juliet*, *Othello*, and *Antony and Cleopatra*, we are stunned by how the world responds to the intense love between two people. More often than not, outsiders intend to do harm to those who are adamantly in love. The excuses that the world use in order to play out its distaste for such unions include, at least in Shakespeare's works, that the lovers are too young or too different or their families do not get along. And yet, true love survives. In my chapter, "Mosher and Shakespeare: On the Immortality of Romantic Love," I explain how, in several of his own works, Mosher explores such a love, one capable of surviving a disappearing wilderness, disapproving parents, and the seeming finality of death itself.

The themes that I undertake to investigate, over the course of my various chapters, are ones that have existed since the beginning of humankind. They are the age-old themes of war and love, the environ-

Introduction

ment, discrimination, and the matter of who we really are beyond the limitations of our physical bodies. Mosher, over the course of his literary career, has drawn upon those same issues as he has placed them into the framework of a Vermont that has held on to its rural independent roots perhaps longer than most other places in America. It is apropos, though, that faced with his own mortality, Mosher would want to see as much as he could of that America which his work so ably represents. And, indeed, this yearning forms the essence of my book's conclusion. In one final attempt, on my part, to tie a Mosher work to that of other great writers, I turn to Twain's *The Innocents Abroad* and John Steinbeck's *Travels with Charley*. Twain traveled to Europe and the Middle East. Steinbeck and Mosher ventured across large tracts of territory within the United States. All three of the authors had already been familiar with dogged determination and hard manual labor when they undertook their extensive trips; and I would like to think that they all would have approved of the undergirding concept of my conclusion which I entitle "'Not Gently' in Steinbeck's *Travels with Charley*, Twain's *The Innocents Abroad* and Mosher's *The Great Northern Express*." None of those authors took lightly what the world has to offer in terms of the trials and tribulations and satisfying moments that, all together, make up the lives of the great majority of the people in the world. That those authors would never stop exploring the depths of such varied life elements—even at a time when others would have felt that to do so was a waste of precious limited time—is a testament to just how dedicated they were to their craft and to the idea that if they gave all they had to the fulfillment of that craft, even down to the last bit of strength and intestinal fortitude, then they could thus provide us with a view of the world that would allow us to learn a great deal about ourselves and understand better how we fit into the continuum of humanity that is as timeless in terms of its vital characteristics as are the works of the authors themselves who, to a large extent, were able to substantially recreate that world in the form of their literary masterpieces.

• I •

First Chancellorsville, Then Gettysburg

Horror, Escape and Restitution in Crane's *The Red Badge of Courage* and Mosher's *Walking to Gatlinburg*

On June 2, 2010, Mosher gave a talk at the Leonard Aldrich Library in Barre, Vermont, and told his audience about visiting the National Civil War Museum in Harrisburg, Pennsylvania, where he came across a particularly striking artifact. The item happened to be a poster from the Civil War era that had been devised to encourage young northern men to enlist in the Union cause. Mosher had, on hand, a projector slide showing the actual poster because he wanted us to see for ourselves exactly what the wording was. It read: "Join now, boys, for a beautiful chance to see some of this world away from home."

Upon examining the poster over and over, for the lengthy stretch of time that Mosher had it up there on the screen for us to see, one could not help but think about just how much the wording on the poster resembled the poster advertisements one sees in the lobby of a travel agency, urging potential customers to purchase tickets for some faraway exotic location to get a break away from ordinary day-to-day life that must begin to seem quite mundane at a certain point. "Mundane" might be exactly the word to describe how most Americans used to live. Before the arrival of the automobile, most people ventured no more than 20 miles, during their lifetime, from the place they were born. In the 1860s, the prospect of being able "to see some of this world" was an enticing idea indeed, along the lines of how someone today might view a round-trip ticket to Paris.

Only, back then it was not a trip to Paris that the poster was advertising. No, nothing of the sort. And making it back home was not a guarantee.

As he contemplates joining the Army, Henry Fleming, the main protagonist in Stephen Crane's novel, *The Red Badge of Courage*, envisions that the Civil War is "one of those great affairs of the earth."[1] It is one of those great military moments in history to rival anything that the Greek poet Homer ever wrote about during his time. For young Henry, the Civil War is a "play affair" in which he "thrilled" at the prospect of participating, for the "glory" to be attained.

Once enlisted, though, the issue that becomes of primordial concern to him is whether or not he, quite contrary to his previous notions about thrill and glory, will instead be so overwhelmed with fear that he will be more inclined to turn and run away in the face of the enemy described to him by older soldiers as "gray, bewhiskered hordes who were advancing with relentless curses and chewing tobacco with unspeakable valor; tremendous bodies of fierce soldiery who were sweeping along like the Huns."[2] And it will not be long before the fighting and killing begins for Henry and, quite different from the "picturesque attitudes" which he had once dreamt about as being the way that soldiers held themselves, he is instead faced with the horror of dead men who, fallen in battle, now "lay twisted in fantastic contortions." Their heads and appendages are twisted in such a way as to make it seem like they had been "dumped" from some place high in the sky, plummeted to the earth and now lay battered and broken upon the battlefield.

Nevertheless, Henry had stood his ground and fought during that initial phase of the battle. Which particular battle it was has been the subject of much scholarly debate. Lyndon Pratt, for example, suggests that the setting for Crane's novel is the Battle of Antietam, a battle that was fought on September 17, 1862, and wound up being the bloodiest single-day battle in United States history. The wounded, dead, and missing, according to one source, reached a total (both sides combined) of 22,717.[3] It was a battle in which the Union claimed victory although they had thousands more casualties than the South; moreover, the North's commanding general, George B. McClellan, was so unorganized as to remind us of Crane's depiction of generals as "stupid" and indeed "idiots" who "did not know what they were about."[4]

• *I. Horror, Escape and Restitution* •

In his 1939 essay, "A Possible Source of *The Red Badge of Courage*," Pratt pointed to the significance of Claverack College in Crane's life. That quasi-military school was in operation from 1779 to 1902. When Crane enrolled there in 1887, there was a particular faculty member on the staff who in all likelihood was at Antietam, though forced into flight as the carnage ensued. Drawing from, among other things, a letter from a student who had attended Claverack during Crane's time there, Pratt puts the pieces together concerning General John Bullock Van Petten and the circumstances under which he and Crane would have most likely engaged in conversation, details of which could have been later fictionalized by Crane in the pages of *Red Badge*. Pratt conveys:

> At Claverack the custom obtained of having faculty members preside over the tables in the dining hall. General Van Petten had charge of one such table, and thus, three times a day, a small group of students would be gathered around him under circumstances which, while assuredly polite, were to a certain degree informal. Under such conditions as these it is not impossible to conceive of the General remembering Antietam.[5]

It is difficult to imagine that Crane—with his keen interest in military history—and General Van Petten could have been at the same educational institution and, even though it was two-and-a-half decades after the battle, not talked about the implications of so many human casualties.

That various elements of Antietam would find their way into *Red Badge* is not so much of a stretch considering this very likely relationship that existed between the general and the future writer. Nevertheless, the weeklong (April 30 through May 6, 1863) Battle of Chancellorsville has garnered much attention as the probable source for the two-day battle that comprises the bulk of the novel. Among other things, the Rappahannock River is mentioned in *Red Badge* and that is the very river that the Union general Joseph Hooker had to cross at Chancellorsville in order to engage the Rebel forces. Then there were the pontoon-bridges and the plank road at Chancellorsville that made their way into the pages of Crane's book, albeit the author declined, in the novel, to give his battle any particular name at all.

Mosher's character, Pilgrim Kinneson, is not exactly like Henry Fleming. He was not attracted to the military because of some romantic notion of "a beautiful chance to see some of this world." But it was indeed a romance, at any rate, that drove him to enlist. He had fallen in love with a girl from his northern Vermont community, but his parents forbade him to marry her because she was a French Canadian Catholic. Her parents likewise forbade her to marry him, and the pain of that whole situation inclined him to seek solace by getting away from it all; the best way to (as the Civil War advertisement poster put it) get "away from home," without having to pay for it, being simply to join the Army.

Most of Mosher's novel involves a quest, on the part of Pilgrim's brother Morgan, to find out what happened to Pilgrim after he joined up and then, at a point, was never heard from again. What we eventually learn is that Pilgrim was at the Battle of Gettysburg, perhaps the most momentous battle of the war where the Union wounded, dead, and missing numbered in the vicinity of 23,055.[6] On the Confederate side, the number was an equally astounding 23,231 who were cited as having been wounded, dead, or missing.[7] As was the case with the Battle of Antietam, the number of casualties, with regard to Gettysburg, can only be approximated. The real numbers will never be known since it was not unusual, in that war, for the dead to be buried quickly, sometimes in mass graves, to prevent the spread of disease. Reflecting on the war, two decades after it had ended, the poet Walt Whitman conveyed the essence of things as he remarked about the places where "nearly *all* the dead are unknown. At Salisbury, N.C., for instance, the known are only 85, while the unknown are 12,021, and 11,700 of these are buried in trenches."[8] In that essay, "The Million Dead, Too, Summ'd Up," Whitman makes specific reference to the Battle of Gettysburg, Lee's flight after the battle had ended, and the "infinite dead" whose remains will never be identified, while with their bodies they nevertheless left a "land entire saturated."

Whitman's depiction is reminiscent of the many scenes in *Red Badge* where soldiers have fallen and we as readers are left to wonder what ultimately became of their remains. As one examines the Battle of Chancellorsville more closely, with its end date of May 6, 1863, and then as one notes how less than two months later the Battle of Gettysburg was engaged, it can be interpreted that the latter event was just an extension of the former, one battle won by the South, the next won by the North, with such a conflation of overwhelming casualties, between the

• *I. Horror, Escape and Restitution* •

two sides that, as Morgan contemplates it, "slavery, the greatest evil mankind had ever devised, was the ultimate issue, but it had long seemed to him that the conflict had acquired a malignant life of its own."[9] Mosher makes it a point to say that even northern Underground Railroad conductors had different reasons for participating in that enterprise, not always because they were staunch egalitarian abolitionists. Sometimes the conductors' involvement was a simple matter of where they just so happened to live.

It is interesting to note, by way of comparison, that many of the young men and boys who fought on the side of the Confederacy were not advocates for slavery. Relatively few actually owned any slaves that they, if indeed they possessed any, would have felt compelled to maintain ownership over. John Curran, in his analysis of Crane's novel, makes the startling observation that throughout all the pages of that work, there is a conspicuous absence of two particular words that one would assume would be on the tongues of at least some of the soldiers who are fighting for the North. The two words that are missing are "slavery" and "union," and instead of certainty about the mission at hand, their minds are filled with questioning:

> Why are they fighting? Can they fight? Have they won? What is their strategy? What role do they have in the battle? Who is directing the battle? What battle is it?[10]

At the actual Battle of Chancellorsville, much of the fighting took place at a spot known as the Wilderness, a heavily wooded area where little else was effective but for men to fix their bayonets and charge one another for endless hours. What occurred can only be guessed at, for it is perhaps as Whitman assessed, that "future years will never know the seething hell and the black infernal background of countless minor scenes and interiors ... of the Secession war; and it is best they should not—the real war will never get in the books."[11] Even as Crane depicts the smoke-filled horrors of his fictional version of the Wilderness and Mosher renders his fictional perspective on the smoke-filled Wheat Field and Devil's Den of Gettysburg, the reality of what occurred at those various battle sites will, as Whitman so adeptly put it, "never be even suggested."

Howard Frank Mosher and the Classics

One wonders, very early on in *Walking to Gatlinburg*, how it is that Morgan seems to know "for a fact" that his brother is still alive. Those brothers have an uncle, Colonel John Kinneson, who knows about the horrors of war firsthand and has come to the conclusion that his nephew Pilgrim is most likely buried in one of the mass graves dug for the unknown dead in the aftermath of Gettysburg. But Morgan holds fast to his belief that Pilgrim is alive, and by the time Morgan has been on his search for a while, we as readers have come to believe, along with him, that Pilgrim is alive, that Morgan is not searching in vain because, in spite of having no evidence to prove it, we become as certain as Morgan himself is that, in spite of the infernal chaos of battle, Pilgrim "had slipped away from it," managed somehow to survive it. Once Morgan does finally catch up with Pilgrim who we learn has relocated, even as the war rages on, to the mountains just outside of Gatlinburg, Tennessee, the question that looms in our minds is just how should we regard this relocation?

To understand what Pilgrim's situation is now, it is useful to consider the point, in Crane's novel, where Henry runs away even though in an earlier skirmish, he had held his own in the fighting. Having survived "the supreme trial" of battle, he was able to rest somewhat, thinking "in deep gratification" what a "fine fellow" he was. But then, the enemy reappeared through "great clouds of smoke" like "machines of steel" or indeed like some "monster" and Henry is "horrified," paralyzed, certain that he is about to be "gobbled" up by the "redoubtable dragons."

One of the crucial issues in Crane's novel is whether or not Henry becomes cowardly at this point. He sees one after another brave soldier "suddenly" stop and run away in the opposite direction of battle. Henry joins suit in what the critic Marilyn Boyer calls "not a well-calculated decision but an instinctive escape from imminent death."[12] In his narrative of the situation, the novelist himself characterizes Henry's retreat as not necessarily desertion but instead a "revelation." Something has been revealed to him that, in all his previous contemplations about war and its consequences, he had not known before.

Nor could Mosher's Pilgrim have anticipated what war would be like. Indeed, killing anyone, or being killed himself, was not what he signed up for. A Harvard Medical School student, his goal was to give

I. Horror, Escape and Restitution

aid to the injured and he was prepared to perform that service for whoever needed his help, regardless of which side they had fought on during the conflict. What Pilgrim was not prepared for, though, was the human carnage to which he would be ultimately exposed, particularly at the Slaughter Pen where the fighting was more intense than this military surgeon "had ever witnessed or imagined." As he is helping carry a makeshift ambulance, piled with soldiers, up a hill toward the tent hospital, that wooden plank ambulance and the men carrying the ambulance are blown to bits and, through the "mist of blood raining" down around him, Pilgrim found himself running "until he could run no more."

Before we too hastily declare Pilgrim to be a coward here, it would behoove us to consider Emily Dickinson's "Poem #3" where she raises the question of what it is, exactly, that makes one person a coward and another person a hero. In that poem, she takes the rather curious position that staying and fighting is a cowardly act while, on the other hand, it is the hero who finds a way out.[13] In *Red Badge*, as Henry turns away from the fighting, he becomes regretful of having done so, because he will now have no chance to receive a wound—a "red badge"—to symbolize his courage. He is in such anguish in fact, at having left the battlefield, that he even wishes he was dead now and "he envied those men whose bodies lay strewn over the grass of the fields."[14] In modern-day terms, one could say that Henry is experiencing post-traumatic stress disorder. The war has taken such a toll on him, psychologically, that what he wishes for, while understandable, is not what is best for him. He has, in fact, run away from death and that is a good thing. He has survived but, like many other soldiers who have had to witness comrades fall in battle, he carries with him the guilt that he is still alive.

Neither Henry nor Pilgrim would have been able right away to grasp the meaning of Dickinson's poem because it would seem to cut entirely against the grain of what one would have thought to be the definition of a "hero." Heroes do not run away from battle. Or, do they? Citing the eminent historian Howard Zinn, Boyer observes that on just the Union side alone, there were well over 200,000 deserters.[15] It would be disingenuous for anyone to summarily declare that each one of them was a coward when in actuality many might have been merely responding to the reality of circumstances which could very easily have included such factors as treacherous terrain, incompetent generalship and, as Melissa Green characterizes it, a sense that they are fighting "a battle which can no longer be identified" with any certainty because of the dual nature of it being an "actual battle on the one hand and a 'moral' battle with the war animal on the other."[16] Both Crane and Mosher provide us with climactic scenes from what was a very real military conflict but, at the same time that they do so, they are offering us glimpses of the irony and indeed the insanity that was also involved in that war.

Why else would Crane refer to many of his characters not by their real names but with descriptives such as "the tall soldier" or "the cheery soldier" or "the loud soldier" or "the tattered soldier?" In many ways, the names are not so much indicative of a particular side in the war as they are reflective of humanity in general. After one particular skirmish, the cheery soldier tells Henry, "I couldn't tell t' save m' soul which side I was on. Sometimes I thought I was sure 'nough from Ohier, an' other times I could 'a swore I was from th' bitter end of Florida."[17] In other words, the cheery soldier—whose name in itself is a contradiction to the setting he finds himself in—is telling the youth, who signifies the primary age group of practically every army since the dawn of time, that he might as well have been a soldier from anywhere in the whole United States.

In his 2007 novel, *On Kingdom Mountain*, Mosher alluded to just such universality as he has Jane Hubbell Kinneson discover a letter written by her father in 1864. As it turns out, her father's name was Morgan, the same Morgan Kinneson who, in *Gatlinburg*, is searching for his lost brother Pilgrim. The letter is addressed to Slidell, an escaped black slave whom Morgan had met and fallen in love with during his search. While they spent much time together, the moment arrived when Morgan had to venture further south and she had to go in the opposite direction, toward freedom. Once back in Vermont, Morgan seeks to re-establish communication with this woman who had figured so prominently in his life. But of particular significance, in that letter, is Morgan's recapitulation of how he aided a Confederate captain whom he found wounded in his barn one evening, having been shot in the leg by his own Rebel compatriot after the two of them had robbed a bank in Kingdom County, presumably for the purposes of adding to the Rebel treasury and diverting attention away from Rebel soldiers elsewhere further south.[18] It is

• *I. Horror, Escape and Restitution* •

ironic that the soldier Morgan found was shot by his own fellow Rebel; and Morgan, from the North, is the one who nurses him back to health. Even more ironic perhaps, though, is how the Rebel whom Morgan nursed back to health had earlier, before the bank robbery, "*done the same for an injured Yankee soldier, hiding in the mountains in North Carolina, named Pilgrim.*"[19] As we consider how that Pilgrim was Morgan's very own brother, we are made to ponder the cyclical nature of things as first Pilgrim cares for wounded Union soldiers at Gettysburg, then a Rebel cares for Pilgrim, then Morgan cares for the Rebel who had cared for Pilgrim. It is almost as if, in some cosmic sphere, they were all on the same side though, in the very real sphere of human existence, those who served on one side were the bitter enemies of those who fought on the other.

Such brutal irony is a reflection of how life has been depicted, going all the way back to antiquity. In Greek mythology, Eris—the Goddess of Strife—is said to have tossed, right into the midst of a wedding celebration, what has come to be regarded now as the Apple of Discord, that thing which disrupts what otherwise would have been a wonderful potential for harmony. Instead, the goddesses Hera, Athena, and Aphrodite all fight among themselves for this apple since they have been told that it rightfully belongs to the one who is the fairest. Aphrodite wins the apple but Athena, out of anger and desire for revenge, sides with Greeks against the Trojans in what will become a 10-year-long war (1194–1184 BC) that need not even have been waged at all.

In what turned out to be a rather unusual coincidence, Professor Michael Schaefer at the University of Central Arkansas offered a course, in the spring of 2003, called "American Romanticism and Realism." One of his texts for that course was *Red Badge*. As fate would have it, the novel was discussed from March 17–28, the period that also marked the beginning of the Iraq War that would officially go on for seven years. In those early days of war, most of Schaefer's students were reluctant to criticize the Bush administration's invasion of Iraq, an invasion undertaken to search for weapons of mass destruction. Some students had friends and family who had been deployed and those students, understandably, in no way wanted to convey any message along the lines of how loved ones might be fighting a war "in vain."

Still, reading *Red Badge* proved helpful in assessing the Iraq War since "many students had remained ignorant of or indifferent to that controversy until the implicit but undeniable connections between the events of *Red Badge* and the situation in Iraq demanded their attention."[20] By the time they reached the end of their discussion about the novel, students had become embroiled in such issues as whether or not indifference to an enemy's humanity robs a soldier of his own humanity and whether or not Henry in particular fails as a human being, in direct proportion to the emphasis he puts on glory in battle over and above the horrors that he himself has witnessed. In *Red Badge*, Henry is able to negotiate his fear of battle as he claims a new persona, so determined to achieve battle glory that his comrades now regard him as "a barbarian, a beast" and a "war devil." It was this aspect of Henry that had so disconcerted Professor Schaefer's class. Henry becomes a "hero" to the point where even his superior officer is stunned, left so amazed that he can only declare, "By heavens, if I had ten thousand wild cats like you I could tear th' stomach outa this war in less'n a week."[21] So, in the contest between fear and glory, it is the latter that seems to have won. The youth, one can now imagine, has been redeemed and has paid restitution for his earlier conduct of fleeing in the face of battle.

By the end of the novel, it would be easy to say that Henry, by virtue of his transformation into hero, should be judged a success in life. And yet, he is still a haunted man, hoping now for "eternal peace," a peace that he had eschewed at the beginning of the novel when he had lamented over whether he would have to "be a man heretofore doomed to peace and obscurity, but, in reality, made to shine in war."[22] Now, he wants endless peace and the very last sentence of the novel offers us no indication as to whether or not he found it since what he sees, through the infinite "hosts of leaden rain clouds," is one "ray of sun" and that solitary ray is off at a distance "over the river."

Mosher brings that issue to bear most profoundly as he has Morgan making his way through Upstate New York, encountering places with names like Fool Hill, The River Styx, Second Coming, and Poverty Ridge. They are desolate places with "dilapidated houses and sagging barns." Poverty-stricken would indeed be the best way to describe the area. It was just the sort of region of the country where Union recruiters could

• I. Horror, Escape and Restitution •

come and effectively sell the Civil War as a "beautiful chance to see" the world. In his essay comparing *Red Badge* to Homer's *Iliad*, N. E. Dunn goes so far as to compare the heroic Henry to Achilles. They both are ferocious in battle but they also, as Dunn continues his assessment, "are fallible human beings caught up in civil war, concerned with moral values but also deluded by their own pride, capable of independent thought yet strongly affected by the values of their respective societies."[23] It was pride that caused Achilles' downfall. Pride that made Pilgrim stalk off and join the Army to pay his parents back for denying him his right to choose whomever he wanted to marry. It was pride that made Henry wish for glory in battle, and pride that made Mosher's Upstate New York young men, who were "clamoring to enlist," choose the prospect of finding glory in war preferable to remaining in their boring rundown homes.

If only they had known, beforehand, what Henry discovers soon after he has enlisted and is awaiting his first taste of battle. It had not taken much contemplation, as the fighting approached, for him to wish

> he was at home again making the endless rounds from house to the barn, from the barn to the fields, from the fields to the barn, from the barn to the house. He remembered he had often cursed the brindle cow and her mates, and had sometimes flung milking stools. But, from his present point of view, there was a halo of happiness about each of their heads, and he would have sacrificed all the brass buttons on the continent to have been enabled to return to them.[24]

From that description, it seems that Henry and his mother were at least a bit better-off than Mosher's Upstate New Yorkers who were prone to go to war. But one imagines that the New Yorkers will come to have feelings nonetheless that are quite similar to those that the youth develops. Like Henry, they will realize that peace should have been the ultimate objective. And once they are back home, they will appreciate, more than ever, what they earlier might have regarded as the nothingness of their existence.

The problem is that many of them will not return home. Indeed, after the Trojan War has ended, we as readers of *The Iliad* are brought to the realization that most of the Greeks, who participated in that conflict, will not make it home. *The Odyssey*, in fact, can be interpreted as one long detailed study of just how difficult it is to get home not just physically, but psychologically and emotionally, after one has gone off to war. Odysseus's wife, Penelope, has suffered beyond measure. Henry's mother, not knowing if her son will live or die, laments, "There's many a woman has to bear up 'ginst sech things these times, and the Lord'll take keer of us all."[25] By the time Mosher's Morgan has arrived in Upstate New York, we can see for ourselves just how well those who have been left behind have been taken care of. In the wake of the men going off to fight, we find "hollow-eyed women, widowed by the war at twenty, gaunt and aged at thirty .... The children looked worm-ridden and rickety."[26] If this is how it is now, while the war is going on, one can only wonder how it will be for those soldiers who do manage to stay alive and make it back to what they once knew as home.

It was men such as those whom Pilgrim would have been doctoring during his time as a "surgeon" on the battlefield. And then he ran away from it all, found his escape in the mountains of Tennessee. Yet, what he had done was a form of desertion, in the face of battle, that would require some sort of restitution, a making up for that action, however much we might want to declare the action as, under the circumstances, being understandable. So, for his restitution, Pilgrim has set up a medical practice in that "primeval forest" where he makes his rounds on an "ancient nag." The would-be Harvard doctor has now dedicated his life to making expert medical care available to those who otherwise would have been among the least likely to have received it. This, for that community, will mean fewer childbirth fatalities, fewer deaths due to simple infections, and the security of knowing that with almost any illness there is the possibility of treatment and recovery.

For those readers who might have felt that Pilgrim was in dire need of redemption after having run away from the battlefield, his medical contributions, since that moment, certainly have fulfilled the need. In a sense, that redemption was Mosher's way of supplying a more satisfactory restitution, for his version of Henry, than what Crane himself had offered in *Red Badge* when he had Henry redeem himself by shifting away from being a deserter and evolving instead into a "war devil" capable of single-handedly turning back the enemy, firing on them without stopping until one of his own discombobulated comrades has to tell him that "there ain't anything t' shoot at" anymore. In fact, restitution for

• *I. Horror, Escape and Restitution* •

Crane's Henry perhaps does not come until a year after the novel was published and that author provided a sequel in the form of a short story in *McClure's Magazine*. The story was entitled "The Veteran," and it documents the last day in the life of an aging Henry Fleming who, at the beginning of the story, finds himself reminiscing about the war for a ready group of listeners who are gathered at the local grocery store.

Among other things, the veteran admits to having fled in the face of battle and he confirms that the events that make up the bulk of *Red Badge* did indeed happen at Chancellorsville. It seems that Henry has made it back, after the war, to the farm life that he had yearned for when he got his first taste of war and learned, rather quickly, that it was not the idyllic world that he envisioned when he had defied his own mother and enlisted. Now, as Crane's short story reveals, Henry can go "peacefully to sleep" at night, having found a solace comparable to what Pilgrim finds in the mountains outside of Gatlinburg.

Mosher's Pilgrim has made his restitution and that achievement likewise seems to have been accomplished by Henry. That is, once we make it all the way through Crane's short story. The tale ends with a blazing barn fire where cows, workhorses, colts, and a drunken man need to be rescued. Of all the citizens who might have performed the rescue, it is Henry who "had gone headlong into the barn, where the stifling smoke swirled with the air-currents, and where could be heard in its fullness the terrible chorus of the flames, laden with tones of hate and death."[27] The fire takes on the appurtenances of war as the flames become "deadly and triumphant foes" that in the end will prove to be the cause of Henry's undoing. But he has performed valiantly before the roof caves in on him as he goes back to rescue colts "in box-stalls at the back of the barn." The scene is eerily reminiscent of how Pilgrim had tried to save wounded soldiers who lay helpless on the makeshift ambulance before being blown to bits.

Henry dies in that short story, his retribution complete, all the more complete since it is only his physical aspect that is gone. The sacrifice that he made will live on in the form of a spirit that offers us more than just a modicum of hope for the future. In the mountains, serving the less fortunate, Pilgrim is also destined to die, his death at the hand of the ubiquitous slave catcher who had been chasing Morgan since when

Howard Frank Mosher and the Classics

that younger brother had first begun his trek from Vermont. The drunken man who started the barn fire became the personification of evil as Crane refers to him as "one who is the weapon of the sinister fates." And Mosher's slave catcher will reappear, some way or another, regardless of how often each physical form he takes on is killed. The fact that mere mortals—such as Henry and Pilgrim—can undertake to engage such an enemy so valiantly is, in the final analysis, what we are left with to hold on to for sustenance as the war between what is moral, and what is not, rages on through the generations.

• II •

Female Vulnerability and Industrialization's Dehumanizing Process in Mosher's *Marie Blythe*, Sinclair's *The Jungle*, Dreiser's *Sister Carrie* and Crane's *Maggie*
A Girl of the Streets

Utterly fascinated by his sprawling 455-page *Bildungsroman* of a novel, *Marie Blythe*, I informed Mosher that, for the purposes of an essay I was working on about that novel, I assumed the factory, at the core of that work, was based on a similar factory that had once existed back at his birthplace of Chichester, New York. Two brothers, Frank and Lemuel Chichester had, in the mid-nineteenth century, been searching for a good place to build their furniture factory and so they carved, out of the rural landscape, a site for the factory's foundation, built their factory, and quickly began attracting workers who not only eked out a livelihood there but contributed, even more, to the factory owner's livelihood, since that factory would wind up building houses for its employees as well as a general store for the workers to make their necessary purchases. Over the course of its existence, ownership of the factory would change hands, but the entrepreneurial concept remained the same as workers poured in to become the human cogs in the grand capitalistic scheme that was begun by the Chichester brothers and then continued on by one William O. Schwartzwaelder who not only renamed the factory after himself but oversaw further expansion of Chichester until the Great Depression ended the whole scheme and the factory wound up being auctioned off right along with the homes where the factory workers were living.

Marie Blythe would seem to be a work drawn directly from that profound chain of events. Entrepreneur Abraham Benedict arrives in the northeastern corner of Vermont with the initial intent of conducting a logging enterprise that winds up flourishing on a massive scale until he gets the idea that instead of transporting lumber upriver to Canada, he can hire skilled and unskilled laborers to build furniture for a market that he envisions as being unlimited. Just as a railroad had been constructed, in 1881, to run right through the real-life town of Chichester, the fictional Benedict sees to it that a railroad is built to accommodate his factory. It will be the means whereby day laborers can be brought in to work, at their unskilled positions, and then transported back to nearby Kingdom Common once their day's work is done.

As for the skilled laborers, their expectations were somewhat greater, for Benedict had promised them not only twice as much money, as they had earned in Grand Rapids, but also "good houses" to live in so as to make their experience reminiscent of a sort of Eden which Benedict himself must have been meaning to reclaim, in the first place, when he chose this particularly rural location to create what would become a quite "prosperous village" that, however, had the rather ominous name of "Hell's Gate," and events surrounding the furniture factory will live up to that name as time moves on and Benedict's son, Abie, takes control of things but with not nearly the morality or the vision that had led his father into that furniture-building venture. Lack of business acumen on the part of Abie, in addition to his evil nature, will cause the factory to go into such a decline that the business and all the homes will have to be put up for auction in a manner not at all unlike what happened in Chichester in 1939.

So, when I told Mosher that I thought the Chichester factory was the model that he used for the factory in *Marie Blythe*, he responded, "Yes, but there is also another one."[1] That was when he drove me to a place not far from his home, parked the car and reminisced back in time

• *II. Female Vulnerability* •

to the spring of 1964 when he and Phillis had interviewed for teaching positions and they had both been successful. One of their jobs, as Mosher put it, reflecting back on those days, was to be effective enough teachers so as to keep students "out of there," the "there" being the factory where we, now in 2010, sat in his car in front of as we ruminated on all the new implications that could be added to the mix for an even more effective analysis of his novel than what using just the Chichester factory as a model could provide.

When Mosher brought it to our (Renae's and mine) attention that even at this point in 2010, workers at the factory were losing their fingers, my mind went back in time to 1906, when Upton Sinclair's novel *The Jungle* exploded on the literary scene, exposing the innumerable horrors of working in the Chicago stockyards where cattle, sheep, and pigs were slaughtered and prepared for shipment to locations throughout the United States. Perhaps the most horrible scene of all, in that novel, was to be found in what Sinclair refers to as "the killings beds," where men covered in frozen animal blood, since there was no heat where they worked, had to butcher the cattle under such dangerous conditions that Sinclair, in his documentary style, conveys, in terms of these men's circumstances, that the

> cruelest thing of all was that nearly all of them—all of those who used knives—were unable to wear gloves, and their arms would be white with frost and their hands would grow numb, and then, of course, there would be accidents. Also the air would be full of steam, from the hot water and the hot blood, so that you could not see five feet before; and then, with men rushing about at the speed they kept up on the killing beds and all with butcher knives, like razors, in their hands—well, it was to be counted as a wonder that there were not more men slaughtered than cattle.[2]

The accidents, to which Sinclair refers, run rampant through the novel. Hands are cut off, fingers are lost through a slow process of blood poisoning, and since acid was used to loosen the sheep's wool and then wool-pluckers had to pull out the wool with their bare hands, that acid would eventually eat away those workers' fingers. Even Jurgis Rudkus, the "big and strong" Lithuanian immigrant who used to always be sure of getting work, and surviving the harshest conditions, suddenly finds himself reduced to the level of ordinariness when a steer breaks loose on the slippery killing bed, a melee ensues with knife-armed men "tumbling over each other," and Rudkus severely twists a tendon in his leg, an unfortunate event that leaves him incapacitated for months.

The reality of the situation becomes that now his wife, Ona, will have to go to work at the stockyard factory, and this is the ominous beginning of a downfall that is best characterized by Sinclair's own narrative statement that the Packingtown area of Chicago, where the stockyards are located, has become a place where "women's bodies and men's souls, were for sale in the market place."[3] It will not be long before Ona realizes this as her boss begins making demands on her of a sexual nature. Since Jurgis is unable to work, the family is depending on her income for their survival, a fact of which her boss is well aware. As Ona explains to her husband, after the tragic event has unfolded, "He knew all about us; he knew we would starve …. [H]e said if I would—if I—we would all of us be sure of work—always. Then one day he caught hold of me."[4] From that female worker's perspective, she had no choice but to give in to her supervisor. Her labor was for sale but it was also in the nature of things that, as Sinclair himself noted, her body would become part of the employment situation bargain.

In what might be regarded as one of its rawest incarnations, Vermont was at one time notorious for its carnival strip shows. The phenomenon was such that MacArthur genius award winner Susan Meiselas, for three straight summers between 1973 and 1975, took her photography skills to various localities, particularly Tunbridge, Woodstock, Essex Junction, and Barton, Vermont. As she followed these shows throughout the Vermont countryside, Meiselas sought to understand the circumstances of these women who were paid very little to take off their clothes for jeering lascivious men who somehow found it acceptable to objectify them in all sorts of demeaning ways, including what amounted to assaults, while the women performed in the crudest manner on a public platform. And then after they performed, there would often be the expectation of sexual favors, prompting a stripper named Lena to lament, in an interview with Meiselas, that regardless how many of the young women might reconcile themselves, with what they were doing, by calling it their first step toward big-time entertainment, in actuality

• *II. Female Vulnerability* •

[w]e aren't professional show girls, we're prostitutes pretending to be show girls. But what else can I do? The only thing I know how to do is dance. I can't be a secretary; I'm not trained for it .... The only thing I can do is dance or be a waitress. Do you want me to be a waitress for the rest of my life? ... the men were the same. I mean, if I bent over a table I had twenty of them looking up my skirt. Old men would come in at six o'clock in the morning. I'm just out of bed, and the first thing they'd think about is grabbing my ass. It seems no matter where I work there's some form of it. I prefer dancing.[5]

Who were those women that the interviewee seemed to present within the realm of a rather broad spectrum? In terms of whom it was that Meiselas interviewed and photographed, they were females ranging from 17 to 35 years of age and "seeking," as Meiselas puts it in her introductory remarks, "mobility, money, something different from what was prescribed or proscribed by their lives that the carnival allowed them to leave."[6]

For all its reputation as a bastion of liberalness and independent thinking, Vermont can be a difficult place to earn a living, particularly for young women who have not had the benefit of long-term planning for their future. As a largely rural state, it is susceptible to limiting the extent to which women can break out of, even if they strongly desire to do so, the patterns of living that have for so long characterized the frontier style of existence. Having herself received a master's degree from Harvard, Meiselas was inspired to create a photographic retrospective that Jim Harrison, in a *Harvard Magazine* article about the photojournalist, describes as her attempt to "expand the context of her uncompromising photographs, presenting a surprisingly complex, compassionate look at these women who, by and large, are simple farm girls trying to make a living as best they can in a seedy world."[7] Though they were engaged in the distinct occupation of stripping, their situation was not all that different, at its essential core, from what Sinclair's Ona was forced to become upon leaving her rural Lithuanian setting for a new life in the stockyards of Chicago.

Critic Orm Overland is partly correct in his assessment that Ona's tragic life is due to the change in her environment from rural to urban, that "an important aspect of the drama of immigration," as experienced by that Lithuanian girl, "was the incongruous meeting of nineteenth-century European peasant cultures with a twentieth-century American urban capitalist and industrial society."[8] I say that Overland is only partly right in that assessment because before Ona had ever ventured to America, she was already a form of prey even to the man who would become her husband. Without having spoken a single word to Ona herself, Jurgis had asked "her parents to sell her to him for his wife—and offering his father's two horses he had been sent to the fair to sell."[9] While still in the Lithuanian wilderness, he had viewed Ona as a worthwhile commodity, and while he is unsuccessful in purchasing her as long as her father is alive, once that father dies, "Jurgis's heart leapt as he realized that now the prize was within his reach."[10] All that stands in the way of Jurgis obtaining his goal, now, is Ona's stepmother and a few other relatives who are nonetheless too poor to resist what Jurgis presents as Ona's best option in life. So, before she had even arrived on America's shores, the prospects for her having a full and happy lifestyle were subject to a certain tenuousness, a tenuousness that was a reflection of the times in which she lived, times that were only further exacerbated by the factory system environment at the core of Sinclair's novel.

Mosher's Marie Blythe suffers a similarly delicate situation. Coming down out of the Canadian woods, in search of a better life, that protagonist's father dies in a logging accident just as he is at the point of getting his family settled in the promising new land. Immediately, we are made to witness the early stages of a downward spiral as Marie and her mother, Jeannine, must now go to work at the "hardest and dirtiest" jobs.

> They hoed out henhouses and scraped stovepipes. They broadcast ashes on gardens and draped rugs over clotheslines and flailed them with brooms. Aggravated by the ashes and soot and dust, Jeannine's chronic cough grew rapidly worse; by the winter solstice, she was leaving a trail of bright red splotches in the frozen snow from her house to the village.[11]

It will not be long before that mother also dies, leaving Marie an orphan at the tender age of ten. For a brief period, the child joins up with a band of gypsies (in actuality, itinerant Italian stonecutters), one of whom advises her to seek employment at the Benedicts' home. When Marie had done the hard and dirty work alongside her mother, it was usually at the homes of German cabinetmakers whom Abraham had imported to work at his furniture factory. Those homes had been particularly

• II. Female Vulnerability •

oppressive for Jeannine in terms of not only the furniture—heavy and dark with stark white antimacassars—but also the curtains and lamps with their dark amber beads, all of which reminded the mother, in a rather portentous way, of what a funeral procession looks like.

Once Marie joins the gypsies, part of her performance routine involves dancing with a bear that, while quite old, is still dangerous enough to "snap at her ears." Operating under the alias of "Mario, the wrestling gypsy boy," she takes on all comers in wrestling matches. All of this takes place in the factory yard, leaving us as readers with no choice but to surmise that these curious forms of entertainment are a direct by-product of the factory system and that she, as a female, even within the somewhat protective society of the gypsies, is nevertheless still vulnerable to being preyed upon by that system. When she actually moves into the Benedict home, to work as an assistant housekeeper, she is not just continuing on with the sort of menial work that has characterized her life, but now—with this new job—she is relocated into the belly of the beast itself.

In the Benedict household, it is not Abraham Benedict she need fear so much as she should be afraid of that furniture magnate's son, Abie, who displays his general sadistic tendencies in an episode where he has managed to trap six rats in a molasses keg. When he drops a cat into the barrel, it manages to kill two of the rats, but the other four are about to "savagely" destroy him until Marie "reached in and yanked him out. Two rats came along, dropping onto the floor and scurrying into the darkness."[12] That left two rats in the barrel and Abie is determined to torture them to death, pouring in bucket after bucket of water until he is sure that they will not be able to touch the bottom of the barrel. Then he rests his elbows on the rim of the barrel, relishing in what to him is a most enjoyable means of entertainment, made all the more delectable because it is something that he himself has contrived:

> At first the rats swam around the sides of the barrel very quickly; but when they realized that they would soon exhaust themselves, they slowed down into a methodical, steady circling. From time to time they raised their sharp-featured heads, like miniature otters looking for a bank to crawl out on ....
> A short while later, the smaller rat crawled up on the other one's back.

> As the stronger animal tired, its circles became tighter. It began to create a little swirling vortex in the center of the barrel. Then the little rat slid off and started to go under, but the big one picked it up by the back of the neck and treaded water until it was just barely able to hold its head up.[13]

The cat was to have been part of the show until Marie interfered, leaving Abie only two rats with which to entertain himself. When Marie threatens to end this entertainment too, wanting to "bang them over the head" with a shovel so that they can die quickly, Abie is determined instead to have the two animals suffer as long as possible.

The depths of Abie's evil character become all the more obvious as he compares those rats to people and declares that both species are "great survivors." The analogy is not lost on Mosher either as he describes the rats in a manner comparable to what human beings might display when they are operating at their most compassionate, first having those rats calculate the time and energy that they will have to allot in order to continue treading water, and then having the stronger rat attempting to save his companion from drowning. This issue of compassion, or the lack thereof, arises yet again in the mind of the reader as the molasses barrel, of Mosher's novel, can be interpreted as the literary extension of what the acid vats at the stockyard factory represent in Sinclair's novel. Workers sometimes fall into those acid vats and, once their bones are fished out, we learn how it is not only animal parts that are made into lard and fertilizer, but human bodies that are also a part of the commodity that will soon be for sale to an unwitting public, with no explanation offered to the family, of such victims, beyond some farfetched tale of how their loved ones had come in to work, gotten a week's wages and then disappeared, leaving no indication of where it was that they were going.

We observe a similar situation in *Marie Blythe* as Marie, forced by circumstances to work at the furniture factory, finds herself at the point of being tossed—by a six-foot, 500-pound co-worker—into a varnishing tank, the co-worker having been paid to do the deed by the man who has now become company boss, Abie Benedict himself who, at this point in the novel, is reminiscent of Sinclair's problematic Master Freddie, a decadent young man who is prone to go slumming, from time to time, and then return to his meatpacking magnate father's mansion where the walls are adorned with all manner of paintings of naked women, from a

· II. *Female Vulnerability* ·

"nymph crouching by a fountain" to "dryads dancing in a flower-strewn glade" to "maidens bathing in a forest pool." Those scenes on the mansion walls, magnificent as they are in all their brilliant artistry, are, from another perspective, merely the pictorial representation of what women, like Jurgis's wife Ona, have to endure at the factory that generates the income so that men like Freddie's father can live as they do and perpetuate the system that is so demeaning to women in the worst of ways.

In writing *The Jungle*, Sinclair drew substantially from Theodore Dreiser's *Sister Carrie*, a novel published six years earlier and having, at its core, the life of young Caroline Meeber who ventures from her rural community of Columbia City, Wisconsin, to make a new life for herself in the big city, Chicago. As will later be the situation with Ona, Caroline found herself working in a factory, in her case a shoe factory where her task consists of one chore that she winds up performing until "her hands began to ache at the wrists and then in the fingers, and towards the last she seemed one mass of dull, complaining muscles, fixed in an eternal position and performing a single mechanical movement which became more and more distasteful until at last it was absolutely nauseating."[14] That tedious work is awful enough, but beyond the work, she also has to endure the "leering" men who proposition her with comments such as "Ain't going my way, are you?" and her own supervisor whom Dreiser maintains has become "a true ogre, prowling constantly about." That boss might very well have been Marie's 500-pound co-worker, functioning under the auspices of Abie himself who, by his very voyeuristic nature, yearns to hear from his co-conspirator, about how Marie was left to fend for herself, trying to swim her way out of a varnishing vat. Just the thought of it all gave Abie the same sort of pleasure he had received upon watching, for the time that he had been allowed, the rats left to drown in the molasses barrel.

Long before he had become the new magnate of the furniture factory, Abie had been growing up and developing right there in the Big House that his father had built as a symbol of achievement in honor of the Benedict name. The scene with the rats in the barrel is one indication of how effectively the evil in Abie was festering, but even before the episode of the 500-pound woman and the varnishing vat, we were witness to how little was the compassion that Abie had for other human beings in general. When Marie was yet a servant at the Big House, she and Abie had gone sledding together but his goal, all the while, had been to create the greatest possible mischief. To that end, he crashed his sled into hers, knocking her off course and in the direction of a steep granite quarry, 100 feet deep. Her sled goes over the edge but she manages to grab hold of a "small birch" and yell for help. Abie takes his time coming and when he does arrive near the edge of the quarry where she is hanging helplessly, he does not offer to help her but instead asks, "Why should I give you a hand?" Marie is shocked, unable to believe what she is hearing and it is Mosher who has to remind us, in explicit narrative terms, that Abie was now "looking at her quite dispassionately, the way he had looked at the drowning rats in the molasses barrel."[15]

With one hand still clinging to the birch, she reaches for a place where she might begin to pull herself up, but she is unable to make even a dent in the solid ice. Squatting to watch closely, like a member in the audience at some sordid carnival sideshow, he hurls taunts at her such as, "Your fingers are turning white," "Hang on with your eyelids," and then finally the egregious question, "Will you take off all your clothes for me tonight if I pull you up here?[16] Marie agrees to the proposition, Abie pulls her up and when they return to the Big House, she keeps her end of the bargain and lets him undress her whereupon he only laughs, declaring her too skinny to do anything with anyway.

The situation of Marie's agreement is interesting since Abie's later rejection of her only increased the mystery surrounding one whom she must have regarded as a would-be suitor, albeit a suitor who has never given her any indication that what he feels for her is love. And yet they do eventually engage in what Mosher refers to as making love, and at one point in the novel they are doing so "at every opportunity." One of the men, whom Meiselas interviewed for *Carnival Strippers*, was "a talker" charged with the task of calling out, to people passing along the walkway, hoping to entice men to come over and watch the show. This one particular talker tells Meiselas how quite a few of the girls got their start in the business because they "met some son of a bitch that they fell in love with. He wanted their money and they went to work. And if she didn't produce more, he went to another chick."[17] Just at the time when Marie is beginning to fall for Abie, in spite of the cruelty that he has exhibited

• *II. Female Vulnerability* •

toward her, we are told through Mosher's narration that he already has "several different girlfriends." He has not yet become the furniture baron of Hell's Gate, but there in the Benedict household, he is already plying his trade, so to speak, the factory having been the means whereby the Big House was created, within which is the means leading toward the undoing of Marie herself.

The complexity of how those factors are interwoven is best understood upon further reflection of that ride Mosher took us on in the summer of 2010, when he showed us the factory with regard to which he and Phillis had been charged with the task of teaching their students well enough so that they would not have to go and work there. One would think that it would be mainly the male students that Mosher and his wife had to be worried about but with the evolution of the factory system, there developed simultaneously a particular feature that would prove a greater danger to the females who, for example in Sinclair's novel, were there for the "men who sought pleasure" and would be in high demand

> so long as they were young and beautiful; and later on, when they were crowded out by others younger and more beautiful, they went out to follow upon the trail of the working men. Sometimes they came of themselves, and the saloon-keepers shared with them; or sometimes they were handled by agencies, the same as the labour army. They were in the towns in harvest-time, near the lumber camps in the winter, in the cities when the men came there; if a regiment were encamped, or a railroad or canal being made, or a great exposition getting ready, the crowd of women were on hand, living in shanties or saloons or tenement rooms, sometimes eight or ten of them together.[18]

That scenario is not so much different from Meiselas's description of the carnival strippers who "work out of a traveling box, a truck that unfolds to form two stages, one opening to the public carnival grounds, another concealed under a tent for a private audience. A dressing room stands between them."[19] The lumber camps and the stockyards, of Sinclair's novel, have somehow created an environment where young women are drawn to facilitate, in sometimes the most lascivious ways, the sexual desires of men who perform the dreariest jobs of an encroaching modern industry. Needless to say in such situations, there is always, for the young women, a lurking danger that could spring forth at any moment at the hands of drunken customers.

Even Sinclair's main protagonist, Jurgis, who at one point in the novel might have been characterized as having as much morality as the best of men, finds himself, after having been beaten down by the stockyards, nodding at a saloon girl whereupon they go upstairs to a room and the "wild beast rose up within him and screamed" as he found himself willing to take advantage of her unfortunate situation. The nature of such circumstances grows even uglier in Mosher's novel when Marie, after having left the Benedict home, ventures out into the world and finds herself applying for a job at a saloon in Pond in the Sky. The name of the village would seem to be synonymous with everything glorious that humankind might partake of within the realm of God-given nature. But nothing could be further from the reality.

The saloon at which Marie is applying for a job is owned by a man named Bull Francis who owns pretty much everything and, not coincidentally for Mosher's purposes, is also the justice of the peace. In other words, he is the law. Whatever he does is part and parcel of a code by which all others will be forced to abide. What he has done, in his saloon, is hang a gilded cage from the ceiling within which the girls he has hired are expected to dance for an array of customers including railroaders, loggers, and salesmen. So, when Marie comes to him for a job, his first question to her is, "How are you at dancing?" Desperate for work, Marie responds that she has been dancing since she was three years old. What she will later learn, however, is that the sadistic tendencies of the customers include cutting and biting the dancers and putting out cigarettes on their bare legs. The full horror of the situation becomes all too clear to her one night when a searing pain comes tearing through her left heel and she spins around to find that one of the drunks has actually reached through the cage and is stabbing at her with his lighted cigar, trying to burn her again.

That scene brings back to mind Meiselas's photo-documentary work and the stripper Lena who tells of the time when "one guy and four of his buddies grabbed hold of me and he pulled a knife, a long knife, and was going to stick it inside me cut me open."[20] Lena would, more than likely, have been seriously injured had another stripper, Patty, not rushed to the scene and "kicked the guy's head." As if drawn from the pages of Meiselas's book, Mosher's Marie renders a similarly

• II. *Female Vulnerability* •

violent response, kicking out two of her attacker's teeth, thus preventing him from doing any more damage to her body. Policemen, who should have felt themselves responsible for Lena's safety, stand by and watch in amusement much the same way that Mosher's Justice of the Peace Francis stands by and watches the heinous goings-on in his establishment.

The ability of the public, and public officials at that, to behave in such a manner has to do with how young women in the situations of Lena and Marie are perfunctorily relegated to a low social status. Lena, thinking back to the time when she first started dancing, remembers how the "townspeople thought I was a whore already—even when I was a virgin, they considered me a slut."[21] Of course, Lena will eventually evolve into prostitution. But even as she does, we are made to ponder what Ona Rudkus's cousin, Marija Berczynskas, had to say about the matter. Jurgis, shocked that Marija has become a prostitute, listens as she offers the stark rationalization that "when people are starving ... and they have anything with a price, they ought to sell it."[22] So many of the Lithuanian immigrants who came over with her have fallen into abject poverty, or even worse died, that the mere fact of her survival is, in a sense, a testament to her success. She goes so far as to tell Jurgis that he should have long ago accepted what the state of things was and supported his own wife's involvement in what Marija has concluded would have been a viable solution for all the economic problems visited upon the Rudkus family including dangerous working conditions, poor housing, homelessness, jail, and ultimately the death of everyone in the Rudkus family except Jurgis Rudkus himself.

Marija presents the situation as one of inevitability along the lines of what we witness in Stephen Crane's 1893 novel *Maggie: A Girl of the Streets* where Maggie's neighborhood is described:

> Long streamers of garments fluttered from fire-escapes. In all unhandy places there were buckets, brooms, rags and bottles. In the street infants played or fought with other infants or sat stupidly in the way of vehicles. Formidable women, with uncombed hair and disordered dress, gossiped while leaning on railings, or screamed in frantic quarrels. Withered persons, in curious postures of submission to something, sat smoking pipes in obscure corners.[23]

Howard Frank Mosher and the Classics

What is being described here is a tenement section of New York's Bowery district, distinct in American history for the poverty and anger and resulting antagonisms and physical confrontations, both within the home and outside in the streets. The novel begins with Maggie's young brother, Jimmie, being pelted by "howling urchins" who are throwing rocks at him for no reason other than to vent the frustrations of their daily life. When that brother makes his way back home, his sister confronts him, accusing him of what she calls "allus fightin'," as if the altercation he was in was all his fault. Having been thusly accused by her, he "struck" her and, while she retreated, he "advanced dealing her cuffs." But it is not just the children who fight this way. The mother, Mary, goes into fits of rage at the least provocation. The father tells Jimmie, "I can never beat any sense into yer damned wooden head."[24] And neighbors, perhaps the same "formidable women" who lean on the tenement railings, muse at the regularity of it all, wondering who's "beatin'" who "dis time."

Not that those formidable women's lives are any different than the lives of the Johnsons. Critic David Fitelson in fact contends "it is self-evident within the novel that violence is the predominant form of human communication."[25] It is against this backdrop that Maggie ventures out to get a job. We are told in the fifth paragraph, of Chapter 5, that she found work in a collar and cuff factory where she, along with 20 other girls, "treadled at her machine all day." In retrospect, we could assume that such a job is not so bad; but before we jump to such a conclusion, it is best to hear what those, of the social worker persuasion, had to say with regard to women who would have been in Maggie's employment situation. One such observer, the Reverend T. De Witt Talmage, laments, in his 1872 treatise *The Abominations of Modern Society*, that in New York City alone, there were "thirty-five thousand sewing girls." Rising before dawn and going on little or no food, they went to factories where they would be severely overworked and drastically undercompensated, without even the five-cents fare to catch a "city-car."

It is of great significance that, also in Crane's Chapter 5, just before he tells us that Maggie got such a job, we are informed that the child Maggie has "blossomed" into a "pretty girl" and men have begun to leer and make comments along the lines of "Dat Johnson goil is a puty good looker." Yet, Maggie must still go out to work. The alternatives, as the Rev-

• *II. Female Vulnerability* •

erend Talmage puts it, are "starvation or dishonor." For Maggie's brother Jimmie, starvation is not an option as he orders her, in the fourth paragraph of that Chapter 5, to either "go teh hell or go teh work," perhaps not realizing or perhaps not caring, as he issues the ultimatum, that the work itself will be just another version of the hell that he suggests is something she should avoid.

Of course, the hell to be avoided, as far as Jimmie is concerned, is the one that exists for girls out on the streets. Such a result would spell the beginnings of a certain death of the soul, a death that, though not biological, would amount to psychological, indeed spiritual devastation. Yet, I find Daniel Cottom's essay "Maggie, Not a Girl of the Streets" quite instructional here. In that essay, he draws parallels between the "grisette"—a feature of French society from the mid-seventeenth through the mid-nineteenth centuries—and Maggie working at the collar and cuff factory. The grisette type, as Cottom describes her, was "always poor, always pretty" and proud of her independence as "a young worker." But then Cottom goes on to say that the grisette nonetheless had a keen awareness of her condition because "she goes to work, she takes pride in her independence—and she knows ... what pride goeth before, not only in Christian homiletics but also, and more compellingly, in the world of modern work."[26] Yes, the biblical Proverbs 16:18 does stipulate that "pride *goeth* before destruction," that word "destruction" meaning many possible forms of devastation, one of those forms of devastation reflected in what Talmage refers to as a "death-groan .... a slow, grinding, horrible wasting away." Such was the fate of Sinclair's Ona, as a young woman in the world of factory work; and such might have been the fate of Mosher's Marie had she not barely escaped.

Indeed, it might also have been the fate of Dreiser's Carrie who, before she got her job at the shoe factory, had tried to get a job at the cap factory, Speigelheim & Co., which was

> a place rather dingily lighted, the darkest portions having incandescent lights, filled with machines and work benches. At the latter labored quite a company of girls ... drabby-looking creatures, stained in face with oil and dust, clad in thin, shapeless, cotton dresses.... They were a fair type of nearly the lowest order of shop-girls—careless, slouchy, and more or less pale from confinement.[27]

That word "confinement" draws our attention back to the furniture factory where Marie begins working and then finds herself about to drown in a Hell's Gate varnishing vat. In her case, the gatekeeper had been Abie Benedict. At Carrie's prospective place of employment, the person who will decide whether or not she gets the job is a foreman who banters back and forth with her over the likelihood of her employment, finally offers her three dollars and fifty cents a week and then, while she contemplates that meager offer, he "look[s] her over as one would a package," as if enjoying, even before she has the chance to work there, the fact that he has already locked her into a cage of sorts where he can enjoy her as nothing more than an object.

Carrie does not work at the Speigelheim company; yet, the shoe factory, where she does eventually work, offers little respite since, as I alluded earlier, the foreman there is not much better than the one at Speigelheim's. Ona's vulturous supervisor had exacted sexual favors from her and, we get the sense, was on the verge of leading her toward prostitution. That process in *Sister Carrie* is altered somewhat and, relatively speaking, more subtle as Dreiser has the foreman, at the shoe factory, touch "the shoulder of one of the girls" as he makes his rounds, lurking like a "shadow," threatening, we might imagine, to fire someone with whom he is not satisfied as he "passed slowly along, eyeing each worker distinctly." Carrie soon loses her job at that factory when she falls ill for three days. She then later gets another factory job that still promises to be no better than where she had worked before. Unlike what was the case with Ona, Carrie will be rescued by a virtual stranger, Charles Drouet, who extends twenty dollars to help her along. At first, she refuses the money but when Drouet tells her to just think of it as a loan, she accepts it but, in doing so, "felt bound to him" as if the loan was a down payment on some long-term transaction from which she will later feel the need to extract herself.

Crane's Maggie evolves into the world of prostitution, and it would seem that Carrie has at least been saved from that. But as Dreiser's protagonist moves from one male benefactor to another, first Drouet and then George Hurstwood, we wonder at the extent to which she has been commoditized by what the critic Charles Harmon calls "the miniaturizing quality of cuteness" that "can plausibly be seen as having very sig-

• II. Female Vulnerability •

nificant cultural ramifications. Indeed, from the broadest vantage, cuteness can be seen as being instrumental to the stabilization of capitalism itself."[28] Dreiser makes it a point to consistently remind us that Carrie is beautiful. That is what has Drouet and Hurstwood competing to win her affection.

But beyond those two men is a whole world of others who are also quick to assess her based on that one characteristic. As she begins her climb up the ladder toward becoming a successful actress, her fate is determined by those such as the manager at the Casino who "judged women as" one might judge "horseflesh." Even after she has become an established actress, she cannot escape evaluations of the sort rendered by a theater critic who only had to say, of her performance, that she was "merely pretty, good-natured, and lucky," luck having been achieved, one might assume, from the prettiness that everyone evidently noticed about her before they noticed anything else. Writing in 1900 for *Century* magazine, the New York City actress Clara Morris declared, "Many a woman who works for her living must eat with her bread the bitter salt of insult."[29] Morris's essay is an eye-opening assessment from one who had been employed in the acting profession over the course of forty years beginning in the early 1860s and, now in retrospect, she was, in that aptly entitled essay "A Word of Warning to Young Actresses," doing just that, "warning" actresses what to beware of, especially actresses of the youthful and pretty variety. What Morris, at one point in her essay, urges is that such actresses, in order to survive, turn a deaf ear "to those hyenas." However much it might seem like Carrie has risen to a level that is above such male response, the reality is that she is but another version of Mosher's Marie Blythe dancing in Bull Francis's gilded cage, another version of the strippers that Meiselas found dancing on the stages of Vermont's carnivals and county fairs.

It is all too much for Sinclair's Jurgis to bear, particularly once he learns that his wife's supervisor has led her down the road to prostitution. Upon receiving that knowledge, Jurgis immediately stalks off to where the supervisor Connor is working and beats him to a pulp, the consequences of which action will lead to his incarceration and a decline from which his family will never recover. In Mosher's novel, Marie's response to Bull Francis's demand that she be a prostitute is not so much different from Jurgis's response to Connor, except Marie does not physically attack her boss. Instead, when Francis tells a group of his dancers that he has arranged for a "special railway car" to take them to the Wenlock camp to give the boys up there a "good time," she boldly rejects the offer, declaring to the boss, "I don't intend to go up to Wenlock or to any other place for that purpose. What the rest of the girls do is their business, but I won't be on that pleasure excursion."[30] She stays and dances at the Pond House while the other girls are carted off to Wenlock, but before the night is over, she is set up anyway and arrested for "soliciting customers," an obvious retaliation on the part of Francis. In fact, it is Francis himself who sentences the accused to a full six months in jail, though solicitation is something that she had never even contemplated doing.

Later in the evening, on that summer day when Mosher had driven us to the factory, I went home and immediately checked my computer to see if there was indeed any such town, in Vermont, that went by the name of Wenlock. I discovered, to my surprise, that it does exist, just 38 miles directly east of the factory. I envisioned young women being shuttled back and forth across that distance, with their aim being to satisfy in various ways the men who worked at those industrial enterprises—the factory and the logging camp. I wondered where the young women might have come from, how many would have escaped if they could have, but might have been just like Marie who wanted to escape her situation but could not, for the life of her, fathom "where to go."

After reaching Wenlock, I then googled all the Vermont towns that Meiselas had visited during those long hot summers of 1973, 1974, and 1975. All small towns. But one in particular, Barton, stuck in my mind for some reason that I could not fathom until I combed the pages of the photo-journalist's book one more time and was reminded that it was Barton where Lena was attacked by five men while she danced, four holding her down while one of them tried to slice her with his knife. This place, Barton, which could so easily and might indeed have been the Pond in the Sky of Mosher's novel where Marie got stabbed with a lighted cigar while she danced in a gilded cage. And while I searched those places on the computer, I pondered all the addictions that I had heard so many girls were enduring in this state that is filled with quite a few small quaint towns that draw tourists from all over the country to

II. Female Vulnerability

marvel at their idyllic beauty. Heroin, I have been told, is the addiction, in particular, from which a large number of young women suffer. But it might as well have been the morphine to which Marija is addicted in *The Jungle* or the alcohol the girls need, in Meiselas's photo-documentary, in order to get up there on the dance stage, or the laudanum to which the "sad girls" in Mosher's novel have become addicted to help them cope with their Pond in the Sky predicaments.

Where was Barton? As I thought of all that, it became more and more imperative to find out, if Wenlock was only 38 miles away from the factory, then just how far away was Barton? When I learned that it was only five miles south of the factory, I suddenly understood just why Mosher had lingered, parked so stoically right in front of the building where men had lost their fingers and perhaps were in need of some kind of entertainment even if performed by souls lost themselves, the men and women together, all participating in a time-worn ritual so that, at least for a moment, they might forget where fate had led them to reside.

· III ·

The Journey to Salvation in Bunyan's *The Pilgrim's Progress* and Mosher's *Walking to Gatlinburg*

As I was interviewing Mosher for this project, it came out that I attended the University of Virginia, a rather famous institution nestled in the Blue Ridge Mountains. Mentioning the school was my way of comparing the Blue Ridge to the likewise wondrous green mountains where the author's home of Irasburg is located. But he made the connection an even deeper one as he explained to me that both the Blue Ridge Mountains and the mountains of Vermont are part of one long mountain range, extending from New England down through part of New York and Pennsylvania, West Virginia, Kentucky, Tennessee, and past Virginia on into North Carolina.[1] Of course, Mosher's characterization of the single mountain range is a geographical fact. Yet, the perspective that it is all just one long mountain range is especially useful, in the literary sense, as one contemplates what the author had in mind with his creation of the character Pilgrim Kinneson.

In fact, more than the mere presentation as a character in Mosher's work, Pilgrim is notable for being someone who disappeared. As Jane Hubbell Kinneson tells it, in *On Kingdom Mountain*, he "ran away to war, and we heard nothing of him until his commanding officer reported him missing in Tennessee."[2] As I mention in Chapter I, the reason he ran off to war had to do with both romance and religion. His parents,

III. The Journey to Salvation

devout Presbyterians, vehemently objected to him marrying a French Canadian Catholic girl. Her parents objected just as vehemently and, according to Jane Kinneson, the girl was so anguished that she "vanished," ran away never to be heard from again. That was when Pilgrim, as a consequence, disappeared too. Shortly thereafter, Jane's father, just a 17-year-old boy at the time, took off in search of his older brother. Jane, however, seems not to have learned much about the details of her father's search, nor for that matter what ever became of her Uncle Pilgrim.

The details would nevertheless be forthcoming in Mosher's next novel, *Walking to Gatlinburg*, where the parental dictates, against matrimony as pertains to the young lovers, are the same as what was revealed in *On Kingdom Mountain*. A significant difference, though, is with regard to which of the lovers disappeared first. In *On Kingdom Mountain*, by Jane's account, it was the Catholic girl, Manon Thibeau, who vanished first. In *Gatlinburg*, however, it is Pilgrim who vanishes first, thereby laying an important foundation for the idea that a great deal of what occurs in *Gatlinburg* is for the purpose of reinforcing some key points evidenced in the English writer John Bunyan's seventeenth century allegorical tale, *The Pilgrim's Progress*. The first part of Bunyan's work, published in 1678, is a recapitulation of Christian's journey from the worldly City of Destruction to the heavenly Celestial City. It was not until the second part of the work, published in 1684, that Bunyan's audience would learn of Christiana's trek to the same spiritual destination. It is thus appropriate that, well over three centuries after Bunyan's Christian "began to run," Mosher's Pilgrim would start his own journey away from a world that held so little promise for the fulfillment of his soul. Mosher's Manon, like Bunyan's Christiana, would be compelled to make the same journey later.

The religious conflict, as presented in *Gatlinburg* with the situation of the two forbidden lovers, is reminiscent of Bunyan's own personal dilemma as he, in 1660, was confronted with the governmental stipulation that he either preach in accordance with the rules of the Anglican Church or not preach at all. King Charles II was particularly worried that preachers of another denomination might actually be only using their religious position to undermine his royal authority. Bunyan was known to have preached anywhere, in a cornfield if necessary, and when he was arrested for doing so, he accepted his imprisonment as the price to be paid for his insistence on spreading the Word in the manner he felt he had been ordained, by God, to do.

Contemporary scholar of religious studies E. Glenn Hinson conveys the depths of Bunyan's decision:

> He paid a great price for his persistence. His second wife, Elizabeth, pleaded three times for his release in 1661, reminding the judge that she had four small children, one blind, who could not help themselves, and "nothing to live upon, but the charity of good people." It is not difficult to imagine how Bunyan agonized over his decision .... The discomforts of a foul prison that had no fireplace and only a straw bed troubled him less than did his family's plight.[3]

Bunyan would ultimately serve a 12-year prison sentence with the greatest irony being that it was all over a disagreement about how a Puritan might want to worship in a country that was dominated by the Anglican religious persuasion. The whole matter was absurd, but then again we are reminded that America was founded by many people who had taken it upon themselves to flee from such religious persecution. The irony persists, though, as we are made to consider that the parents of Mosher's Pilgrim, in all likelihood, are descendants of immigrants who fled Europe in pursuit of religious freedom and yet those parents did not believe quite enough in religious freedom to accept the marriage of their son to a woman who was Catholic.

It was Pilgrim who fled Kingdom County, Vermont on a quest that would take him through numerous dangers and lead him headlong into the Civil War and then, once he was miraculously extracted from that conflict, lead him into further dangers; however, it is through Morgan's journey, in pursuit of his brother, that we experience the significance of a process that Mosher feels is essential for his reader to absorb as the means whereby we ourselves might be able to arrive at the most important destination to which any human could ever aspire. In a sense, Morgan's search is our own search in much the same way that Bunyan had advised, at the beginning of *The Pilgrim's Progress*, that "this Book will make a Traveller of thee, if by its Counsel thou wilt ruled be."[4] Bunyan had meant for his text to be, through a series of parables, a look at how one who undertakes to be successful, in the Divine quest, must proceed.

• III. The Journey to Salvation •

Likewise, Morgan's quest is a parable, for though he is in search of his brother, the search has a much deeper meaning, a meaning akin to the painstaking progress that Bunyan's pilgrim achieved, rendering that text a spiritual guidebook within which one receives information on certain strategies whereby the traveler can successfully negotiate the treacherous terrain that Bunyan so accurately characterized as the "wilderness of this world."

The Christian walk is filled with all sorts of dangers, not the least of which is the Christian's own psychological pondering on what the mechanism will be for his salvation. The simple resolution to that issue is that Christ died for the sins of the world and if one believes that, and conducts himself accordingly, then he is thereby saved. And yet in spite of the apparent simplicity, many are inclined to ask questions about the nature of the journey and why it seems, far from being simple at all, a rather arduous journey from both a physical and intellectual standpoint. One must, in the final analysis, rely on faith and this is what, in our all too human state, is inclined to sometimes waver.

Another specialist in religious studies, Benjamin Berger, acknowledges this difficulty and accordingly maintains that "Bunyan does not portray Christian as a man of unshakable faith or even of particularly staunch belief."[5] It is a quite profound commentary that this Christian who left behind a wife and children, to take this journey, is nevertheless not one who is possessed of "unshakable faith." This is what, in Berger's mind, lends a necessary suspense to Bunyan's novel because, from a Calvinist perspective, the goal of salvation has already been preordained for Christian, but the literary quality of the novel is achieved because "the dynamics of the text, as one might call these peaks and valleys which spot the novel, consist of Christian's movements between faith in the divine and cognizance of his own innately human imperfection."[6] Indeed, the "peaks and valleys" serve as metaphors, for the Christian struggle, as they indicate the trials and tribulations that Bunyan's pilgrim must face, those same "peaks and valleys" becoming, in Mosher's text, not only symbolic of the struggle but also, quite literally, the range of mountains extending from the northernmost parts of Vermont down through the mid–Atlantic states and on into the South, encompassing so much of what comprised the United States during the Civil War era.

It does not take long, once Bunyan's pilgrim has undertaken the quest for salvation, for him to arrive at the foot of a place called Hill *Difficulty*, the manifestation, in physical terms, of what the author sought to convey about just how hard it is to achieve the goal of heaven. In Matthew 19:24, Jesus had warned the disciples, "It is easier for a camel to go through the eye of a needle, than for a rich man to enter into the kingdom of God." In other words it is hard for someone, who has acquired vast worldly possessions, to simply give it all away even if it is Jesus who is telling him that this is the way to heaven. When the rich young man is instructed, by Jesus in Matthew 19:21, to "sell that thou hast, and give to the poor, and thou shalt have treasure in heaven," that young man chose to hold on to his worldly goods in lieu of what seemed, to him, a much more vague type of treasure to be acquired at an equally vague point in time.

But it is not just the rich who have this difficulty. The apostle Paul, in Romans 3:10, declared to the breadth of the world, "There is none righteous, no not one." That profound declaration speaks to the very innate nature of a sin-sick world that, without the benefit of spiritual guidance, is doomed as Paul puts it so bluntly in Romans 6:23, declaring, "For the wages of sin *is* death."

We witness a choice being made by Bunyan's pilgrim as he elects to stay on the straight and narrow path. Others, two characters in particular named Formalist and Hypocrisy, have jumped a wall to get where Christian is, preferring to take this short cut that they have heard of as having been pursued "for more than a thousand years." And now as they stand alongside Christian at the foot of Hill *Difficulty*, they too seek the kingdom of heaven with its eternal life, but they also observe that this hill is "steep and high" and so, in accordance with how these two men are by nature, they look for shorter, easier routes, one of those routes having been named *Destruction*, the very thing the apostle Paul in Romans 3:16 declared, contrary to being a legitimate route, as actually being an impediment to the successful Christian's progress.

One of the things that Bunyan conveys about the Christian journey is that the road indeed is narrow. Making his way up Hill *Difficulty*, the Christian pilgrim begins running but then grows weary and falls asleep, this state of rest being a condition that the dutiful Christian can

• *III. The Journey to Salvation* •

ill afford since evil is all around him, waiting for the opportune moment to strike. Christian receives this message, as he sleeps, with a voice "saying, *Go to the Ant, thou sluggard; consider her ways, and be wise.*"[7] Having been told, essentially, that he is a lazy pursuer of the Christian way, this pilgrim is thus jolted into wakefulness and "sped on his way" along the narrow path that stretches out before him toward the hill's summit.

The potential to be distracted from the path is one that Mosher evinces in *Gatlinburg* as he has Morgan go off in search of a moose for supper, leaving his Underground Railroad passenger, Jesse Moses, vulnerable to be captured by slave hunters. In presenting his own version of the righteous path that a man should take, what better issue to raise, in conjunction with humankind's multitudinous moral dilemmas, than the circumstances of slavery and the Civil War? In handling those issues in his novel, Mosher has the benefit of a setting, Vermont, with a rather striking history. Having abolished slavery in 1777, Vermont was fertile ground for the establishment of Underground Railroad stops, conducting slaves through the mountains on toward freedom in Canada. When the Fugitive Slave Act of 1850 was passed into law, to be applied to the whole United States, the Vermont state legislature deemed it an abhorrent law and, before the year was out, had passed its own Habeas Corpus Law making it hard for the Fugitive Slave Act to be enforced within the state's borders.

What the Fugitive Slave Act demanded of states was for law enforcement officials to assist—once an escaped slave had made it to the North—slave catchers in recapturing that slave. Not only were northern officials forced to assist slave catchers, but ordinary citizens were also required to assist or else be subjected to a fine and possible imprisonment, whether those ordinary citizens believed in slavery or not. I asked Mosher, "So, if slave catchers came into Vermont, ya'll wouldn't have helped 'em?" With not the slightest hesitation, the author gave me an answer in the clearest terms: "Help 'em! We'd a shot 'em."[8] In my entire interview with Mosher that day, it was his most abrasive comment, as if he had to say it that way, in that particular tone as a response to what, I now understand, was an unretractable insult.

Morgan loses track of the moose and is heading back toward the cabin, where he has left Jesse, when he hears two gunshots and, like Bunyan's pilgrim at the foot of Hill *Difficulty*, is jolted back to a state of alertness. Like that Christian of Bunyan's novel, Morgan has some instinct for the straight and narrow path that he should be on. The latter character's distraction, with the moose, is not much different from Bunyan's Christian who falls asleep on his mission only to be awakened to the evil all around him, in Morgan's case that evil being the slave catchers who, while Morgan was out hunting moose, have killed Jesse. Bunyan's pilgrim had sped up the hill and now it is Morgan who, upon hearing the gunshots, "SPRINTED BACK UP the mountain": and, in spite of the path being completely covered with snow, is able to nevertheless detect that path by looking at the "narrow opening" between the tops of the trees, that narrow path being Mosher's version of the narrow road that Bunyan's pilgrim must adhere to if he is to ever make his way to the Celestial City.

Transporting escaped slaves along the Underground Railroad stops becomes a metaphor for the narrow road to salvation, but it is quite significant that Morgan, at this point in the novel, is a mere 17 years old, still a child who is substantially in need of guidance. He has learned much about life from his older brother Pilgrim, but not nearly as much as he needs to know, and thus begins his journey to find out what exactly became of that brother who went off to war after having been denied the opportunity to marry Manon. Word was that Pilgrim had been at the Battle of Gettysburg and was now somewhere in the mountains near Gatlinburg. The path is no longer a northerly one as Morgan is now determined to go in a southerly direction along what Mosher would assert is just one long mountain range, one long path that, albeit linear in nature, is more importantly a moral trail upon which the individual must stay as a necessary part of his spiritual development.

Literary critic Kathleen Swaim points to the complexity of that development in *The Pilgrim's Progress* as she examines, in the novel, a character named Evangelist. Evangelist may have been based on Bunyan's own spiritual mentor, John Gifford, who was for a long time the pastor of St. John's Church in Bedford, England. In Bunyan's novel, Evangelist is the one who, early on, offers the pilgrim direction and is able, Swaim argues, to:

• III. The Journey to Salvation •

demand the hero's trust and mediate his acceptance of the call to adventure.... He gains Christian's trust and willingness to leave behind all that has been familiar and safe in favor of a dangerous unknown future. Christian is isolated, lost, diffusely anxious, socially and psychically disoriented until his herald's catechizings force him to articulate his contradictory feelings, reenvision his predicament, and transmute his negative motivations to a positive one.[9]

Morgan, in *Gatlinburg*, is likewise disoriented as he flees from one of the slave catchers. It is then that he encounters a "country priest" who just so happens to be riding in a rather mysterious sled pulled by two bay horses. This priest is Mosher's version of Bunyan's Evangelist, and the priest is apparently directing Morgan toward where some of the most brutal battles of the Civil War are being fought. Morgan, as I indicated earlier in this chapter, had been heading north, and so the priest had urged him to change his course, advising him, "You're headed in the wrong direction, I must tell you."[10]

That is when Morgan painstakingly writes a letter to his parents, announcing that for a time, that he himself is uncertain of, he will be gone away from home so as to pursue the heavenly course. It is what Bunyan's Christian had to do when he left his wife and children behind in order to undertake a journey that was more important than even them. It is what Christ Himself provided in Matthew 19:29 when he stipulated, "And every one that hath forsaken houses, or brethren, or sisters, or father, or mother, or wife, or children, or lands, for my name's sake, shall receive an hundredfold, and shall inherit everlasting life." By undertaking his search for Pilgrim, Morgan is forsaking mother, father and homeland for a task of paramount importance. The quest Morgan undertakes, that is learning the road that his older brother took, is in essence the younger brother being involved in the effort to save his own soul, a journey that indeed every person must undertake for himself. And the journey is one that must substantially be made alone.

Bunyan's pilgrim, traveling along his mountainous path, encounters numerous evil foes that, quite often, are found in the lower valleys of his route. In the Valley of Humiliation, he battles the formidable Apollyon, an arch devil, who is at the point of killing Christian until, drawing upon his faith, the pilgrim gives him a "deadly thrust" with his sword, dispensing of that evil "for a season." At the Valley of the Shadow of Death, fiends envelope Christian and are at the point of tearing him to shreds until, drawing on prayer, Christian is able to escape. At Vanity Fair, the pilgrim is imprisoned on trumped-up charges and then put on trial with a jury consisting of members with names like Cruelty, Live-Loose Lyar, and Enmity, with the trial itself being presided over by a judge with the name of Hategood. But through the gift of "he that overrules all things," Christian escapes that situation too.

Morgan, on his journey, is faced with the prospect of having to fend off entities who are just as vicious as the worst of Bunyan's villains. *Gatlinburg*'s Steptoe, for example, boasts of having killed "more than a dozen young girls and keeping their bodies preserved in a Pennsylvania icehouse so he could violate them repeatedly."[11] Dr. Surgeon brags that by "introducing infection into open wounds, conducting unnecessary amputations and prescribing lethal dosages of arsenic drops he had killed more Union and Confederate soldiers than any ten roaring cannons."[12] As had been the case with Bunyan's pilgrim negotiating his way through some of the most heinous evils of the world, Morgan must be ever vigilant so as to survive the atrocious tactics of people like Steptoe and Dr. Surgeon who, at various points of the novel, in some form or another, seem about to catch up with our hero.

As I have indicated before, Bunyan's tale is substantially allegorical and it serves us well to consider Mosher's novel in a likewise vein, as a tale meant to convey some deeper message beyond the mere details of its characters and settings. One of the more striking bits of evidence for this approach to reading the latter author's work is when Morgan encounters a tortoise that, rather uncannily, is able to talk. Even more uncanny is the fact that his name is Pilgrim. Morgan had been on the verge of eating the tortoise until that animal exchanges, for his life, both the promise to tell Morgan where to look for his brother and the promise to explain how the town, where they are now, first got its name.

During his lecture at Aldrich Library, Mosher offered an explanation for how the tortoise came to be included in the novel. As he was driving along, on a research trip near Gettysburg, a snapping turtle was crossing the road, so the author pulled over, stopped the car, got out, picked the turtle up, and was about to carry it to safety on the other side

• *III. The Journey to Salvation* •

of a fence, when another driver pulled up, shouting, "Put that reptile down!"[13] This other driver had misunderstood Mosher's purpose in picking up the turtle and thus we are given, by the author himself in recapitulating that story, the means whereby a tortoise got to appear in *Gatlinburg*.

As it turns out, the town where Morgan now finds himself is a place called Mason Or Dixon, a play on words intended to represent the historic Mason-Dixon Line which supposedly separates the northern part of the United States from the southern part. The line was established by surveyors Charles Mason and Jeremiah Dix, to resolve a boundary dispute over a problem that was discovered in 1681, that problem being how if the then existing border between Maryland and Pennsylvania had been allowed to stand, then the city of Philadelphia would have been in the former colony instead of the latter. Mason and Dixon's four-year surveying project resolved that problem, but the absurdity of the prospect that Philadelphia might have wound up in Maryland is actually just a reflection of the more general absurdity that a line drawn between two colonies, as a way of dividing the future country in two, would have been thought of as a necessity.

In telling his story, the tortoise—legendary in world culture for his wisdom and longevity—conveys the tale of how there were once two Alexander brothers, one named Mason and the other named Dixon. They settled the town but then argued for more than 40 years over what to call it. Should it be called Mason or should it be called Dixon? Here they had been living in a town created out of nothing, arguing the whole time over what to call it until "finally old man Mason Alexander, who was upward of ninety, walked up to his tottering brother and shot him down in the street to settle the dispute once and for all."[14] As bold an act as that was, it still did not settle the dispute. In fact, later that evening Dixon's oldest son, bent on getting revenge against his uncle, shot and killed him, establishing a feud that would carry on within the Alexander family for four generations, decimating that clan and rendering the town, that the Alexander brothers had worked so hard to settle, now a place that was unlivable for either their progeny or the progeny of anybody else.

The tortoise's story about Mason Or Dixon is reminiscent of the mythic tale of how Romulus and Remus founded the city of Rome but then argued over which of two hills should be the site for that city. Romulus built a fence (or wall, depending on which version of the legend is being told) to establish a boundary around his hill. When Remus leapt across the boundary, Romulus killed him and thus the city, that they jointly established, received its lasting name from the brother who was able to survive what was actually a ridiculous conflict, no less ridiculous in fact than the imprisonment of Bunyan for practicing a different denomination of Christianity than that which was espoused by the leadership of England. No less ridiculous than the idea that two sides of one country would fight across the boundary of an artificial line and engage themselves in a four-year-long bloody conflict, viewing that as an alternative better than resolving the matter peacefully before half a million people got killed.

Like so many of the guides in Bunyan's text, the tortoise of Mosher's novel provides spiritual guidance through his allegorical tale. But, as is the case with the guides in Bunyan's work, the tortoise gives geographical direction too, telling Morgan where to go to inquire further about his brother Pilgrim. Pursuing the direction that he has been told, Morgan encounters Jesse Moses's granddaughter and together they come upon one of Thomas Jefferson's black sons, now an old shoemaker living quietly on a Virginia hillside. With Jefferson having never freed his black children's mother, historians are coming to question more and more what was the nature of the relationship between that slave owner and Sally Hemings. For example, legal scholar Annette Gordon-Reed offers the following analysis:

> We might say that if a master really loved a slave, he would free that person so that there was no master-slave relationship. We may think this because we have a romantic idea that love makes people unselfish, strong, and brave enough to stand openly against all convention. Sometimes it does, and sometimes it does not. Many white men have acted (and do act) selfishly and cowardly in their relationships with black women. This does not mean that none of these men had (or have) feelings that we would not recognize as a form of love.[15]

There are many ways that one might interpret what must have been a complex situation that existed between Jefferson and Hemings, but from

III. The Journey to Salvation

the perspective of their son, as Mosher presents him, it was a profound tragedy that Jefferson did not free her and all of his other slaves. Had he made such a bold move, other Virginia statesmen would have followed his lead and once the war broke out, the state of Virginia would have been so inclined in the direction against slavery that it would have remained with the Union even while the southernmost states were seceding. Consequently, Robert E. Lee would have accepted President Lincoln's offer of a military appointment and then defeated the Confederate Army in a matter of months, sparing the country the trauma of an elongated civil war from which it, in all likelihood, will never completely recover.

As far as Mosher's version of Jefferson's black son is concerned, the nation's third president might well have saved us from the Civil War had he but acted differently, in his own time, with regard to the issue of slavery. He wished to be on the side of righteousness but, like Mr. By-Ends in *The Pilgrim's Progress*, wanted also to "jump in my Judgment with the present way of the times whatever it was."[16] Often when white slave owners are analyzed, from a retrospective historical standpoint, it is suggested that they were nothing more than the product of their times, limited by social custom. But what Bunyan's Christian insists from By-Ends is that—if he wants to travel with him and his companion Hopeful—he "must go against Wind and Tide." As it turns out, this is something that By-Ends is unwilling to do, declaring instead, "I shall never desert my old Principles, since they are harmless and profitable."[17] Christian and Hopeful continue on their journey toward salvation, leaving By-Ends behind to consort with others of his ilk, Mr. Money-love and Mr. Hold-the-World who is in particular agreement with By-Ends and urges, "Let us be wise as Serpents .... let us be content to take fair weather along with us."[18] Needless to say, By-Ends and his companions will not make it to the Celestial City, perishing as they do at the Hill Lucre silver mine, perfect examples of what can happen when one ignores the warning that Christ gave His disciples, in Matthew 16:26, "For what is a man profited, if he shall gain the whole world, and lose his own soul?"

Having one's soul saved is what is at the heart of both *The Pilgrim's Progress* and *Gatlinburg*, and the shoemaking son of Jefferson gives us some insight into how this is done as he asks Morgan to deliver some shoes, he has made, to Robert E. Lee, to be worn by Confederate troops so they will not have to go barefooted. Morgan's initial reaction is to not want to be of any assistance whatsoever to Lee's troops. Nevertheless, he feels compelled to honor the cobbler's request if for no other reason than payment for the kindness that the old man has rendered him. Viewed a certain way, one might be inclined to conclude that the shoemaker is betraying the Union cause. But viewed another way, what the shoemaker is doing is preserving his own humanity.

We learned, in *On Kingdom Mountain*, that after Morgan had returned to Vermont, from his search for Pilgrim, he came upon one of the Confederate culprits of the St. Albans bank robbery. Morgan secretly nursed him back to health, although he "never did trust the fellow," and helped him escape into Canada from where he presumably found his way back to the South. In that novel, Morgan expressed how, in spite of "befriending" the Rebel captain he did not feel that he had "transgressed" in any way since he had been raised under the family credo that one should be a friend to *all* mankind. Jefferson's black son might be said to be functioning with a similar sense of duty to mankind as he cuts against the grain, of the conventional wisdom of his times, in order to give shoes to the needy, that giving having been done for the simple reason that his position as a shoemaker makes it possible for him to do so and it was the proper thing to do for someone who calls himself a Christian.

Bunyan's Christian, at the point where he meets By-Ends, has already established a relationship with Hopeful that amounts to a "brotherly covenant" on the journey to the heavenly city. It is a curious matter, however, that Hopeful only appears after Faithful, Christian's previous companion, is executed by authorities at the town of Vanity. The witnesses who testified against Faithful were Envy, Superstition, and then finally Pickthank who explained to the judge how Faithful had spoken against the gentry of the town, those gentry including a sordid assortment of individuals with names such as Vain Glory, Carnal Delight, and Lechery. The death, of course, is not really the end of faith, for faith, in the final analysis, has only been transformed as is evidenced with Christian seeing "a Chariot and a couple of Horses, waiting for *Faithful*, who (so soon as his adversaries had dispatched him) was taken up into it, and straitway was carried up through the Clouds, with sound of Trum-

III. The Journey to Salvation

pet, the nearest way to the Celestial Gate."[19] By killing off this allegorical version of faith, Bunyan is providing his own interpretation for I Corinthians 13:13, where the apostle Paul instructs the church, "And now abideth faith, hope, charity, these three; but the greatest of these is charity." By having Faithful meet the end that he does, in *The Pilgrim's Progress*, Bunyan is seconding Paul's declaration of just how important charity is, for it was Paul, in I Corinthians 13:2, who himself stipulated in the profoundest of terms that "though I have all faith, so that I could remove mountains, and have not charity, I am nothing."

In the third verse of that same chapter, Paul acknowledges those who give of themselves to feed the poor. Paul then draws a fine line of distinction that is very much similar to what Mosher seeks to convey in his analysis of the Underground Railroad when he has Morgan, reflecting back on the various conductors and stationmasters he has encountered, remark "how each conductor seemed to have a different reason for helping fugitives reach Canada and how, in some cases, those reasons had little to do with a hatred of slavery or a love of universal freedom."[20] Paul expressed that if he were to feed the hungry, but not do it with a charitable spirit, then it "profiteth me nothing." In the case of Underground Railroad conductors, it can be assumed that there were indeed some conductors who had no particular love for blacks, or their rightful place of equality within the spectrum of humanity, and nevertheless they helped slaves get out of the South and on the road to freedom. While there were conductors who held a firm belief that all human beings were born equal in the eyes of God, there just as certainly were other conductors who transported slaves as a means of giving in to a certain type of vanity. This last type of conductor, in spite of outward appearances, actually lacked the prerequisite intent for charity that Paul had in mind when he spoke of such charity as being above and beyond even faith and hope.

Margaret Soenser, in assessing gender roles in Bunyan's work, argues "that spiritual authority rests ultimately with men in *The Pilgrim's Progress* is apparent from the narrative shift half way through Part 2, away from the immediate concerns of Christiana's 'progress' and toward guide Great-heart, who, in the remainder of the text, seeks out and vanquishes four giants."[21] Christiana, whom I mentioned earlier, is Christian's wife who, "some years" after her husband started off for the Celestial City, undertakes the journey for herself and, with the aid of her guide Great-heart, takes on quite a few physical challenges along the way. Not only taking on physical challenges, she also, even before she had begun the journey, had the intestinal fortitude to fend off an objecting Mrs. Timorous. Mrs. Timorous had not wanted Christiana to go whereupon that latter woman, referring to her husband declares, "I am now as he was then; nothing will serve me but going on Pilgrimage."[22] It will be remembered, moreover, that it was Christiana herself who was something of a guide for Mercy who was at first a reluctant traveler but then winds up becoming a shining example of charitable giving, investing particularly in the poor as she defends herself against the worldly pretender to religion, Mr. Brisk, who desired, more than anything, that she become his wife. When Brisk inquired as to how she could possibly gain any benefit from working so hard for the poor, Mercy replied, "I do these things … that I may be rich in Good Works, laying up in store a good Foundation against the time to come, that I may lay hold on Eternal Life."[23] That certainly does not sound like someone who lacks in spiritual authority. In fact, it sounds exactly like what Paul had in mind when he wrote in I Corinthians with regard to the real meaning of charity.

This issue of authority also arises in *Gatlinburg* with a character named Mercy Johnson, a runaway slave whom Morgan saves from horrible abuse at the hands of northerners. Mercy had run away from a Tennessee plantation, made it to the North where she was sexually abused and, upon being rescued by Morgan, vowed to go back south to the plantation from which she had previously escaped. One might be tempted to conclude, from that scenario, that Soenser is correct about spiritual authority resting with men, considering how it is Morgan who tells Mercy that he has an idea that is better than going back to the plantation. But what we are also told about Morgan at this point is that he is a man at war with his "former self," a man who is as much in search of direction as is his companion Mercy. As he had done with a previous female companion, Birdcall, he will leave Mercy with a woman named Mother Bremmen who lives high up in a tree because she has decided to "shun the earth" with its inherent evil. Mercy, in Mosher's novel, will

• *III. The Journey to Salvation* •

ultimately receive direction from a source similar to that from whom Bunyan's Mercy receives her direction, the guide in the case of both of those women being yet another woman who herself is divinely inspired.

That sense of divine female inspiration is a trope with which Mosher is particularly comfortable as he, in *On Kingdom Mountain*, has Morgan's daughter Jane, an elderly woman herself by this time, perceive the Holy Trinity in a cluster of three chestnut trees. One of the trees is hollow and in that hollow is the body of an immaculately preserved Civil War soldier. How the soldier came to be preserved and who he is exactly is a mystery, but Jane quickly suggests that he be called Pilgrim, not because she thinks he is her father's brother but because of the universality she believes should apply in terms of the human quest, in general, for salvation in a sin-filled world.

At a much earlier point in time, indeed in *Gatlinburg*, Morgan had asked Jefferson's black son whether or not a man named Pilgrim had passed by this way, to which the cobbler answered, "No man that I know of named Pilgrim traveled this way lately headed either north or south. Yet I have met many a pilgrim on many a long hard progress."[24] Within that cobbler's response is perhaps the most direct reference that Mosher offers to Bunyan's novel, but just as importantly, the cobbler brings to mind Jane herself for whom it was not so important whether or not the Pilgrim in the chestnut tree was Union or Confederate as much as the shared humanity that, within the context of the Holy Trinity, he represents. Similarly, we are made to ponder, when the cobbler says he has not seen Morgan's brother in particular, whether it is more important that there have been "many" pilgrims along the way for whom geographical direction—north versus south, for instance—is not as important as is the direction that their soul is taking.

Lodged on Kingdom Mountain until her final days on earth, Jane had arranged to have carved, on her tombstone upon her death, words with which Bunyan's Mercy and Mosher's cobbler would have been in complete agreement. There on her tombstone are the words, "Live each day not as though it is your last, but as though it is the last day of the lives of the people you meet."[25] It can be quite a task, trying to live each day to the fullest, as if it is your last. How much more incredible it would be to dedicate oneself to treating others as if they were in the midst of their last day on earth. One can only imagine the extraordinary amount of kindness that would be kindled if people en masse treated each other with such a degree of altruism.

I was so overwhelmed by the phrasing of the epitaph that, immediately after Mosher finished his Aldrich Library lecture, I went up to tell him that it was among my favorite quotes in all of his books. That was when he informed me that it was one of his wife's sayings whom he had stolen it from and given voice through the fictional character Jane. When I spoke later with Phillis Mosher, herself, I verified that it is indeed one of her sayings. My curiosity now peaked even further, I asked if she indeed lived that way, to which she answered, "I try."[26] As our interview proceeded, I learned some of the details of how, over the years, she has taken into her home quite a few people (adults and children) who were in need of not just physical sustenance but the kind of emotional and spiritual nourishment that can only be gleaned from someone who believes in putting into action the words that would become Jane's epitaph.

It is useful here to consider what another scholar, Sylvia Brown, had to say about *The Pilgrim's Progress* being an offshoot of the Bible. She argues that

> the ultimate proof of the fertility of the Word is that it can produce more words. This image of the breeding, multiplying text extends beyond scripture to all spiritually efficacious books. The Bible reproduces the body of Christ through the spiritual rebirth of its readers, but it can also spawn other evangelizing texts, able to carry the transcendent Word, which may do the same reproductive work. Sermon texts, books of practical divinity, spiritual autobiography, instructive allegories like *The Pilgrim's Progress*: these are often simply called "good books" and their goodness lies in their fertility.[27]

The Pilgrim's Progress is a text that was, of course, heavily influenced by the Bible. For example, a refrain from the former text, "Blessed is the man that feareth always,"[28] is clearly meant to reiterate the message of Psalms 112:1 wherein it is stated, "Blessed is the man that feareth the Lord." The mere fact that Bunyan's primary travelers are named Christian and Christiana is perhaps the most glaring proof that events in the Bible were the driving force behind Bunyan's work.

• *III. The Journey to Salvation* •

As she is nearing the end of her journey, Christiana meets up with Mr. Valiant-for-truth whose own parents had tried to stop him from setting out for the Celestial City. Valiant-for-truth confides, "Why, they told me that it was a dangerous way; yea, the most dangerous way in the World, said they, is that which the Pilgrims go."[29] Mosher's Pilgrim is further evidence of just how dangerous the journey is. While we, as readers, do not see much of Pilgrim's trek in detail, we do see what his road must have been with all of its attending dangers, for the brother Morgan was following in Pilgrim's Underground Railroad conducting footsteps up in Vermont and we saw how the younger brother barely escaped death at the hands of the devilish slave hunters. As he journeys south in search of his older brother, he experiences kindness from some people but he also encounters the devastating aftermath of kangaroo courts, raids on civilians, and military battles so bloody that it is hard to comprehend how anyone could say it was their side that was the victor.

By the time he has reached the Blue Ridge Mountains of Virginia, Morgan is making his way, quite delicately, along a "series of ridges called Satan's Staircase," so wondrously beautiful and yet so potentially deadly as, further along, he comes to "peaks" in those same mountains that are a "devil's puzzle of tier upon tier separated by deep gulfs and troughs and roughs splaying out in every direction."[30] The phrases "Satan's Staircase" and "devil's puzzle" are not inadvertent terms employed by Mosher but they are intended to convey the same sense of things that Bunyan meant to impart as he had his pilgrims trek through the Delectable Mountains where there awaited Knowledge, Sincere and the divine shepherds but also Ignorance, Mistrust and Guilt. Having arrived at the Delectable Mountains, pilgrims are in sight of the Celestial City and yet they are as much in danger as they had ever been.

Morgan eventually finds his brother Pilgrim high up in the Smoky Mountains just outside Gatlinburg, Tennessee. The older brother had chosen to stop here in performance of that part of the mission similar to what Bunyan's Mercy was compelled to do in giving her time and energy to helping the poor. It is what Jefferson's cobbler son did as he made shoes for the unfortunate soldiers of Lee's army. High up in his "delectable" mountains, Pilgrim gives his gift of expertise to those who had the least access to medical care.

Howard Frank Mosher and the Classics

Yet, like Bunyan's Delectable Mountains and Mosher's Blue Ridge Mountains, the Smoky Mountains are equally dangerous. In fact, some version of a slave hunter is still on Pilgrim's trail, regardless of how determined the medical practitioner is to settle down into a self-sacrificing, peaceful existence. When Mosher's Pilgrim is finally felled by a gunshot fired by the slave hunting villain, it seems at first to be a tragedy beyond redemption. Morgan had traveled so far to find his brother and then, once locating him, must watch him leave this world in such a brutal way. But just as was the case in Bunyan's novel, Mosher's Pilgrim should not be thought of as dying but instead as just moving away from a place that, in the words of Bunyan's Hopeful, "notwithstanding all the righteousness thereof, is in a state of condemnation."[31]

• IV •

Good, Evil, and the Mystery of Life in Mosher's *Disappearances* and Melville's *Moby-Dick* and *Billy Budd*

Disappearances, Mosher's first published novel, is a work that traces the vanishing of William Bonhomme's family, a process that began with his ancestor, René St. Laurent Bonhomme who had come down out of Canada in 1796, on a brandy-smuggling expedition and wound up establishing the village of Kingdom Common, the first institution in that village, of course, being a local tavern. When he decided to disappear, many years later, he asked his granddaughter Cordelia to take one last trip with him on Lake Memphremagog, that body of water signifying a hybrid, being partially located in Canada and partially located in the United States. It is significant that René's granddaughter is named Cordelia because in asking her to go along with him, he is able to perceive what Shakespeare's Lear could not ascertain about his daughter Cordelia who, though declining to profess her love to him verbally, actually loved him more than did her two sisters who only professed love so as to acquire vast portions of his kingdom.

It will indeed be René's last trip, that we know of, because at a certain point while they are paddling north on the 27-mile-long lake, he tells her to stop, whereupon they eat lunch and, afterwards, he appears to have drifted off to sleep. Cordelia quietly leaves to go pick some blueberries but, when she returns, the old man and the canoe are both gone. As that story is being recounted to William ("Wild Bill") by his father ("Quebec Bill"), the boy William leaps to the conjecture that René must have drowned and then was buried back at the homestead where there is a gravestone with René's name on it and the dates of his birth and death. Quebec Bill, however, corrects his son, telling him the truth about the headstone:

> "He ain't under it, Bill. He could have set the canoe adrift and then went off in the woods. A man could easy enough get turned around in these big woods even today. Old René wouldn't have though, not unless he meant to. Maybe he meant to. However it happened, they never found a trace."[1]

This ability to disappear is one that Cordelia will in time acquire, and thus one is made to wonder whether that capacity is more a blessing or a curse. Quebec Bill had himself mastered the art at the age of 16 when he shot two men and then disappeared for many long years, venturing far and wide, from Boston to Seattle and then back eastward to Denver for a while until he decided to return home to Vermont whereupon he would learn that all eleven members of his family were gone, themselves all disappeared.

Mosher's novel is set in the year 1932, which is quite some time before Wild Bill will declare that Kingdom County "had disappeared" and that America itself "is disappearing." And yet, this process of disappearing was begun perhaps—just as Melville's Ahab had declared to Starbuck of their hunt for the whale Moby Dick—"a billion years before this ocean rolled." It was on the second day of the chase that Ahab had rendered that statement to his first mate, after the White Whale had disappeared into the sea for the second time, presaging the final day of the chase when practically everyone and everything will disappear, sent by Moby Dick down into the oceanic depths, leaving only Ishmael alive to tell the story that, having been told in all its vivid detail, still winds up being more a mystery than the revelation we as readers might have wished for.

Just as Captain Ahab felt compelled to undertake his search for the great White Whale, Quebec Bill is compelled to make his journey back to Canada for the whiskey that he will be able to bring back, across the border, into Vermont and then sell so that he will have the needed funds to continue the operation of his farm. Prohibition is in force, so such an undertaking is illegal, but it is the only way, after he has tried everything else, for him and his family to survive. William S. Gleim, in *The*

• IV. *Good, Evil, and the Mystery of Life* •

Meaning of Moby Dick, characterized Melville's novel as "fundamentally a parable on the mystery of evil and the accidental malice of the universe. The White Whale stands for the brute energies of existence, blind, fatal, overpowering, while Ahab is the spirit of man, small and feeble, but purposive."[2] That universe, to which Gleim refers, is of course indecipherable and yet mankind has been engaged, throughout the millennia, in the effort to not only survive but to also glean at least a modicum of understanding about the realm within which he exists, why he is here and what exactly is his mission.

In the throes of the Great Depression, Quebec Bill's mission ostensibly is to go get the liquor, bring it back, sell it and thereby get the money that he needs. But when one considers how this whiskey-running operation has been going on for more than a century, all the way back to the time of René Bonhomme, the mission takes on the appurtenances of something quite similar to what Melville's Ahab had inherited. Before electricity became a widespread commodity, whaling was one of the largest enterprises in America just as whiskey-running, at one time, was one of the largest enterprises in the northernmost part of Vermont. And just as *Disappearances* is about much more than just people disappearing or the enterprise of running whiskey, so too is *Moby-Dick* more than the story of a sea captain's quest to gain vengeance against the whale that bit off his leg.

The name "Ahab" itself is problematic. Looking at it from a biblical perspective, he is regarded as one of the most evil of Israel's kings, having married the less-than-moral Jezebel and then gone so far as to allow himself to fall so much under her influence that he becomes a pagan worshipper. Afterwards, he accepts her idea for acquiring land even though it will mean not only the death of the previous landowner but also the deaths of that landowner's heirs. Nevertheless, God offers Ahab numerous opportunities to repent, and indeed he finally does go through the motions of repentance. Yet, the moral of this story is that there is something in man that cannot entirely avoid his own evil nature, and so God, though putting off for a time His retribution against Ahab, will inevitably invoke retribution against this king who remained, until the end, still not quite able to adhere to the expectations that God had laid out before him.

Howard Frank Mosher and the Classics

As preordained, King Ahab will die in battle against the Syrians and be made, in essence, to disappear from the face of the earth. Melville's Captain Ahab is described in the novel as suffering from monomania, so focused is he on finding the whale. The captain calls himself "more a demon than a man" and even earlier he had pronounced, "I'm demoniac." But before we declare him as being simply evil, which is how King Ahab is so often characterized, we must examine the captain's complexity, for while he does indeed declare himself a demon, he is also, as he himself puts it, like "Adam, staggering beneath the piled centuries since Paradise."[3] Melville's Ahab is obviously embroiled in inner turmoil, burdened as was Adam in all his human imperfection; and so we find the captain pleading to the stars, "Oh God! That man should be a thing for immortal souls to sieve through!"[4] What we are left with is a fundamental incongruity: the body of man, which must die, serving nonetheless as the receptacle for what we call the spiritual aspect of ourselves that we have not even the capacity to understand. This is why one of the primary benefactors of the Pequod can only say, in this regard, that Ahab "ain't sick; but no, he isn't well either .... He's a queer man ... but a good one. He's a grand, ungodly, god-like man."[5] That fumbling for words, through the mouth of Captain Peleg, gives voice to the contradictions that comprise the makeup of all mankind.

Moby Dick is just as unfathomable. At one point, Ishmael calls him a "mysterious monster," but then later he says that the animal's "mystical brow" is the signification of God. In exploring such ambiguity, Melville was quite fortunate to have had the example of a sperm whale to convey his message. In his chapter "Of the Monstrous Pictures of Whales," he goes into great detail explaining how so many visual depictions of the whale have been wrong, some portraits having him look like a dolphin while other portraits have him looking like a squash. Even Oliver Goldsmith's *An History of the Earth and Animated Nature*, a popular resource during Melville's time, showed the whale as looking like, in Ishmael's words, an "amputated sow."

We now, in contemporary society, have the technological equipment to see exactly what the whale looks like without having to actually go on a whale hunt which, Ishmael is quick to remind us, is so risky an endeavor as to likely end in our deaths. During the early 1840s, Melville

· IV. *Good, Evil, and the Mystery of Life* ·

himself was a sailor aboard the whale ship Acushnet and so had the advantage of seeing for himself "precisely what the whale really looks like." Yet, even that is not enough for an understanding of who the whale is. The author gives a great deal of detail to the process, once a whale is captured, of skinning the animal and extracting, from it, the blubber and spermaceti. But that whale is still a mystery, from its multi-faceted tail to its "broad firmament of a forehead" that consumes one third the length of its body.

Ishmael, the voice for Melville, draws our attention to that head as being especially intriguing in terms of the features that are either missing altogether or at least so situated as to render this sea mammal something destined to represent the supernatural. It has "no proper nose" and yet it can smell across vast distances. It has no ears and yet it can fathom, with a certainty, the numerous and varied ocean sounds. Its mouth is located under the head and is undetectable unless the animal projects itself entirely out of the water. And then there are the eyes, located distinctly on either side of this massive head, disconnected and yet so focused as to be "ubiquitous," allowing the whale to first submerge itself and then calculatingly reappear with "swiftness to the most widely distant points." When Ishmael tells us, further, that the White Whale not only moves swiftly from place to place but is capable of being in two places, "in opposite latitudes at one and the same time," then we as readers are moved to wonder, all the more, whether this "largest inhabitant of the globe" is mainly good or, on the contrary, mainly meant for evil.

This question of good versus evil is the quandary that we are faced with in *Disappearances* when we first encounter Carcajou whom the narrator observes was "the biggest man I had ever seen." That word "carcajou" is actually another name for the North American wolverine, but the wolverine itself is, in the words of Quebec Bill, "part bear, part skunk, part wolf. All of them and none of them."[6] Thus begins a mystery that will consume so much of the book as to make the relationship between that mysterious entity and Quebec Bill perhaps the most important one for our consideration. When we learn that Quebec Bill is twenty years older than his wife Evangeline, we are reminded of Captain Ahab's own "young girl-wife" whom he left to go whaling, just one day after their marriage. Both of those women are, like Faith in Nathaniel Hawthorne's

1835 short story "Young Goodman Brown," reluctant to let their husbands venture off and yet powerless to actually stop them from going out into the world where evil, in some form or another, is an ever present part of the reality.

In fact, when Carcajou first appears, it is to hijack liquor from two monks who are paddling in a rowboat, about to make a delivery for funds to keep their monastery functioning. These monks are significantly named Brother Paul and Brother St. Hilaire. The biblical Paul is credited with having written at least 12 of the Bible's epistles while the nineteenth century French deist Étienne Geoffroy Saint-Hilaire believed in God but also believed that man had to make his own way through a world that had laws of its own. The theoretical conflict between Paul and Saint-Hilaire finds itself reflected, though in quite a different way, in the two monks' differing perspectives with regard to the issue of smuggling liquor, a situation that only deepens in complexity with the arrival of Carcajou who might be said to represent an even greater evil—hijacking their liquor—than that evil personified in the monks who are merely violating the strictures of Prohibition. Brother Paul calls liquor-running an "ungodly business," to which Brother St. Hilaire responds with some consternation, "This ungodly business is going to put the monastery on a paying basis."[7] The conversation itself brings back to mind the distinction to be drawn between the deist Saint-Hilaire and the Apostle Paul, one drawing upon the laws of the world to make his point, the other drawing upon the word of God. When Carcajou arrives to, in a manner of speaking, settle the dispute, we are left wondering, as had been the case with Moby Dick, what exactly to make of it all.

Quebec Bill and his son are watching, from shore, as Carcajou is robbing the monks, and that father would have shot at the thief but for the fact that the monks were in the line of fire. Yet, even more interesting than that is how matter-of-factly Quebec Bill responds to the appearance of Carcajou in the first place, much like how Captain Ahab rather consistently renders the query to whatever ship's captain he encounters out on the sea: "Hast seen the White Whale?" Discarding his quadrant and compass, which prove ineffective as instruments to chart his direction, Ahab relies on some inner resource, combined with old "sea charts" and "log-books," to ascertain where Moby Dick will be. That captain had

· IV. *Good, Evil, and the Mystery of Life* ·

been on course, since the beginning of his journey, in the direction of the White Whale; and thus it is that when Quebec Bill calmly states, "Here he comes now," when Carcajou appears, the encounter seems to be what one might well have expected as the purpose to which Quebec Bill, for his whole life, had been assigned.

A further striking aspect of Carcajou is the color of his hair. As Wild Bill describes it, "his hair, which was totally white, fell out from under his cap over his shoulders and down his back to his waist."[8] The Wolverine, in the form of Carcajou, appears very much to be a man, but his large size and long, flowing white hair are reminiscent of the message conveyed by Melville in his "The Whiteness of the Whale" chapter wherein the author acknowledges that the color white has long been associated with ideals such as "gladness," "beauty," and even that which is holy. And yet, declares Ishmael with regard to this whiteness, there "lurks an elusive something in the innermost idea of this hue, which strikes more panic to the soul than that redness which affrights in blood."[9] We are left, by the end of that chapter, to wonder whether all the other colors are "but subtle deceits ... allurements," covering up "the charnel-house within," those colorful hues having been produced by "the great principle of light" that is in essence a "shroud" that the great White Whale has come to represent.

As it turns out, Carcajou is in competition with the LaChance family, a clan that consists of eight brothers, their father, and two uncles. Hoping to eliminate Carcajou from the hijacking business, the LaChances set fire to the cabin where Carcajou and his gang of albiners are holed up. After the cabin has been burned to the ground, the LaChances begin poking around in the embers, thinking that the whole gang had burned up inside when all of a sudden "Carcajou and his white boys sprung up out of the root cellar where they said no human man could possibly have survived and mowed down five of them on the spot with machine guns, including the father and uncles. The ones that made it to the woods said all the while the machine guns was a-clattering Carcajou was laughing a laugh like they never heard before and never wanted to again."[10] Before it is all over, four more of the LaChances are killed, leaving only two of that family left to report that Carcajou was "no human man." So, what exactly is he, if not a human? As he laughs his way hideously through the slaughter, he is like the White Whale who wreaks destruction on Ahab's crew, boat by boat, "satisfied" on day two of the chase "that his work for that time was done," taunting old Ahab to dare come at him again, something the tortured captain, through some mysterious design of Fate, must be compelled to do.

Unaware of all that has happened, Quebec Bill's brother-in-law Henry Coville is persuaded, by the surviving LaChances, to rob Carcajou. It is Bill who informs Henry of how Carcajou killed the LaChances. The LaChance brothers' goal had been to manipulate Henry into taking a chance on stealing from the potentially devastating inhuman. Put another way, first the LaChances try to kill Carcajou who, in turn, kills most of the LaChances, the survivors of whom employ Henry to rob Carcajou. That chain of events, as absurd as it might seem, is no more absurd than Ahab's recognition, near the end of Melville's novel, that "we are turned round and round in this world, like yonder windlass, and Fate is the handspike."[11]

Once he has been made aware of the reality of the situation, Henry seeks to avoid what Fate has ordained and he adamantly declares, "This run is off.... We're going home." The brother-in-law is to Bill what Starbuck is to Ahab. Before the first day of the chase, Starbuck pleaded, "No more! It is done! We head for Nantucket! Come my Captain, study out the course, and let us away!"[12] By the end of the second day, Starbuck is begging Ahab to stop chasing the enigmatic whale:

> "In Jesus' name no more of this, that's worse than devil's madness. Two days chased; twice stove to splinters; thy very leg once more snatched from under thee; thy evil shadow gone—all good angels mobbing thee with warnings:—what more wouldst thou have?—Shall we keep chasing this murderous fish till he swamps the last man? Shall we be dragged by him to the bottom of the sea? Shall we be towed by him to the infernal world?"[13]

The Parsee is that shadowy figure to which Starbuck refers when he declares "thy evil shadow gone." But it would be much too simple a matter to say that, once Moby Dick has submerged the Parsee underwater, evil is thus eliminated. Paul, in Romans 7:25, put it this way in terms of a certain complexity: "with the mind I myself serve the law of God; but with the flesh the law of sin." Such a duality is present as Captain Ahab offers up a Spanish doubloon to the first person who sights the White

· *IV. Good, Evil, and the Mystery of Life* ·

Whale. On that coin are three mountain "peaks as proud as Lucifer" while at the same time they are "peaks, that almost seem the Trinity." As Ahab considers the coin, in all its golden roundness, we begin to understand exactly how much it signifies the world with all of its inhabitants, a world where good and evil arise in ways that, in terms of trying to draw a clear distinction, really turn out to be not so clear at all.

When examining a novel such as Melville's *Billy Budd*, the distinction between what is good and what is evil would seem to be a rather clear one. The critic Robert Narveson relies substantially on Revelations 12:9–10 to make his point that John Claggart is the representation of evil, for in that passage the accuser has been cast out of heaven and, as Narveson argues, "it should now be clear that in choosing the name *Claggart* Melville has managed to suggest ... that there is something vaguely unpleasant about the person bearing it, and that the person is to be associated with Satan."[14] The accuser in those biblical passages is "that old serpent, called the Devil, and Satan, which deceiveth the whole world" and thus "the accuser of our brethren is cast down, which accused them before our God day and night." Claggart is the master-at-arms aboard the H.M.S. *Bellipotent*, who as soon as the foretopman Billy Budd is impressed into service, has evil intentions. It is not long before he will accuse Budd of conspiring to commit mutiny which, in times of war such as these, could result in a death sentence for the accused. Narveson further asserts that "the common word for an accuser in German is *Anklaeger*; in Dutch it is *aanklager*. The German root word *Klaeger*, meaning 'complainer,' is very similar in pronunciation to *Claggart*."[15] Considering that Claggart, as his name suggests, is of "mysterious" origins, it would thus not be unreasonable for one to conclude that not only are those origins foreign—that is, not English—but also that his intentions are tied to an evil nature.

Melville himself would seem to make the same argument as, in Chapter 11, he offers us his own narrative contemplations about evil as pertains to Claggart. In trying to reach conclusions, he draws upon, for assistance, John Calvin, Plato, an unknown mentor whom he refers to as "an honest scholar," and even Ann Radcliffe whose 1794 *The Mysteries of Udolpho* influenced Jane Austen as she wrote *Northanger Abbey* (1818), a novel in which good people—at least in the mind of *one* of the characters—suddenly turn into villains. After all his ponderings, in that Chapter 11, the narrator comes to conclude that there is a certain ambiguity, and possibly an insanity, involved; and as far as Claggart is concerned there exists "the mania of an evil nature, not engendered by vicious training or corrupting books or licentious living, but born with him and innate, in short 'a depravity according to nature.'"[16] Thus, as far as Melville is concerned, evil is not learned from books or even from one's own experiences, however horrendous they might be; but, instead, the capacity for evil is something that is an integral part of man's "innate" condition.

A vital source for the creation of *Billy Budd* was most likely the events that occurred aboard the American ship the *Somers*, in 1842, when a young midshipman, Philip Spencer, boarded and was immediately confronted with, as James Fenimore Cooper reported in his book *The Cruise of the Somers*, "the first development of that prejudice which met the young officer, almost as soon as he crossed the gangway of the brig to join her."[17] On that ship, Claggart had his alter ego in the form of First Lieutenant Gansevoort who, as would later become a turning point in Melville's novel, charged Midshipman Spencer with conspiring to mutiny. Cooper further attests that Gansevoort's "own version and opinion of the alleged project, was sent among inferior officers; and, long before the sun went down, it became the subject of 'dry' joking among some of them .... it is important, as illustrative of the blundering rashness of the lieutenant, and of the eagerness with which any tale against *Mr. Spencer* would be received."[18] The sense we get from Cooper's report is that Gansevoort was intent not only on falsely accusing Spencer but also spreading that accusation in the form of gossip, a story that others aboard the ship will help him disseminate with a certain "eagerness" and even humor. Cooper is quite specific, furthermore, in conveying that this gossip-spreading phenomenon was pretty much complete "long before" sunset which only serves to reinforce, for us, just how eager others, aboard ship, were to have a part in the spreading of the tale, with no concern for veracity, only that they are on the side of self-preservation in the midst of a brewing human storm.

That storm is brewing also in *Billy Budd* as Claggart's general bad feeling toward the young sailor begins to spread, like a congenital sick-

• *IV. Good, Evil, and the Mystery of Life* •

ness, among many of the crew "with whom [Billy] had never exchanged a word, his position in the ship not bringing him into contact with them, these men now for the first began to cast upon Billy ... that peculiar glance which evidences that the man from whom it comes has been some way tampered with, and to the prejudice of him upon whom the glance lights."[19] Men, with whom Budd has had virtually no contact, have nonetheless come to adopt the feeling of resentment that perhaps began with Claggart but, then again, perhaps had always been there within the gossiping men lurking, just as Red Whiskers, aboard the *Rights-of-Man*, had been lurking, waiting for the right moment to attack one whom he thought of as a "sweet and pleasant fellow," that was Budd himself. In that instance, when Red Whiskers attacked, Budd "[q]uick as lightning ... let fly his arm" and gave his assailant a "terrible drubbing," the major difference between Claggart and Red Whiskers being that one man was a superior officer, with built-in authoritative influence, while the other man was, more or less, Budd's equal. We are told, after Red Whiskers has been beaten, that he now loves Budd. Either that or he is a "hypocrite" in the matter, a possibility that looms just as dangerous, for Budd, as when the older man decided to hit the "Handsome Sailor" in the first place.

In his essay "'Too Good to Be True': Subverting Christian Hope in *Billy Budd*," Lyon Evans, in reference to Red Whiskers, observes that "it is not very likely that the gangleader of the ship, soundly beaten in a fight, and in front of the other men, would subsequently love the person who had whipped him."[20] Evans goes on to suggest that it is not love that Red Whiskers and some of the other members of the crew feel for Budd, but instead fear. It is, in fact, quite intriguing to watch, on the *Rights*, as shipmates of Budd darn and wash his clothes, and the carpenter "at odd times" works on a chest of drawers. It reminds one of the high school scene, in more modern times, where the star athlete is loved not because he is nice but because he is stronger and more popular than anyone else and thereby entitled to have others doing favors for him on a regular basis. His girlfriend is the pretty cheerleader of whom other girls are, at once, envious and admiring. Budd, with his physical power and uncommon beauty, is the athlete and the cheerleader, all rolled into one, and thus not the Christ-like figure that many readers of the novel see him as being, but instead a man who at times seems to be innocent but who, in actuality, has serious flaws in his character.

Melville, in the novel, likens Budd to the "beautiful woman in one of Hawthorne's minor tales." We can speculate that the minor tale, to which Melville has reference, is "The Birth-mark" (1843) where the beautiful Georgiana has but one flaw that is a small red birthmark, in the shape of a hand, on her cheek. Her husband Aylmer, who is a brilliant scientist, concocts a potion that will remove the mark but as the mark slowly fades from his wife's cheek, she dies. It is significant that Aylmer had earlier had a nightmare in which he cut out the mark and then kept on cutting all the way to her heart. That nightmare, combined with the later death of Georgiana, would suggest that such a mark, or imperfection, cannot be absolutely eliminated any more than the imperfection in man can be eliminated, because mankind is not only not all good but he, even as evidenced by the best among us, is still possessed of a certain evil that one would have thought existed only in the worst of us.

Georgiana has her birthmark and, for Budd, the imperfection is a stutter that Melville describes as a "striking instance that the arch interferer, the envious marplot of Eden, still has more or less to do with every human consignment to this planet of Earth. In every case, one way or another he is sure to slip in his little card, as much as to remind us—I too have a hand here."[21] There can be little doubt that what Melville is saying here is that the same entity, that caused the Fall of Adam, exists in us all. In his essay "Melville's Snake on the Cross: Justice for John Claggart and *Billy Budd*," Jonathan Yoder points to ambiguity in Melville's presentation of Claggart but then urges us also to consider that "Billy's characterization is equally ambiguous—with a dominant signal subverted by secondary signs that Billy joins Claggart as a human mixture of good and evil."[22] One of those signs is Billy's stutter. Another sign, however, is that when Claggart falsely accuses Budd of conspiring to commit mutiny, Billy's "cheek looked struck as by white leprosy." It is quite telling that the "white leprosy" appearance is on his cheek, for it reminds us where Georgiana's birthmark was and what it represented.

But perhaps even more profound a comparative example is the biblical Miriam, sister of Moses, who criticized him for marrying an Ethiopian and, as a consequence, was punished by God and "*became* leprous,

• IV. *Good, Evil, and the Mystery of Life* •

white as snow" (Numbers 12:10). One imagines that Georgiana could have had a long and productive life, even with the birthmark serving as a reminder of the presence of evil. In Miriam's case, though, it is not a minor blemish but the contagion leprosy which will surely consume her entire body, probably sooner rather than later. The "white leprosy," for the moment, appears only on Budd's cheek, but it is important to note that it is leprosy which is likely to spread over his entire body, metaphorically speaking, as it will literally spread over Miriam's body. That image of spreading leprosy brings us back to a consideration of the whiteness of Melville's whale and the whiteness of Mosher's Carcajou. And in that consideration, we are once again brought to the issue of ambiguity or what Evans calls "the problematic man." Whiteness would ordinarily symbolize positive attributes along the lines of what Ishmael had indicated when, in *Moby-Dick*, he noted that it is usually associated with things such as "gladness" and "beauty." Yet, we recall, Ishmael also warned us that in such whiteness "lurks an elusive something ... which strikes ... panic to the soul." By the time we reach the end of *Billy Budd*, we are presented with two quite disparate perspectives on the now deceased Handsome Sailor. One version, of the events in question, labels him an "assassin"; the other version insists he was "incapable ... of willful murder." And it is some middle ground, between those two versions, where we find ourselves searching for the elusive truth. What we do learn from *Billy Budd* is that the evil in the matter is far closer to us all than what we would have liked to think.

During his Aldrich Library lecture, Mosher made the startling announcement: "Anyone who tells you fiction is not based on real people is a liar."[23] It was not the words themselves that were startling, but how the author said them so adamantly from a personal perspective, drawing from his own ancestry to make a critical point. Then he put a slide picture up on the screen to show us what was left of a building that had been practically blown to pieces. Most of us in the audience were shocked to learn what the author had actually conveyed some months earlier in an interview that he gave to accompany the release of *Walking to Gatlinburg*. In the novel, we follow Morgan Kinneson on his quest, against the odds, to find his missing brother but, as Mosher informs in the interview, "Morgan's chief antagonist, the villainous minstrel Ludi Too, was inspired—I'm sorry to say—by my great-great-grandfather, who attempted to murder his own family by dynamiting their home while they slept. Fortunately, great-great-grandpa was the only casualty, though the ancestral home looked like a runaway locomotive smacked right through the middle of it."[24] Mosher repeated something along those lines at the library talk, and one could feel the tension mounting in the audience at the thought that right here before us stood one of the nation's most gifted contemporary writers who had had a great-great-grandfather who had tried to kill off as much of his own family as he could.

One learns, over the course of time, not to ask too many personal questions. So there were questions indeed about the matter that the audience dared not ask. It was enough that the speaker had already shared so much with regard to his family background. But what we wanted to ask were questions such as: Was your great-great-grandfather insane? Was there any prior evidence that he was capable of doing such a thing—any warning? Were there others in your family who were so inclined, albeit to a lesser degree? Such were the questions we might have asked but we respectfully refrained and so left it all a mystery.

Then again, perhaps not so much a mystery, but as simple as what Paul stated when he said, in Romans 7:14, "I am carnal, sold under sin." One of the more enlightened characters, in James Weldon Johnson's 1912 novel *The Autobiography of an Ex-Coloured Man*, develops the point a bit more when he says that "evil is a force, and, like the physical and chemical forces, we cannot annihilate it; we may only change its form. We light upon one evil and hit it with all the might of our civilization, but only succeed in scattering it into a dozen other forms."[25] That white mentor to the novel's black narrator has particular reference to slavery and how the Civil War did not really destroy the evil institution but just "changed it" into other forms of hatred, not unlike how the escaped slave Babo, in Melville's 1855 novella *Benito Cereno*, is capable of doing great harm, both physical and psychological, not only to the ship's Spanish captain but also to blacks who were imprisoned on the ship. The captain had been a willing participant in the evil of slavery, but now that he has become the captive, a certain kind of evil will be perpetrated against him. By the time Babo has undertaken the deceptive strategy of conquering not one but two ships, it is difficult to assess the very nature of

• IV. Good, Evil, and the Mystery of Life •

evil as pertains to one man, Babo, who had been a victim of slavery and the other, Captain Cereno, who had been merely transporting the slaves without having really contemplated, as far as we can tell, all the intricacies of racial difference.

This idea of evil having been disseminated into "other forms" is evidenced throughout Mosher's work. One scene, in *Gatlinburg*, has Morgan Kinneson encounter the slave owner, Arthur Dinwiddie, upon whom the tables have been turned and he is now the captive of his former slaves who are busy torturing him while he is hung up in a cage. The former slaves are "holding a court" after which they will certainly kill him for his numerous crimes against humanity. When Morgan intervenes, chaos ensues with one of the former slaves manning a Gatling gun, accidently blowing up the boiler of a nearby cotton gin, forcing the slaves to plunge into the river where they are gunned down by "whooping" Union soldiers who took it upon themselves to shoot indiscriminately at "anything that moved." We are appalled at that chain of events, perhaps even questioning Mosher's authorial motive in having the Union soldiers themselves possessed of so much evil. One questions Mosher's motive until we remind ourselves that the author, in his writing, has not exempted anyone from the capacity of doing evil, including—from among our greatest presidents—George Washington, Thomas Jefferson, and Abraham Lincoln.

As important as it is to acknowledge that Mosher is an accomplished artist, it is also important to acknowledge that he is, equally, a gifted teacher. Not the kind of teacher who tells you how to think, but one who offers up a tale of life and then asks what your impressions are, much like Melville's Bartleby who, when asked to explain his behavior, only answers, "I would prefer not to." At his library lecture, Mosher referred to the slave catchers, in *Gatlinburg*, as five of the most evil people who ever lived, and we in the audience would have been quick to agree with that assessment but for the grin on the author's face that accompanied his statement as if he had just told us a riddle that he himself had not yet been able to figure out. His great-great-grandfather had tried to murder his own family and the implication was that the most evil character in *Gatlinburg*, Ludi Too, was based on that ancestor of Mosher's. But Ludi Too is also Oconaluftee, a name that Mosher came up with because he saw it, by happenstance, on a road sign during his travels. Mosher showed us a slide of the road sign and then said that once he saw the word, he knew that he would use it to portray an evil character. Why that particular word? one might ask, when there are hundreds of such intriguing words that the author encounters on his various travels. And why something so innocuous as a road sign, of the sort that he must have seen thousands as he drove, from place to place, along the byways of America?

This giving of different names to one entity is also reflected in the character Arthur Dinwiddie, that slave owner who is simultaneously Anno Domini or simply A.D., which could be interpreted to mean literally everyone born after the death of Jesus. While most of us would not wish to be associated in any way with a slave owner, we must nonetheless ask ourselves, considering that name A.D., if our capacity to do bad things is just as strong as that which was possessed by Dinwiddie himself who stands, in the metaphysical sense, for all our forebears in need of some salvation. If we are in some way meant to be similar to a slave owner, then we are just as likely meant to be similar to the slave catcher Ludi Too who, as we near the conclusion of *Gatlinburg*, claims a kinship with Morgan Kinneson, calling him "dear son" as he begs him to go ahead and inflict the mortal wound. When Ludi goes so far as to insist, "You must not forsake me in my hour of need *because you are me*," Morgan reacts with the profound exclamation "No!"[26] Morgan had come to the mountains, just outside of Gatlinburg, ostensibly in search of his brother Pilgrim, but even more importantly he has come here in search of himself. The harsh reality that Morgan is confronted with is stated quite well, in symbolic terms, by the critic John Matteson who draws a vivid connection between the White Whale and Melville's Captain Ahab:

> What Ahab can never grasp is that he and the whale are part of each other, spiritually wedded by their shared malice. The unity between Ahab and the whale is made clear by the fact that Moby-Dick has consumed Ahab's leg and that Ahab's new leg is fashioned from whale ivory. It is as if Ahab and Leviathan have traded parts and now belong to each other.[27]

We could quarrel with Matteson about whether or not Ahab grasps the connection between himself and Moby Dick. Considering that sea cap-

· IV. Good, Evil, and the Mystery of Life ·

tain's single-minded purpose, and the accompanying torment he suffers, one is certainly inclined to believe that he understands something just as Morgan himself must be beginning to understand the meaning of Ludi Too who never dies but just waits, with "great faith," knowing that Morgan "would arrive."

It is the same faith that Carcajou has in Quebec Bill Bonhomme, that he eventually will arrive. Henry Coville understands he cannot stop his brother-in-law. Even at the point where they have temporarily lost their weapons, Henry accepts the reality, acknowledging, "I know that won't stop you, Bill. I know nothing won't stop you."[28] Quebec Bill understands now that he has been set up, by the surviving LaChance brothers, to hijack whiskey from the hijacker Carcajou. Having not been dealt with honestly by the LaChance brothers, Quebec Bill is now intent on keeping the proceeds, from the sale of the eight thousand dollars' worth of whiskey, all for himself, Wild Bill, Henry, and Rat Kinneson who, in some ways, is like Melville's blacksmith Perth who found himself aboard Ahab's Pequod after alcoholism "robbed" him of everything from wife and children to home and the job that had formerly provided him with what once was an excellent lifestyle. Rat's rudimentary farmhand life leaves much to be desired as was the case with Perth whose "landed world" ultimately became so repugnant that he withdrew from it entirely and decided to go "a-whaling."

That Perth is an everyman figure, in *Moby-Dick*, becomes clear as we consider how he is but one of a varied assortment of men contracted to be part of the Pequod crew, ranging in nationality from French, Sicilian, Danish, English, African and Chinese, to Americans of the white, black and Native American persuasions. They might be said to represent the whole world, humanity that is, for as the critic Henry Myers stated the matter, in 1942, Melville did not "suppose that any gulf separated the whalers from ordinary people.... To Melville the repeated actions of the whalers—the search, the pursuit, the kill, the trying of the oil, and cleaning of the ship—seemed perfectly representative of life."[29] Myers is able to draw the connection between whalers and ordinary people because, as I have mentioned, whaling in those days was one of America's leading industries. Whalers were indeed everyman, an everyman specifically represented by Captain Ahab since, by the time of the second day of the chase, we are specifically told that, of the crew, "they were one man, not thirty." Whatever it is that Ahab represents, the whole crew is joined with him in that goal of first finding the White Whale and then attempting to destroy it.

Such is the quest of Quebec Bill as pertains to the villainous Carcajou. As reluctant as Bill's gang might have been to follow him at first, they are like the Pequod crew who are able to suppress their "fears and forebodings" and let the "growing awe of Ahab" dominate their psyche. They indeed have become one person for whom fulfillment in life has become synonymous with killing Moby Dick at all costs. As Quebec Bill's gang is escaping with the stolen liquor, Carcajou pursues and it is the son, Wild Bill, who shoots the Wolverine full of buckshot. One would think that Carcajou is now dead, especially since Quebec Bill assures his son that such is the case, that "half of Carcajou's face had been blasted away."

Yet, Wild Bill is not so sure that Carcajou is indeed dead. In spite of his father's protestations, the younger William cannot help but wonder why, when he shot the white-haired hijacker, he did not fall down but instead "just turned away" when such a shot should have "lifted [him] completely off his feet." So, now we see how Carcajou *should* have been burned alive by the LaChances and then, upon reappearing, *should* have been killed by a load of buckshot that was delivered directly to the head by Wild Bill. Those situations are very much like how Ishmael describes Moby Dick, "that after repeated, intrepid assaults, the White Whale had escaped alive ... that though groves of spears should be planted in his flanks, he would swim away unharmed."[30] By now, one thing is certain. Just as whale oil had not been the ultimate purpose of Ahab's quest for Moby Dick, whiskey is not the real goal of Quebec Bill's journey into Canada. In fact, less than halfway through Mosher's novel, "every bottle of whiskey" has been lost in the chaos of first a canoe chase, then a car chase, then a train hijacking by Quebec Bill himself who, when Carcajou appears this time, "skewered" him with a pike pole.

Actually, Quebec Bill attacked Carcajou in this way because the big white man was aiming his pistol at Wild Bill who thought he was being confronted by an officer of the Royal Canadian Mounted Police but found himself instead

• IV. *Good, Evil, and the Mystery of Life* •

staring into the face of a monster. Huge chunks of flesh had been torn away from it. The right ear was hanging by a few shreds of cartilage. Part of his right nostril was gone. The right eye socket was a leaking gelatinous pulp. His beard was stiff with dried blood. I could see a row of stubby dark side teeth through a hole in his cheek. When he opened his mouth to laugh I realized that he had no cheek at all.[31]

The two Williams as well as Henry and Rat all jump from the brakeless locomotive just before it derails, piling "seventy tons of steel" on top of the Wolverine, prompting Quebec Bill to declare that at least now they "don't have to worry about him no more." But Carcajou returns, again and again, as if he was the great White Whale reincarnate about whom Ishmael had already warned us that if he seemed injured even to the point where he spouted "thick blood," a person should not believe his own eyes because "such a sight" as a battered and bloodied Moby Dick "would be but a ghastly deception."

We will recall that on the second day of the chase, Moby Dick drags the Parsee down into the watery depths and Starbuck feels that, with this occurrence, Ahab has been freed from what had been tormenting him, and can now return home to Nantucket. But, shadowy figure that the Parsee was but one indication of, it can only be surmised that the captain will always be surrounded by phantoms that "seemed fresh formed out of air." Centuries before the birth of Christ, the Parsee was historically an adherent of Zoroastrianism, a religious faith wherein it was believed that the supreme god, Ahura Mazda, created twin spirits, one of whom sought truth and light while the other pursued lies and darkness. Now, Melville's modern-day Parsee has been dragged down to the depths by Moby Dick but he has not been eliminated from the face of the earth. In fact, as much as he was entangled with Moby Dick by the whale-line, it was actually more in the captain, Ahab, that the Parsee saw himself as a tormented soul trapped in between the poles of good and evil.

Truth be told, such is the fate of all humankind, negotiating that territory between the polar opposites of morality and immorality. And the gray area between those two poles is vast and perhaps sometimes indiscernible along the lines of how the critic Geoffrey Sanborn characterizes it, that "in *Moby-Dick* ... cannibals out–Christianize Christians, madness speaks reason, and the pursuit of evil turns out to be the pursuit of God."[32] Thus Queequeg, the pagan, is decent; Pip, the black idiot, has "heaven's sense"; and Moby Dick himself, even while wreaking destruction along the way, is possessed with a certain nobility.

It is quite interesting how, when Carcajou appears on the runaway train, he is in possession of a pistol and is shooting wildly in all directions until he shoots Quebec Bill in the leg, the same appendage the White Whale had bitten off of Captain Ahab. Even so, we are told in both instances how much the victim admired his adversary. Private True Teague Kinneson, in Mosher's 2003 novel *The True Account*, is confronted with his own version of Carcajou and Moby Dick, and it is with no small degree of affection that this Kinneson refers to his adversary as the Gentleman from Vermont, a devilish figure who is about to make off, at least as the private tells it, with the soul of Ethan Allen. A battle ensues that is not unlike what Captain Ahab and Quebec Bill experienced with their respective evil aspects. Recounting the details of his own confrontation, Kinneson describes:

> I shot him. After I shot him I stabbed him. And after I stabbed him I tried to grapple with him with my own two hands. But it was all in vain. It was like shooting and stabbing and grappling with a man-shaped wisp of steam.[33]

That is how intangible and yet how real the Gentleman is, that he can be in one place, at a point in time, disappear and then, however much he might seem to be mortally wounded, reappear some vast distance away.

Wild Bill is carrying his wounded father home when Carcajou reappears. The son takes hold of his hatchet and strikes at him, causing a "chunk" of the villain's head to "fly out and land in the snow." Quebec Bill is ecstatic, relieved that Carcajou has finally been undone. But deep down inside, the father knows that Carcajou is not dead. On he walks, the son who by now is not just carrying his wounded father, but "generations of my ancestors." Aunt Cordelia, who had earlier disappeared into a rock, now reappears, standing on a knoll, taking careful aim with René Bonhomme's musket. She will hold off Carcajou, for the time, while the boy continues carrying his wounded father.

Cordelia, established at this point in the novel as a metaphysical

• *IV. Good, Evil, and the Mystery of Life* •

figure herself, will have to shoot Carcajou, but not before she recognizes him as William Goodman, one of many William Goodmans who have proceeded down through her family line. Like Hawthorne's Goodman Brown, that name William Goodman can mean at least a couple of things. The term "Goodman" was once the manner in which all men were addressed, just as today we use "Mister." Added to that is the fact that Hawthorne's "Brown" and Mosher's "William" are names so common in American culture that they could be said to represent the entirety of mankind, notwithstanding that Goodman Brown is, as it turns out, in close alignment with the devil; and William Goodman, the familial precursor of Quebec Bill, is ultimately just another name for Carcajou.

Quebec Bill disappears, right while he is being carried by his son. Critic Wayne Burke interprets that situation thusly: "The final scenes of the novel seem to lean in favor of Cordelia's statement that the children are determined to assume the sins of the father, rather than Rat's declaration (made before he too disappeared) that the sins of the fathers would be visited upon the children."[34] In a way, both Rat and Cordelia are right. The proximity of time makes it easy to see how the sins of the father, Quebec Bill, can have an impact upon his son. We think back to Mosher's own great-great-grandfather who tried to blow up his family, and we wonder what the impact, though unspecified by the author, had been upon succeeding Mosher generations. Mosher was coy about the issue in his interview, but the impact of that great-great-grandfather, in his heinous action, could have certainly been no less profound a feature in the lives of later generations than, say for example, someone with an ancestor who killed his own brother while the brothers fought against one another in a civil war. Rat's declaration, that the sins of the fathers would be visited upon the children, has all but been proven in the aftermath of our own War Between the States.

On the other hand is Cordelia whose perspective is very much in line with how Captain Ahab thinks about his life as he is determined to find the White Whale upon whose "hump" he has piled the "rage and hate" of all the generations. As I indicated earlier, Ahab is far more all-encompassing than just one man; he is, as Henry Myers puts it, "representative man" who is different from the common man only in terms of "intensity." Quebec Bill is likewise representative man and as they both,

Howard Frank Mosher and the Classics

Ahab and Quebec Bill, disappear from our midst, we are left with no choice but to take up their quest and find out what, from among our own previous lives and predecessors, still hovers above like a curse, to be explained if by no other means than by the "fiery hunt" itself which, though beyond our human comprehension, must still be undertaken.

· V ·

"The unmitigated temerity to 'feel sorry' for a white woman" in Lee's *To Kill a Mockingbird* and Mosher's *A Stranger in the Kingdom*

In Harper Lee's novel, black Thomas Robinson is accused of raping white Mayella Ewell; he is tried, convicted, and sent to the Enfield Prison Farm, 70 miles away from home. His lawyer, Atticus Finch, had tried to keep his spirits up before he was taken away, but the prospect that his conviction might be overturned, upon appeal, was not something Robinson believed could ever happen, and so, while in the exercise yard at the prison, he supposedly made a mad dash and was shot 17 times just as he "went over the fence." We will never know whether or not it really happened that way because the only perspective we have on that chain of events is the one we receive, indirectly, from the guards who did the shooting. If it was their intention to shoot him, whatever the situation, then that is certainly not something they would have relayed to their superiors to be passed on down through the system to the point where Robinson's lawyer would be informed.

We question that killing, particularly because the exercise yard, where Robinson was shot down, is the size of a football field. One would think that would have been enough space for the guards to have noticed whether or not a prisoner had it in his mind to try and escape. Or maybe it was just as the guards said, that he made a charge for the fence "right in front of them" and they did indeed shoot over his head "a few" times as a warning before they had no choice but to shoot at him to keep him from escaping. Following that scenario, one could argue that Robinson was determined to make one final desperate attempt to gain control over his own destiny. Having already been convicted, and having little faith in any appeals process, he told his lawyer, "Good-bye, Mr. Finch, there ain't nothin' you can do now, so there ain't no use tryin'."[1] Those sound like the words of a man who had all but given up on any hope of getting justice and peace in this world and was ready to plunge on into the next world where his chances of finding those things would, at the very least, be just as good as what he had been allowed in the world that he was leaving.

In fact, for all his talk about having had such a "good chance" upon appeal, it was Finch himself who had, even before the first trial, told his daughter Scout that there was no chance of winning because "we were licked a hundred years before we started." It is 1935, in small town Alabama and, while rules of evidence have always existed for application in courts of law, there exists a quite different code, in *To Kill a Mockingbird*, that the critic Claudia Johnson describes as "the law in its broadest sense: familial, communal, and regional codes; those of the drawing room and the school yard; those written and unwritten; some that lie beneath the surface in dark contradiction of established law."[2] It is this broader law that Robinson found himself in the clutches of, a long-held southern code that, once entangled in it, Robinson understood there was hardly a chance he would ever escape.

Of course, Robinson did not rape Mayella Ewell; he never did commit that violation. However, when he accepted her offer for him to do chores for her on a regular basis, without taking into consideration her desperate need for affection, he did violate a code. It is the code alluded to by historian James McGovern when he states, "It is doubtful if any black male growing up in the rural South in the period 1900 to 1940 was not traumatized by a fear of being lynched."[3] Perhaps McGovern's word "traumatized" is a bit strong in terms of how he applies it to all black males growing up in the South during the time to which he refers. Yet, it is important to consider a notice that appeared in both *The New York Times* and *The Atlanta Constitution*, on November 23, 1922, wherein it was reported that—between the years 1889 and 1922—3,436 people were

• V. *"To 'feel sorry' for a white woman"* •

lynched in America, the overwhelming majority of whom were black men.[4]

To cast such a shadow over black male existence was not so difficult at all. In a lecture that he gave in 1923, at the National Conference of Social Work, in Washington, D.C., the sociologist Charles Johnson said that there are three cardinal beliefs that the American public holds with regard to African Americans, and these beliefs "may be said to control in one form or another most of the thinking about Negroes: first, that they are mentally inferior; second, that they are immoral; and third, that they are criminal."[5] Concerning that third belief, Johnson elaborated further on how society has long adhered to the notion that "Negroes are criminal by nature. An alleged peculiar emotional instability predisposes them to crimes of violence, particularly sex crimes."[6] When one considers how such beliefs were dominant, among the white population of Lee's 1930s Maycomb, Alabama, it is not so hard to fathom how the broader unwritten codes, to which Professor Johnson referred, actually came about, branding blacks with a second-class citizenship status with roots in slavery that would later grow into the means whereby blacks would continue to be treated badly long after the institution of slavery had ended.

D. W. Griffith's 1915 film *The Birth of a Nation* is a prime example of racist stereotypes being perpetuated across the broad social spectrum. Based on Thomas Dixon's 1905 novel *The Clansman*, the film has a scene where a black Union soldier (actually a white actor in blackface) lustfully chases a white female through the woods until she is cornered at the edge of a cliff. Preferring death as opposed to being raped by a black man, she hurls herself over the precipice. In another part of the film, we watch as a black politician progresses to the point where he is in the United States Congress, only to learn that what he had really been desirous of all along was to be in a position where he could force himself upon yet another white female. Clearly, a lot of the message of that film was that white females were in danger from the threat of an emotionally unstable marauding band of black men with one thing on their minds.

The presumed need to protect white women was a factor that gave rise to the Ku Klux Klan, but one of the blatant "contradictions of established law" was how thoroughly imbued with KKK doctrine was the legal system itself. So strict was the code against black male/white female relationships that even when such relationships were consensual, the repercussions could be dire. Such was the case of Willie McGee, in 1940s Laurel, Mississippi, who was sentenced to death and executed, having been accused of rape, by a white woman who had had to explain to her neighbors why McGee's truck was parked nearby at 4:30 a.m. In 1931, in Slick, Oklahoma, Jess Hollins had consensual sex with a white woman who, according to Hollins' attorney, "had voluntarily gone with Hollins and had cried rape only when unexpectedly confronted by her brother-in-law when she and Hollins returned to the road."[7] Hollins was sentenced to death but, upon retrial, received a life sentence which he accepted with some sense of relief and did not care to risk another retrial, fearing that a "future jury might" again "give him the death penalty."

More recently, in 1973 Tarboro, North Carolina, three black men were accused of raping a white woman even though the preponderance of the evidence suggested that the sex was consensual. Morris Dees, one of the founding attorneys of the Southern Poverty Law Center, took up the case of "The Tarboro Three" and was told, with regard to their first trial, that "all the folks at the courthouse had laughed at the defense of voluntary consent because it was assumed, as a matter of law, that a white woman would never consent to sex with a black man."[8] In a court of law, the idea is that both sides have to present evidence in order to try and prove their case. But, evidently, among the things that did not have to be proven but instead was simply accepted as legal fact, without need for any argument, was that white women do not agree to have sex with black men. That was also what the journalist Carl Rowan discovered as having been the prevailing sentiment as he was investigating the case of Willie McGee and was informed, by one "Negro professional man" that he interviewed, how the court would "just refuse to believe that any white woman would *want* to lay with a Negro. And if she does, it ain't voluntary. It's rape."[9]

One can imagine, then, how simple a matter it was for Victoria Price and Ruby Bates to convince law officials that they had been raped by nine teenage black boys while they were all aboard a freight train making its run between Memphis and Chattanooga. Several white boys had been aboard the train at one point, had tried to force the black boys

V. "To 'feel sorry' for a white woman"

off and, having failed, were themselves forced to jump from the train. The white boys immediately reported, to a local sheriff, what had happened and the train was stopped at Paint Rock, Alabama, whereupon the two white females had to quickly come up with some explanation so as to explain the situation. What they came up with was a detailed account of how they had been raped by the nine boys, including a 12-year-old who wound up, however, being the only one of the nine who was found not guilty, in a court of law, and so was not sentenced to die in the electric chair. Of the boys who were sentenced, three were 16 years old; another was only 13.

James McGovern's assertion that black males living in the rural South between 1900 and 1940 were traumatized, by the reality of these circumstances, is indeed overstated. If that many men had been traumatized it would have amounted to a paralysis of the sort that the black race as a whole would not have been able to function in any meaningful way, let alone continue to push forward in their ongoing efforts for more freedom, a process that would find its culmination in the Civil Rights Movement of the 1950s and '60s. It was not so much that black men in the first half of the twentieth century were traumatized, but they were for the most part extremely cognizant of exactly how things were and knew to be particularly careful whenever, and wherever, the issue of a white woman was concerned. "Leave the white girls alone" was not just the mandate handed down by racist white men, it was also the admonition passed down from wary black mothers to their young black sons who might otherwise have been possessed of a certain inquisitiveness that, if pursued, could end in the pursuer's ultimate detriment.

Tom Robinson passed by the Ewell yard every day going to and from work. And "lots of times," Mayella Ewell would call out for him to come into the yard to do some chore or another for her, for which he charged nothing because, as he put it during his testimony on the witness stand, "I was glad to do it." Again and again, he went into the yard to help this 19-year-old woman do her chores because he was a kind-hearted person who saw that the burden of work around the house lay squarely on her shoulders with her receiving virtually no help at all from either her widowed father or her seven younger siblings. Robinson had, in a manner of speaking, been hidden even further down a back road—

behind the town dump—than the poverty-stricken Ewells, and so that black man took it upon himself to come out, from the place where he had been relegated, and express his humanity to someone he saw in great need.

It is not so farfetched, perhaps, to consider Robinson's situation as being similar to that of the Frankenstein monster that, due to his unacceptable physical appearance, spends his life on the fringes of an intolerant society when one day, as the monster himself recounts,

> I was scarcely hid, when a young girl came running towards the spot where I was concealed, laughing, as if she ran from some one in sport. She continued her course along the precipitous sides of the river, when suddenly her foot slipt, and she fell into the rapid stream. I rushed from my hiding-place; and, with extreme labour from the force of the current, saved her, and dragged her to shore.[10]

The monster could have stayed hidden in safety, but how even less human would he have been had he just watched while a child wound up drowning? The monster was posed with an irreconcilable dilemma much like that with which Robinson was faced. However, their quick responses, in terms of coming to the aid of someone in need, should give every indication, to us, that they did not see their respective situations as having been a dilemma at all. The realization of the consequences for their actions comes later. For the monster, it is when a man appears, ripping the girl from his arms and then shooting him, leaving him with a "wound, which shattered the flesh and bone." For Robinson, it is when Mayella accuses him of raping her and, while yet telling that lie, can look at him with such a sense of indignation "as if he were dirt beneath her feet."

That was the same Mayella Ewell who had beckoned Robinson into her yard lots of times to the point where one day she went even further and ushered him into the house under the pretense of having some indoor chore for him to do. Then once she had gotten him inside, she began hugging and kissing him, that is until her father appeared on the scene, forcing her to provide some explanation for what was going on. Robinson probably knew then that he was doomed, understood more starkly, than he had ever fathomed before, the extent to which he had violated the unwritten code, making it so that by the time he was sitting

• V. *"To 'feel sorry' for a white woman"* •

in the courtroom he had, in the "secret courts of men's hearts," already been convicted, and as Scout herself comes to understand, "Atticus had no case. Tom was a dead man the minute Mayella Ewell opened her mouth and screamed."[11] That was Mayella Ewell and that was 1930s Alabama.

The question we are posed with, in Mosher's *A Stranger in the Kingdom*, is whether things are all that different in the 1950s in the uppermost reaches of New England. We will recall that Vermont was the first state to abolish slavery; it sent more men, per capita, than any other state to fight in the Union Army during the Civil War. It would almost seem like heresy to suggest that what happened to Tom Robinson—both in terms of his place in society and his status in a courtroom—could also happen to a black man in Kingdom Common, Vermont.

The quiet dignity of Robinson was brought to our attention most succinctly with Scout Finch's observation that "Tom Robinson's manners were as good as Atticus's." That is how a child saw the two men. The typical adult could, more than likely, draw from that observation and conclude that, but for the difference in their skin color, they would have been afforded a similar respect from the general society. One could say that Mosher, in his novel, extends this notion of integrity to a level even greater as he offers us black Walter Andrews who is a stellar human being in too many ways to count. He took salutatorian honors as a history major at the University of Toronto. Afterwards, he enrolled in seminary where he graduated first in his class. In addition, he was an accomplished boxer, making it all the way to the Olympics, competing in the heavyweight division.

In more recent years, he was a chaplain in the Royal Canadian Air Force in which capacity he had received "medals for bravery" in World War II and the Korean Conflict. So, it is no wonder that the United Protestant Church of Kingdom Common was willing to hire him sight unseen on the basis of a telephone interview. As for what Andrews' particular interest was in the Kingdom, he was a widower with a 17-year-old son and he was looking for a nice, quiet rural environment to finish raising him. Before coming to the Kingdom, he had envisioned "Vermont to be one of the few remaining places where folks obeyed the law and helped their neighbors in times of need and assiduously minded their own business the rest of the while."[12] Coming from Montreal, life was now going to take on a slower pace, for both him and his son, slower and more peaceful than what living in the city had allowed.

It would not be long, though, before the dream of a peaceful life began to erode. At the Kingdom County Fair, one of the white villagers, Bumper Stevens, hurls vicious epithets at both Andrews and his son, calling the son "Step'n Fetch" and calling the reverend "Nigger." With one quick jab, the reverend breaks the offender's jaw and then escorts his son away from the scene, but we know that what has just occurred is only the beginning. Before all is said and done, in the novel, the reverend will have to pull out his service revolver and fire it at a white man who is about to attack him further after having already emptied his shotgun into the "glass transom above the parsonage door."

As bizarre as that all sounds, it is not too much different from what happened in the author's hometown of Irasburg, Vermont, in the summer of 1968. That was the year that the Reverend David Lee Johnson made his cross-country trek from Seaside, California, to Vermont because, as reported in *Life* magazine, he was "longing now for a new home in the northern U.S., to get his children away from the racial turmoil in the Seaside schools."[13] All was going quite well until, on the night of July 18, two carloads of young whites drove past Johnson's house, with one of the youths firing a shotgun at the home as the car drove pass. The youths turned around to make a second run, this time shattering a window as they drove pass. But the reverend returned fire, emptying a full clip from his nine-millimeter, semi-automatic Lugar pistol, and the youths, fearing for their lives, sped off into the night.

One of the consequences of that night was that Vermont state troopers were assigned to guard the Johnson house and, at first, they did their job so well that the reverend was inclined to write a letter praising their efforts. Then came the night of July 22, when one of the officers working the graveyard shift claims to have seen something take place that struck a nerve with his colleagues and evidently struck a nerve with some others in the community. What this trooper claims to have seen was a "white girl lying on the couch with ... Rev. Johnson.... At this point ... the Reverend turned ... and motioned with his hand at me and whispered 'get out.'"[14] It bears mentioning, at this point, that in addition to the Johnson

V. "To 'feel sorry' for a white woman"

family—Johnson, his wife, their three children, and a grandchild—there also lived a young white woman and her two white children. If the reverend had been committing adultery with the white woman on the living room couch, it would have been an odd place, considering the circumstances, to do such a thing. But aside from all that, what business of the trooper's would it have been?

Well, as it turns out, it would have been some business of the trooper's because of what Title 13, Section 201 of the Vermont Code provides, that "a person who commits adultery shall be imprisoned in the state prison not more than five years or fined not more than $1,000 or both." So, there was a law against committing adultery. The problem, though, was that no one had been tried under that statute in over a century, and even then the case was not brought by legal authorities but by a wife who had felt so spurned by her husband that she took it upon herself to bring charges.[15] Now, over a century later, charges were about to be brought again, and the prime witness would be the white woman in Johnson's house who, back in Seaside, had been a next-door neighbor, having recently won custody of her two children, following a bitter divorce.

Obviously, Johnson had not paid heed to the unwritten code about interacting with a white woman. He has now been accused of adultery, facing five years in prison and is looking more and more like Harper Lee's Tom Robinson who lawyer Finch, in his closing argument, contends only committed the violation of having "the unmitigated temerity to 'feel sorry' for a white woman," forgetting, when he offered his assistance to Mayella, that if it ever came down to his word against hers about anything, he would fall victim to the prevailing "assumption—that *all* Negro men are not to be trusted around our women."[16] For his lapse in judgment, Johnson would find himself as much cornered by the legal system as if he had been the beleaguered Tom Robinson who had done nothing more incredulous than help out a neighbor in need.

As charges were being drawn up against Johnson, the white woman, with whom he was supposed to have been having an affair, signed the following statement:

"On July 22, 1968, I got up from my bed and went downstairs. I walked to the front living room. David Johnson, Sr. was awake and downstairs.... We were having intercourse for only a few minutes when the door into the living room opened partially. I saw an arm in the opening and Mr. Johnson waved his arm at the fellow to close the door."[17]

That statement is strikingly similar to what the complaining state trooper said happened. The trooper saw the reverend's hand and the white woman saw the trooper's arm, all behind doors that were only partially open. But then several days later, the woman recanted the statement that she had previously signed, that signature having been rendered under duress in the presence of three "goading" white detectives, one of whom provided the actual wording for the document and then placed it in front of her with the choice—that was really no choice—to either sign it or not. That was then, but she wound up later signing something that sounded quite different, a document that read as follows:

> "This statement is being given to contradict the statement given to the Vermont police or investigator or whoever the gentleman was who wrote the statement for me to sign. There was no sexual relationship between Rev. Johnson and I.... I thought that even if I said nothing had happened between us they would not have taken my word. Also, at the time the statement was wrote for me to sign I was nervous and upset and was not given a chance to think clearly of what I was saying or signing."[18]

She had good cause to be nervous as she found herself treading on an assortment of delicate thin lines. There was the reverend that had brought her and her children to Vermont, and whose house she was still living in. There was the reverend's wife who must have once served as a valuable source of support. Then there was the white community of Irasburg and its legal system that, like any other legal system, was no better or worse than the community that it served.

One could argue that the white woman in this case was quite brave in recanting her statement. What, for example, would have become of Mayella Ewell if she had withdrawn her accusation against Tom Robinson and proclaimed that she and so many others had been wrong in their treatment of a black man who had done nothing more questionable than "feel sorry" for her? Odds are someone would have killed her and there is a strong likelihood that it would have been her own father who did the deed. At the Orleans County courthouse in Vermont, the white woman, operating on the advice of her lawyer, pled *nolo contendere*,

• V. "To 'feel sorry' for a white woman" •

which meant she was not pleading guilty but she was not going to go through the process of defending herself either. So, she was fined, charged court costs and sentenced to 6–12 months at the women's reformatory in Rutland. For its part of the compromise, the court suspended the sentence and she quickly got herself and her children out of Vermont, never to return.

As for the youths who had shot at the reverend's house, law authorities methodically moved away from an investigation of them and instead were now involved in an all-out investigation of the reverend, including his personal finances, his military record, and what he was doing with a semi-automatic gun. But the absurdity of the whole situation was beginning to draw unwanted attention beyond the borders of Vermont. The white woman, who might have been a witness, was no longer there; and the trooper, who at first said he saw the Reverend Johnson and "the white girl lying on the couch," was now saying "that intercourse was either being contemplated, or in progress, or recently completed."[19] With the evidence against the Reverend Johnson being so unreliable, at this point, the state was forced to drop the charges. But the damage had already been done and it would not be long before the Johnsons, too, would be packing up their things and heading on.

In Mosher's novel, the Reverend Andrews responds to the racial attacks with a sense of grace and dignity, but then something happens that will prove to be just as threatening to him, and his son, as anything that was ever experienced by either Lee's Tom Robinson or the reverend who ventured cross-country to make a go of calling Irasburg his home. James Kinneson, one of Kingdom Common's newspaper editor's sons, takes it upon himself to deposit, at the doorstep of Andrews, a 17-year-old vagabond girl who was about to become a stripper for the "Paris Revue girlie show." Though she had hopes of going to Hollywood and becoming an actress, she was actually being groomed, by the Paris Revue proprietors, to be a dancer along the lines of what we saw happen to Marie Blythe when she got a job working at Bull Francis's Pond in the Sky saloon. She was under the assumption, when she applied for the job, that she would merely have to dance, only to learn later that, every night, she will be hung from the ceiling in a gilded cage, helpless to the whims of sadistic men who have it in their mind to bite and cut and put out their cigarettes on the flesh of young women so desperate, in their lives, that they are forced to accept the abuse as a condition of their employment.

At the Paris Revue show, "there was a brutal quality about the men and a dreadful grim yet cheery resignation in the submission of the women."[20] What we learned, from Susan Meiselas's *Carnival Strippers*, is that the women in such shows are often regarded as "whores" by the general community, and that certainly is how at least one of the girls is referred to, in *A Stranger*, when the authorities raid the strip show and, in a sense, save the 17-year-old who, primed by her employer to perform a lascivious act, had been dressed up in "some sort of costume, with a tear halfway up the side." She was saved temporarily, by the raid, but then not completely saved because she still had no place to go where her safety could be guaranteed. Bad men want to exploit her, and the good men, who might have been willing to help, are powerless to do so because of the jealousies harbored by women in the Common who resent her for the threat she represents in terms of her youth and beauty. The newspaper editor, Charles Kinneson, in "an Open Letter," written in retrospect after events have occurred, rails against the community in terms of how it handled the situation:

> No one else stepped forward to help the girl, the outcast, the stranger. Oh, we didn't form a mob and try to stone her or ride her out of town on a rail. Those aren't our tactics here in God's Kingdom these days. We just said to each other, maybe a little baffled, "But what has she to do with us? A girl from the tent show? What has she to do with us?"[21]

The editor's other son, Charlie, does help to the extent that he can and, of course, James helps too, by escorting her to the parsonage. But it is the reverend himself who helps most when she comes to the door and "knocked softly, three times." Having heard of her difficulty, he offers her in and, at that moment, he is Tom Robinson charging nothing from Mayella Ewell as he takes on the burden of doing her chores. When Andrews welcomes Claire LaRiviere into his home, one has to contemplate long and hard about which of them is really the "stranger in the Kingdom," just as Lee's *Mockingbird* leaves us in a quandary as to who is more the mockingbird that it would be a sin to kill, Robinson or the reclusive Boo Radley "shut up in his house" for a quarter of a century

• V. "To 'feel sorry' for a white woman" •

"because he wants to stay inside." Radley slips out, from time to time, to do his kind deeds; but he does not linger, knowing as he does how the world responds to people who are different.

Unfortunately, Andrews does not have the option of withdrawing into his own little world. Even above and beyond what he might have felt was his obligation from one human being to another, it is literally his job to "feel sorry" for people in need, particularly someone who approaches him for assistance. It just so happens that the person in need, this time, is a 17-year-old would-be stripper and as soon as she moves into the parsonage, the assumption, throughout the community, is that he has brought her into the confines of his home for the purpose of having sex. It is this perspective that enabled the jury, in *Mockingbird*, to convict Robinson for rape, the perspective that enabled a Vermont state trooper, and then others, to believe the Reverend Johnson brought a white woman, and her children, across the country just to have sex with her even as his own wife, his children, and his grandchild were in the same house, right upstairs asleep.

As circumstances evolved in Irasburg, during that summer of 1968, Johnson became more and more a person of interest in terms of whom the police wanted to investigate. Similarly, the spotlight begins to shine more brightly on the Reverend Andrews once Claire is an established guest in his household. Like Johnson, Andrews has to use a gun to protect himself and, at that point, he becomes even more a person of interest than the man who had threatened his life. Just as the authorities knew all along who attacked the Reverend Johnson's home, *A Stranger's* Kingdom County sheriff Mason White is comfortable with the Reverend Andrews' assailant but not so comfortable with the black reverend himself who had taken a white female into his home and then defended that home with a firearm that has now suddenly become a legal issue. "Why would a *reverend* need a handgun in the first place?" White poses that question to the newspaper editor. "Who is he, anyway? What was his real reason for coming down here, where there isn't another of his kind for fifty miles around?"[22] And as we listen to his words, we wonder to what extent those concerns of the sheriff were the concerns of Kingdom Common as a whole.

Those concerns reach a boiling point when Claire LaRiviere is found lying dead at the bottom of a granite quarry. Also at the scene is the Reverend Andrews' recently fired gun. Charged with murder, the reverend is carted off to jail as the community's fears become even more exacerbated than before. The reverend, in many of their minds, is not just a sexual deviant, he is a murderer, killing his young female house guest to cover up his illicit relationship with her, particularly since she was, as it turns out, at least one month pregnant when she died. The man who had gone out of his way to visit the sick and elderly, and had assumed the duties of the high school baseball coach when the regular coach fell ill, was now a piranha of the most frightening sort along the lines of what John Carlos Rowe says, in his analysis of *Mockingbird*, that "modern western societies are often based on superstitions and ritualized practices as fantastic as those in so-called primitive or archaic communities."[23] We can look back in history and find communities, the "so-called primitive" ones, where outcasts, of one type or another, were burned at the stake and stoned to death. Some were fed to lions and nailed to crosses for practicing their religious beliefs. Positing Maycomb, Alabama, as an example of "modern western" society, Rowe suggests that there are still "cultural forms" or indeed rituals that communities adhere to and live by that make them not distinct from a savage history but, instead, examples of how the savagery rages on in spite of the veils that are applied to make such communities seem to be civilized. We are witness to just such a ritual as we watch Andrews fall from his once-distinguished pastorate, down through the societal ranks, all the way to where he seems destined to become a mere convict.

    Just as Atticus Finch proves that Tom Robinson did not rape Mayella Ewell, Charlie Kinneson is able to prove that the Reverend Andrews did not kill Claire LaRiviere. Resolvèd Kinneson, a cousin of Charlie's, claims to have seen Andrews and Claire having sex but then, upon Charlie's cross-examination, Resolvèd has to admit that he never saw the reverend's face, just "his bare feet and bare legs was sticking out under her." It turns out that it was not the reverend who was engaged in sexual intercourse with Claire, but it was instead the reverend's son. Both of those children being strangers in the Kingdom, they had turned to each other for some consolation as a means of surviving the circumstances the Kingdom had presented them.

• V. "To 'feel sorry' for a white woman" •

Charlie still has the task of finding out who killed Claire, a task that he accomplishes rather handily when he gets Frenchy LaMott to reveal that, one night, he saw the church sexton, Elijah Kinneson, stealing a gun from the top desk drawer in the reverend's study. It was Elijah who killed Claire, partly due to his jealousy over no longer being afforded the status of pastor, although that was never a position for which he had been considered on any permanent basis. The main reason, however, that he killed Claire was so that he could frame the Reverend Andrews for the murder and thereby prevent him from investigating the death, a half century earlier, of the first black man to have lived in the Kingdom, the Reverend Pliny Templeton.

Templeton was born a slave and grew up on a plantation in Georgia. While a slave, he had made something of a career out of attempting to escape, having run away five different times before he had reached the age of 20. The editor's grandfather, Charlie Kinneson, also known as "Mad Charlie," was a compatriot of the legendary John Brown and, like Brown, despised the institution of slavery. Meanwhile, Pliny had garnered something of a reputation himself as someone who was determined to keep on trying to escape until ultimately he was either dead or free. The reputation reached all the way into the mountains of Vermont where Charlie was devising a plan to catch the murderous slave hunter Satan Smithfield. In order to catch him, Mad Charlie needed bait, so he got word to Pliny to try and escape one more time even though the slave master had threatened, if he did try again, to set Smithfield on his trail. Nonetheless, Pliny escaped and made his way on up toward Vermont, drawing out Smithfield whereupon Charlie shot the slave hunter "point blank in the heart."

With Charlie's help, Pliny would enroll at Middlebury College and then, upon graduation, make his home in the Common where he would build and administer Kingdom Common Academy and teach there for 40 years. Then tragedy struck in the form of a disagreement between the two best friends. The Academy had been built under the auspices of the Reformed Presbyterian Church but, as time passed, the school "drifted away from strict RP dogma" and, in effect, staged what might be thought of as a revolt against an "entire *way of life*" that, to put it simply, represented a generations-long stand-off against obtrusive government. Pliny, on the other hand, seemed to be blending not just education but also government-related activities into the religious belief system of the Common, activities such as holding public office and serving in the military. Pliny Templeton is Mosher's fictional representation of Alexander Twilight, the Vermont-born politician, clergyman and educator who miraculously constructed, with massive granite stones, Athenian Hall in Brownington. He resigned his pastorate at the affiliated church for reasons similar to what made Templeton split from the Reformed Presbyterian Church. Of Twilight, Mosher would profoundly declare, "I think he had more faith in education than he had in religion."[24] That was how the author put it during my interview with him as we stood in the shadows of Athenian Hall, marveling at the majestic structure. But, in actuality, Mad Charlie's perspective on the split might have been just as valid, or indeed invalid, as Templeton's position; and the consequences of their disagreement become just as ludicrous as when the brothers Mason and Dixon Alexander, in *Gatlinburg*, work together long and hard to establish a town only to wind up bickering over which of their names they should call it. Mason and Dixon were "upward of ninety" when their argument reached its bitter climax and, likewise, Pliny and Mad Charlie are well into their golden years when their debate comes to its disastrous end. Retracing, in *A Stranger*, the progression of the conflict between Mad Charlie and Pliny, the newspaper editor Charles Kinneson apprises the Reverend Andrews:

> "Finally, in 1900, when Pliny and my grandfather were both old men, Pliny declared himself a United Presbyterian and tried to disaffiliate the Academy from the church, partly in order to get that piano into his school. A number of the trustees supported him. An equal number didn't. They met to vote in closed session and Pliny cast the decisive ballot to break from the church. Afterwards, my grandfather came over to the parsonage and there was a terrible row between the two friends. The upshot of it was that poor Pliny Templeton shot himself that very evening, after which my grandfather went totally insane and spent the last two years of his life in the state lunatic asylum at Waterbury."[25]

The editor got most of the story right. Pliny wanted a piano at the Academy while Mad Charlie and others, of the Reformed Presbyterian faith, did not want the piano, so Pliny and his followers broke away, establishing a United Presbyterian sect within the Common community. What

V. "To 'feel sorry' for a white woman"

the editor got wrong, however, was with regard to how Pliny died. He did not kill himself but was shot in the back of the head twice, by Mad Charlie himself, in brutal response to what he concluded was the ultimate act of betrayal, by someone he assumed was his "beloved friend."

This was the truth that the Reverend Andrews was about to uncover. Elijah was Mad Charlie's son and when it seemed that Andrews was on the verge of finding out that Mad Charlie had murdered his own best friend, the sexton took it upon himself to kill Claire and then watch while the community blamed Andrews, a stranger whom they didn't really know that well but, it was beginning to seem, was a man from whom it was necessary to protect white women. But for Mad Charlie's lawyering great-grandson, ironically named Charlie Kinneson too, Elijah would have gotten away with it.

After Tom Robinson has been killed, in *Mockingbird*, Maudie Atkinson tries to console the lawyer's son, telling him that at least at times like these, when we've got to put somebody up, "we've got men like Atticus to go for us." And yet, how much consolation is that, really, particularly for Robinson's wife and three children? As Finch had done in *Mockingbird*, Charlie Kinneson, in *A Stranger*, provides Andrews with extraordinary legal representation, at one point in his summation, to the jury, rendering what is likely one of the most profound commentaries ever to be found in American literature. Remarking on Elijah's hatred for the Reverend Andrews, the lawyer stressed, "The most unfortunate and dangerous thing about any kind of human intolerance is that you find it wherever there are humans, because, ladies and gentlemen, it's potentially as much a part of the human heart, including yours and mine as its opposite, tolerance, and we have to guard against it every single day of our lives."[26] It was a tremendous challenge that Charlie made not only to the jury but a challenge laid out for the whole Common community and perhaps for the entire world.

We have men like Finch and Charlie Kinneson to go for us and yet there is something still lacking, shortcomings best personified as we observe what ultimately becomes of the novels' most critical characters. In *Mockingbird*, Finch gets re-elected to the state legislature; Robinson is dead. In *A Stranger*, Charlie Kinneson moves on to become county prosecutor and then a federal judge; the Reverend Andrews dies in 1966, fighting in the Vietnam War, the third war he had fought in service to his country. In Irasburg, the community goes on, but the Johnsons are nowhere in sight. Just the empty structure where they once lived. I cannot shake the eerie feeling I have as I stand in front of the house that was shot into all those years before. "That place is haunted" is all I can bring myself to say to Mosher, though I am not quite sure what to make of my own words. "Ghosts are still there,"[27] the writer answers me solemnly, his only explanation as we turn and make our way down the forlorn road.

• VI •

The Technique of Humor in Twain's *Huckleberry Finn* and Mosher's *The True Account*

On the dust jacket of Mosher's 2003 novel, *The True Account*, Carl Hiaasen praises how "Howard Mosher calls to mind the best of Mark Twain—mischievous, touching, and very funny." Cathie Pelletier, on the same dust jacket, goes so far as to remark, of Mosher's novel, that "this may well be the first true American picaresque novel since *Huckleberry Finn*." That latter reviewer goes quite far out on a ledge, figuratively speaking, in declaring *The True Account* to be the "first true" such novel since Twain's classic masterpiece. To say that it took 119 years for anything, along the lines of *Adventures of Huckleberry Finn*, to have been done again is indeed quite a stretch. But through Pelletier's extreme assertion, we do get the point which is that very few authors possess the level of creative ability that even vaguely reminds us of what Twain was capable of doing, as evidenced by his 1884 novel that, though humorous at times, is also about the institution of American slavery. With Twain, one is confronted on more than one occasion with the question of how two apparently disparate aspects, such as humor and slavery, can ever be ultimately reconciled.

In his essay "What's Funny About *Huckleberry Finn*," Sacvan Bercovitch acknowledges, "The first shock is that the novel is funny at all. The slave-hunt serves as both metaphor and metonymy for the world it portrays: *Huckleberry Finn* describes a slave-hunt undertaken literally, collectively, by an enslaved society, a culture in bondage ... and accordingly characterized by violence, mean-spiritedness, ignorance, and deceit."[1] In Huck's hometown of Langlem, Missouri, ignorance abounds, especially with regard to the less-than-human status to which blacks have been relegated. And we need look no further than Huck's own father for an example of mean-spiritedness that has escalated all the way to the point of arbitrary violence. But it is deceit, to which Bercovitch refers, that so much seems to dominate the novel and dominate it in such a way as to leave us at times splitting our sides with laughter even as we wonder what to make of it all.

It would better serve us to separate the issue of "deceit" from the other descriptive terms provided by Bercovitch. Violence, mean-spiritedness, and ignorance have extremely negative connotations, but I would suggest that deceptiveness need not necessarily have so negative a meaning. In fact, within certain contexts, it can be viewed as a positive characteristic such as is conveyed in the ancient African folktales involving Kwaku Anansi, the trickster spider who finds ways to survive amongst other creatures of the animal kingdom, larger and stronger than him, and capable of killing him on a whim if they so desire. In one such tale, "Spider and the Crows," Anansi is able to eat, during a famine, by courteously entering into the midst of a flock of crows and stealing figs from them, those figs having secretly been stuck to him by the beeswax he has smeared on his "hindquarters."

In that same story, Anansi at a certain point finds himself in the middle of a lake, surrounded by crocodiles; but he is able to survive by convincing them that he is their long-lost relative, claiming:

> "I'm one of you. Don't you know that everyone has been searching for me for years? I ran away in the days of your grandfathers, when I was very small. And no one has ever found me. You are the first of my family members I've met."[2]

It is an engaging tale he tells, evoking much sympathy from the ordinarily dangerous crocodiles who, under the spell of Anansi's fascinating story, have become so accommodating that they arrange for him to be a guest in their community, specifically in a hole up on the bank where they lay their eggs. Suffice it to say, Anansi will eat those eggs and, in doing so, he provides us with yet another example of how one so small and physically weak, as he, can nevertheless survive quite efficiently even during a famine.

• VI. *The Technique of Humor* •

But interwoven in the message of the story, a story that is serious in many ways, are situations evoking great humor as when Anansi displays supreme politeness, in backing away from the crows, when the whole time he is just sneaking away with a fig attached to his hindquarters. Humor is applied again, by the teller of the Anansi tale, as he conveys how "the crocodiles themselves cried crocodile tears," lamenting over the spider's circumstances as they offer him a comfortable place to stay where he, unbeknownst to them, will quickly eat the future offspring.

In Mosher's second memoir, *The Great Northern Express* (2012), Mark Twain himself has been conjured up as a traveling companion who instructs his literary heir, Mosher, that "what mainly ails fiction these days ... is that most of you newfangled writers have forgotten how to be entertaining."[3] Yes, a story can be possessed of what one might call a plot, and it sometimes has dialogue and a setting, and it might be said to convey a message. But what Twain would have us remember is what Mosher himself, speaking through Twain, reminds us; and that is, for all the seriousness of authors so great as even Shakespeare and Dickens, there is never anything boring about their works. Such a literary trap was avoided because those authors were not reluctant, when the time arose, to use humor as an essential device.

Helpful in understanding this perspective is Twain himself who, in his 1897 essay "How to Tell a Story," instructs us that "the humorous story depends for its effect upon the *manner* of the telling ... only an artist can tell it ... [t]he humorous story is told gravely; the teller does his best to conceal the fact that he even dimly suspects that there is anything funny about it."[4] Twain wishes to distinguish humor from, on the other hand, comedy and wit. Those last two techniques, in the author's estimation, draw so much attention to themselves that the practitioner practically comes right out and says that he is trying to be funny. The artist of humor, however, leaves his audience wondering if they should laugh and wondering why, after all, the story was told in the particular way that it was, which brings us back to Bercovitch's point about "shock." How can a novel about slavery be humorous? The question is such a lingering one, when it comes to Twain, that well over a century after *Huckleberry Finn* first appeared on the scene, many readers still wondered if, and how much, the author was a racist himself.

Howard Frank Mosher and the Classics

As pertains to that question, it may not help Twain's cause that in his autobiography he waxes sentimental about blackface minstrelsy, reflecting, "I remember the first Negro musical show I ever saw. It must have been in the early forties. It was a new institution. In our village of Hannibal we had not heard of it before and it burst upon us as a glad and stunning surprise."[5] Twain indicates that blackface minstrelsy arrived in Hannibal, Missouri in the 1840s. However, the historian Karen Sotiropoulos suggests that the entertainment form actually began a decade earlier as she describes:

> White men had blackened their faces in the 1830s, thereby beginning white America's love affair with blackface minstrelsy, but the widespread success of popular amusements at the turn of the century seared these images into the American psyche. With the introduction of mass production, stereotyped imagery appeared everywhere from song sheets to food labels, making the blackface minstrel a permanent part of the American landscape. Over the years, minstrel imagery has reflected and reinforced white supremacy and has caused black America immeasurable pain. Yet shortly after the Civil War, black performers capitalized on white America's desire for minstrel shows, marketing themselves as authentic "darkies" and Ethiopian delineators.[6]

To some extent, Sotiropoulos is correct in her assertion that blackface minstrelsy "reinforced white supremacy" and consequently "caused black America immeasurable pain." Furthermore, it did indeed become such a popular art form that turn-of-the-twentieth-century black entertainers such as George Walker and Bert Williams utilized the technique—painting themselves in blackface, that is—to garner for themselves extraordinarily lucrative careers along the lines of what white entertainers such as Al Jolson and Eddie Cantor were later able to do.

The problem for me, though, is that Sotiropoulos and many other scholars, including Eric Lott in his thought-provoking treatise *Love and Theft: Blackface Minstrelsy and the American Working Class* (1993), either ignore or minimize the extent to which black minstrelsy was a distinctly African American creation. This is something that Charles Perdue drilled into his folklore students in the early 1970s at the University of Virginia. To entertain themselves, black slaves would dress up in the cast-off finery of their masters, and then strut around poking fun at their masters' customs and manners. When the white version of black

VI. The Technique of Humor

minstrelsy developed in the nineteenth century, it was a matter of whites imitating blacks who had been merely imitating the otherwise ordinary manners of their masters. Blacks had turned those ordinary manners into humorous presentations. After the Civil War, when blacks put the bootblack or burnt cork on their faces and hands to present, for the American audience, their own version of formalized minstrelsy, it was the culminating link in a cultural chain, the situation being now one of "blacks imitating whites imitating blacks imitating whites."

That was how Professor Perdue would state it, whether it be in his "Introduction to Folklore" class, "Studies in Folklore," "Folklore in America," or "Folklore in Virginia." And when he said it, he said it with a straight face so that we did not know whether or not to laugh at the absurdity or mourn the twin tragedies of discrimination and misrepresentation that are the essence of how black minstrelsy has been perceived and presented throughout the many years of its existence. Twain would have admired Perdue's poker-faced characterization, and the best evidence I can offer for drawing that conclusion is located in the author of *Huckleberry Finn*'s "Notice" to readers as they are about to start their reading of the novel. Twain admonishes, "Persons attempting to find a motive in this narrative will be prosecuted; persons attempting to find a moral in it will be banished; persons attempting to find a plot in it will be shot." We know, of course, that we will not be prosecuted, banished, or shot if we do commit what would seem to be increasingly serious offenses. In fact, we are prone to laugh at the thought that we could be shot for seeking to discover the plot of any story, an exercise that critics, as a whole, have been engaging in over the course of centuries as they conducted their varied analyses in the pantheon of literary artists. Yet, we do not know how hard we should laugh because, as Twain warned us in "How to Tell a Story," there is some degree of gravity involved and part of the task, for us, is to ponder just where graveness ends and humor begins. Many people laugh when they are uncomfortable; others are far too serious about everything. Both of those aspects would seem to be defense mechanisms that provide us with no indication of what humor and seriousness are, let alone how they might be used to benefit the thinking process. The task of artistically presenting such a distinction to be drawn was therefore undertaken by Twain; and for something that has ironically been called a children's tale, it has left us unclear and uncomfortable for the well over 100 years that it has been in print.

Mosher's novel *The True Account* is similarly complicated. It is the tale of a Vermonter who, in 1803, approaches Thomas Jefferson, requesting permission to explore the Louisiana territory that the president has just purchased from France. It just so happens that the Vermonter, along with his 15-year-old nephew, seems to have already journeyed through the territory, having undertaken "the trip backward" as he puts it, since he made a point of sailing around the coast of South America and up the Pacific to begin his own expedition.

The problem, however, is that this Vermonter, the same Private True Teague Kinneson that I mention in Chapter IV, suffered what seems to be a brain injury, received back when he was "with Ethan Allen at Fort Ticonderoga" in 1775. So, much of what the private says is called into question in much the same way that Twain's character Jim's commentary is so often called into question. Just as was the case in *Huckleberry Finn*, where it is a teenage boy who is narrating the story, in *The True Account*, it is Kinneson's nephew who is telling the story, so events are relayed from his perspective even though, as was the case with Huck in Twain's novel, the journey to be undertaken involves a boy in the process of developing by virtue of his experiences with someone who would have been thought, by society at least, to be incapable of advising anyone.

As readers of *The True Account*, we are placed in the delicate position of having to judge a person who might be, for want of a better way to put it, mentally challenged. So, when he says the things he says, are we free to laugh or do we maintain a stoic literary posture? I am not so sure it is even helpful, here, to consider what Mosher himself had to say when I told him that I really enjoyed reading *The True Account*. His response was simply, "Yes, I had a lot of fun writing that one."[7] He had fun writing it; I had fun reading it; but I still wonder how much, exactly, am I allowed to laugh?

Kinneson is described as having "clothes and gear [that are] those of a knight-errant, consisting of chain mail, a belled night-stocking over a copper plate in his head, a red sash, and galoshes worn high or low as the occasion requires."[8] It is 1803, but he is dressed as a knight would have been dressed during the Middle Ages, and perhaps even somewhat

VI. The Technique of Humor

stranger than such a knight because the private is wearing not boots but galoshes and, from time to time, he pops open an umbrella or pulls out a trumpet to give "a long blast" or brandishes a musket so old that we wonder what its true purpose is. That description brings to mind how Twain, in his autobiography, describes the minstrels who performed in Hannibal:

> Their clothing was a loud and extravagant burlesque ... the minstrel appeared in a collar which engulfed and hid half of his head.... His coat was sometimes made of curtain calico with a swallowtail that hung nearly to his heels and had buttons as big as a blacking box. His shoes were rusty and clumsy and cumbersome and five or six sizes too large for him.[9]

In instances when white men painted themselves in blackface and wore the ludicrous clothes, it would have been easy to characterize the performances as simply racist. But what should we make of those instances when blacks performed in blackface? Even as late as 1981, the African American actor Ben Vereen received numerous complaints for having performed in blackface just in honor of the early actor Bert Williams's performances. And yet, one has to wonder about a character like Ralph Ellison's Dr. Bledsoe who, angry one moment, can readjust his "angry face like a sculptor, making it a bland mask, leaving only the sparkle of his eyes to betray the emotion that [the narrator] had seen only a moment before."[10] What blackface is, in essence, is a mask. We are troubled by it and thus decline to laugh nowadays, whether it is a white person or a black person who wears that mask. But a question remains as we hear Kinneson being referred to as the "runaway uncle" who, at times, is inclined to warble an implausible refrain, "Tooleree, tooleree, toolerlee," and at other times speaks from behind what can only be taken as a kind of mask itself.

Kinneson is too often referred to by that term, the "runaway uncle," for us not to draw some connection between him and Twain's Jim, the "runaway slave." As Mosher and I discussed the issue of insanity as it pertains to our two families, he asked me whether or not a particular uncle of mine had died in an institution. When I replied that as far as I know he did, Mosher went on to explain why he had asked the question. It turns out that a relative of his had been committed to an insane asylum. This relative was determined to run away and kept trying, although he would always be caught and brought back. Then, one day another relative of Mosher's came to visit the patient and was told, by the staff, that he had disappeared, the staff wanting the visiting relative to believe that this time the runaway had been successful and could not be found. Mosher's visiting relative, though, until the day he died, tried to prove that the institution had somehow authorized the patient's murder and, as a victim, he was secretly buried somewhere on that institution's grounds.[11]

My point is that just a few short generations ago, people who were declared insane, and subsequently institutionalized, could face horrors beyond what many of us could ever imagine, horrors that, like slavery, would warrant someone feeling the need to escape if they had been unable to avoid being put there in the first place. In his essay "Jim and Mark Twain: What Do Dey Stan' For?," Stephen Railton suggests that Jim, by the end of the novel, has been relegated to a clown-like status because, after all, Twain did have to accommodate his late-nineteenth-century white audience. Railton goes on to assert that by having the story told through Huck's childish "uncivilized voice," that audience does not necessarily have to "add up the implications of his experiences." There was a "truth" to be told, argues Railton, but even "by setting Huck loose to record how whites treat blacks, not to mention how they treat each other, Twain knew that he was pushing at the very limits of his license as a humorist."[12] What Twain could say exactly, and how he could say it, explains, in large part, the words of his "Notice" at the beginning of the novel, that anyone who even tries to find a moral in the narrative will be banished. To be sure, there are many morals to be garnered from the novel, but that is for the reader to ascertain for himself. Twain's primary mission is to make sure that his audience listens intently as he undertakes the task of telling the tale in the most interesting way that he can, which means that humor at times will be necessary even if it does butt up against what many of us, as readers, would design to declare as serious matter of the kind that is inappropriate to present in a humorous manner.

In his discussion of Faulkner's trilogy—*The Hamlet* (1940), *The Town* (1957), and *The Mansion* (1959)—Percy Adams maintains that "the humor in the completed trilogy is not there just for its own sake, nor is

• *VI. The Technique of Humor* •

it inadequate or damaging to the plan of the total work. Taken out of context much of it is uproarious farce, but all of it is more successful when read as an element of structure or as development of a theme."[13] As with *Huckleberry Finn*, there are plenty of themes or morals that one could find in Faulkner's trilogy, and that is not necessarily a bad thing. However, where I agree with Adams most, especially as pertains to *Huckleberry Finn* and *The True Account*, is with regard to humor all in itself as an "element of structure" that is key to those novels' success as works of art.

Not only is the humor filtered throughout both of those novels, but humor serves as the sturdy beginning and end of the works. *Huckleberry Finn* opens with the "Notice" and ends with the Evasion chapters, so humorous that critics such as Railton have labeled them a flaw that "trivializes the novel's issues." When I asked Twain scholar Robert Lamb how he thought I should perceive the novel's ending, he reminded me, first, of how keenly aware Twain was of what was going on in the post–Reconstruction era and, second, how the apparent reduction of Jim into a burlesque figure was a reflection of how blacks had startlingly lost ground during that phase in American history.[14] Considering Lamb's thoughts on the matter, we are evidently left by Twain to ascertain for ourselves just who Jim is, even in terms of his relationship to Huck whom he regards as his friend but whom Lamb asserts is really "so much more," this so much more being a matter that I will return to later.

Humor looms as a curious structural device near the end of *The True Account* as well, as we find Kinneson having, for a third time, accidently sewn his thumb into some "pink and yellow silk cloth" while he is making something that neither we nor his nephew can ascertain. After having experienced all manner of good and evil in his adventures, throughout the novel, he is preparing a hot-air balloon which he will ride in alone toward what Mosher's own wife Phillis, through the character of Yellow Sage Flower Who Tells Wise Stories, informs will be "many wonderful new adventures." There will be more stories in store for Kinneson and if his old attire and newly built means of transportation are any indication, those coming stories will be filled with humor even as the tragic parts remain.

Yet, as we near the novel's end, Kinneson offers us the same element of complexity that Railton suggests was the case with Twain. Railton spoke about how Twain had been able to "push" at the limits of his license as a humorist by using Huck to tell the story. It is Huck, for the most part, who records how whites treat blacks as well as how whites treat each other. A prime example would be Huck's own father, pap, who is capable of raining down abuse on his son to the point of literally making him a prisoner. There would seem to be nothing funny about such abuse, but then again we must remember Twain's own words from "How to Tell a Story" where he insists that humor is necessary, but dependent on the *manner* of the telling. Thus Huck tells the story of his abuse:

> Every little while he locked me in and went down to the store, three miles to the ferry, and traded fish and game for whisky and fetched it home and got drunk and had a good time, and licked me. The widow she found out where I was by and by, and she sent a man over to try to get hold of me, but pap drove him off with the gun, and it warn't long after that till I was used to being where I was, and liked it, all but the cowhide part.[15]

Huck has no desire to return to the Widow Douglas's home because he does not want to become "sivilized." But then, he does not want to be beaten either, or locked up like a wild animal in captivity. And many readers are disturbed upon learning how the boy came to like living with pap, readers who are disturbed at the tragedy while at the same time having to cover their mouths to keep from laughing as they listen to him, quite innocently but also linguistically adept, refer to his being beaten, not as a whipping, but simply "the cowhide part."

At the end of *The True Account*, as Kinneson is humorously working on his balloon, he takes on a subject for discussion so serious as the devil himself. He tells his nephew, "I have concluded that the more important struggles in this world are not those between us mortals and the Devil, or even between Good and Evil. Rather, the more difficult conflicts are those between human beings."[16] It is as if the devil, particularly what we know of from biblical reference, has been removed from the equation as, even without devilish assistance, we are capable of treating each other quite horribly. Then we are told that Kinneson "gave the bell on his cap a vigorous jingling," that bell being the harness bell attached to the end of his red woolen night-stocking that covers the copper crown that itself covers the head injury, the one that presumably

• VI. *The Technique of Humor* •

lessened his mental capacity. But if he is of lessened mental capacity, then it is a rather intriguing lessened capacity because he, of all people, is the one who renders the most profound pronouncements about life. "Our lives are mighty paradoxes," he tells his nephew at one point, that uncle jingling his stocking-cap bell as he speaks, a bell that we had already been told was there to remind him, and presumably remind us all, that none of us can escape the extent to which "all men are fools."

And that means *all* men. Mosher, as had been the case in *Gatlinburg*, is not inclined here, either, to even spare United States presidents. At the beginning of *The True Account*, we see Thomas Jefferson pulling Kinneson's nephew aside to ask if he would be willing to trick his uncle into believing that he is headed in the direction of exploring the Louisiana territory while actually heading back north toward Vermont. That nephew, Ticonderoga Kinneson, never believed he could pull off the trick but nevertheless tells Jefferson, "It is possible." Uncle and nephew are able to extract, from Jefferson, a stallion, a mule, forty dollars, and the president's good wishes for the supposed expedition. Ti (the nephew's nickname) does try to sway his uncle toward the north, but the surprisingly perceptive uncle demurs, insisting that they need to proceed "due *west*, into the mountains, to elude any pursuers who might still be on the track of a 'runaway uncle.'"[17] Private Kinneson will undertake his own Louisiana Purchase expedition, regardless of Jefferson's lack of legitimate support. But that specific mission is no more the core essence of Mosher's story than Jim's escape from slavery is the ultimate meaning of *Huckleberry Finn*. Otherwise, Twain would not have had the escaped slave venture toward the deep South to make his getaway.

In their escape, Jim and Huck encounter two shysters, the younger one claiming to be the Duke of Bridgewater, the older one claiming to be the King of France. Huck, in turn, conjures up an elaborate tale of his own to explain what he, the white boy, and Jim, the black man, are doing traveling together. The king and duke even ask Huck directly, "[W]as Jim a runaway nigger?" to which Huck calculatingly responds:

> "Goodness sakes, would a runaway nigger run *south*?" … "My folks was living in Pike County, in Missouri, where I was born, and they all died off but me and pa and my brother Ike. Pa, he 'lowed he'd break up and go down and live with Uncle Ben, who's got a little one-horse place on the

river, forty-four mile below Orleans. Pa was pretty poor, and had some debts; so when he'd squared up there warn't nothing left but sixteen dollars and our nigger, Jim. That warn't enough to take us fourteen hundred mile, deck passage nor no other way. Well, when the river rose, pa had a streak of luck one day; he ketched this piece of a raft; so we reckoned we'd go down to Orleans on it. Pa's luck didn't hold out; a steamboat run over the forrard corner of the raft, one night, and we all went overboard and dove under the wheel; Jim and me come up, all right, but pa was drunk, and Ike was only four years old, so they never come up no more."[18]

Notice that there are no tears, from Huck, as he tells this tragic story about his family and how "they all died off." Needless to say, the king and duke do not take the time to show any sympathy or even offer their condolences. They just set about the task of planning how best to function in the midst of their own uncertain circumstances.

They fancy themselves actors and, as such, they fall right into the minstrelsy category. They will stage their own version of *Romeo and Juliet,* and then *The Royal Nonesuch,* counting on the citizens living in small towns, up and down the Mississippi, not to know the difference between a legitimate Shakespearean performance and an old baldheaded bearded man dressed up in night clothes to play the role of the teenage lover, Juliet. The king and duke are, in fact, able to pull off their deception for a while, collecting quite a bit of money in the beginning, which begs the question not only with regard to those theatrical performances but also with regard to how much *Huckleberry Finn,* as a whole, should be thought of as just one long minstrel show with Huck sometimes in the role of Sarah Mary Williams and Jim sometimes in the role of the ignorant nigger taking his cues from Huck on when he should speak and when he should shut up. It is minstrelsy at its best since the audience does not know exactly how to respond. The whole matter of how much to laugh or, on the other hand, how much to cry becomes a never-ending cyclical issue that defies any simple explanation as humor and tragedy are the two inextricable parts of a whole that, even in our intense contemplations, are prone to leave us baffled.

In *The True Account,* Private Kinneson had not really needed Jefferson's forty dollars. Long before venturing out to Monticello, the Vermonter had been working on a play that, for more than 20 years, he had been calling *The Tragical History of Ethan Ellen, or The Fall of Fort Ticon-*

• VI. *The Technique of Humor* •

deroga, and it had on occasion been performed before relatively large audiences. Interestingly enough, once he takes the production to New York City, he receives a review that at first renders him angry and then reflective about what a new title for his play should perhaps be. Writing for "the *Times*," the reviewer lambasted the play as being "the greatest farce ever written. Juvenile in conception, violent in execution, puerile, nay, prurient, in its attempts at humor, and in the most vile taste, *Ethan Allen* violates all known principles of composition. Characters are thinly drawn, nor do their actions flow from human nature, but rather from the diseased imagination and self-conscious extravagances of the author."[19] Ti informs us that his uncle had "styled" the play a tragedy because he felt that Allen had been "undervalued" in history and indeed should have been America's first president. In fact, that leader of the Green Mountain Boys did contribute substantially to the nation's origins, from the time when he walked out of Connecticut to fight for the New Hampshire Grants settlers' freedom to establish that territory, to his taking from the British, without firing a single shot, the fort in Ticonderoga. Yet, the *Times* reviewer found the play about Allen to have been silly, overly sexual, extravagant, and with characters so thinly drawn that we wonder if what Kinneson has rendered, for his audience, verges on caricature or, on the other hand, just something that the audiences cannot understand in terms of the full complexity.

I am reminded, here, of a brisk winter evening—February 26, 1972—when I took the walk from the University of Virginia campus to attend the Lions Club's 30th Annual Minstrel and Variety Show, an experiment that I decided to undertake since it was related to one of the subjects we had been reading about in the "Studies in Folklore" class. What struck me most about the show was a character named "Dirt Cheap" Wallace, a white man made up in blackface with a swallowtail coat along the lines of what Twain described, in his autobiography, as how the minstrels were dressed in the first such show to arrive in Hannibal, Missouri. Wallace's bowtie was at least four times as large as what would seem normal, and his nappy wig highlighted the bulging white eyes and broad white-lipped grin, indeed the supreme caricature of a human being.

I had been advised by my fellow black students, at the University, not to attend. They anticipated that the show would be an insult not just to me but the entire black race. I certainly understood their perspective. Yet, now in retrospect, I am not sure how to feel about the participants in the show; I hesitate to declare them all racists, just as I hesitate to declare Twain a racist even as I ponder the extent to which, in Stephen Railton's words, Twain may have "sold Jim into burlesque" and transformed him "into a comic stereotype." Perhaps I would have been satisfied to conclude that such is what the Lions Club sponsors had allowed to occur with "Dirt Cheap." But when the comic "Dirt Cheap" let down the mask long enough to deliver a serious complex-filled rendition of "Ole Man River," I was confused once again about exactly how I should feel, for what does a white man, albeit in blackface, really understand about being "tired a livin' but 'feared a dyin'?" And yet, the song coming from the caricature was as full of humanity, in all its extensive value, as anything I had ever heard before.

As I read, in *The True Account*, how the *Times* reviewer found Kinneson's characters to have been "thinly drawn," including, I would imagine, the character of Ethan Allen himself, I am brought to consider how much that reviewer might have misunderstood Kinneson's words as conveyed through the characters' dialogue presentations. Kinneson deemed his theatrical production a tragedy, but the reviewer contends that the play is "hilarious," and "the greatest farce ever written." Perhaps the disparity, as between Kinneson's intended creation, and the reviewer's response, is a tribute to the complexity of the real Ethan Allen. At any rate, Kinneson has no problem, at a point, simply altering the title—a significant alteration and yet perhaps not so significant at all—from *The Tragical History of Ethan Allen* to *The Most Comical History of Ethan Allen*. The title of the play has changed but the content of the play is the same and that, when one ponders what the difference between tragedy and comedy might be, is a paradox of vast, perhaps irreconcilable proportion.

The human mind, body, and soul, all combined, is a quite complicated entity, but I am no less guilty than others in wanting to assess the aggregate of those parts in a far too simplistic manner, which is why I had to ask flat-out, of Professor Lamb, if indeed Mark Twain was a racist, to which Lamb responded "no" and then added, as if the presentation

VI. The Technique of Humor

of Jim was the focal point of how one should arrive at a conclusion: "One thing you have to remember is that Jim is a master of the minstrel mask. He wears the mask so well that, for about 100 years, critics didn't know it was a mask."[20]

It reminds us of another Jim, the one in *Invisible Man* who tells the elaborate tale of how he committed incest with his daughter. For quite some time, literary critics believed that he actually did commit the act. Even the novel's narrator is aghast, wondering, "How can he tell this to white men...? I looked at the floor, a red mist of anguish before my eyes."[21] That narrator is embarrassed, believing, as many readers once did, that not only did Jim Trueblood commit the sin of incest and then the social sin of telling his story to whites, but that he also is indeed the personification of evil as far as the novel is concerned. We were quite anxious to roundly condemn him until the critic Houston Baker explained that "the main character in the Trueblood episode ... is both a country blues singer ... and a virtuoso prose narrator ... one must first comprehend, I think, the sharecropper Trueblood's dual manifestation as trickster and merchant, as creative and commercial man."[22] Twain's character Jim is commercial in the sense that he has stolen himself away from his master and intends to work so that he can, first, buy his wife's freedom and then they, together, can work hard enough to buy the freedom of their children. Ellison's Jim is some distance removed from slavery but not so far removed that he will not have to be—like the spider Anansi and Twain's Jim in the midst of powerful adversaries—a trickster extraordinaire.

Twain's Jim has accomplished an extraordinary feat by escaping from slavery, but perhaps just as extraordinary is the long-term trick that he plays on Huck himself, letting him believe that pap is still alive and someone Huck needs to continue to run away from, thus allowing Jim the white escort that will increase the chances of his own escape continuing to be successful. That strategy, in itself, disproves the theory that Jim is but an ignorant nigger. Nor, as I addressed earlier in my discussion of Kinneson's experience with Thomas Jefferson, is the former just the "daft" victim of a head injury suffered at Ticonderoga. The story of how he got the injury is suspicious, but then as he proceeds along the trail, navigating his way through the Louisiana territory, we find him to be at least as adept a storyteller as Twain's and Ellison's Jims. Spinning, to the Sioux Indians, an elaborate yarn about who the members of the Lewis and Clark expedition are, Kinneson says they are Martians who must be handled with "moderation" because "if the Sioux harmed them, far more would descend from the skies—more than the buffalo of the plains, and fiercer, too."[23] Kinneson goes on to warn the Native Americans that one of the first things those Martians "would no doubt" do is confiscate all their hemp, a gift that Kinneson had given the Sioux to insure his own safe passage. When one thinks about how often Native Americans have been tricked out of their land with meager gifts, including alcohol, it is easy to see how someone might argue that an author should not make light of the mind-altering drug factor that was systematically involved in whites taking control of land that once belonged to Indians. However, it has to be acknowledged that such events took place and as we watch, in Mosher's novel, the Lewis and Clark expedition being allowed to pass on through, we wonder whether the events, leading up to their safe passage, are more tragic or comic or indeed an inextricably linked combination of both artistic attributes.

Kinneson will actually save the Lewis and Clark expedition many more times, the members of which he views nonetheless as his competitors in a race to the Pacific. When Lewis learns that this is how the private perceives the situation, he retorts angrily, "We are engaged in no race, but the most serious of enterprises in the interest of our country."[24] Kinneson, at that point, does not respond directly to Lewis, but once both Lewis and Clark are "out of earshot" he takes the opportunity to instruct his nephew, with regard to Lewis's statement, that "we would all do better to take ourselves less seriously by one half."[25] That "one half" designation is a curious one, prompting us to conclude that the other half can indeed be serious, leaving us, however, still contemplating the extent to which there must be a trick involved in the dichotomous process.

We can be sure, though, that the young charges, under Private Kinneson and Twain's Jim, respectively, have achieved a high level of skill in the endeavor of applying such multi-faceted trickery. Excited about acquiring freedom, Jim tells Huck, "You's de bes' fren' Jim's ever had; en you's de *only* fren' ole Jim's got now."[26] However, when I asked Lamb if Jim and Huck were friends, his response was, "So much more than that.

VI. The Technique of Humor

Jim was a *father* to Huck, his mentor, his protector, his conscience."[27] Lamb went on to explain that society would never, at that time, have allowed Jim to be Huck's "father" even though he serves that function in terms of the novel's events.

Among other things, Huck has indeed mastered the art of lying. He is, as I mentioned earlier, Sarah Mary Williams when he needs to be, but then upon finding himself caught up in the middle of the Grangerford-Shepherdson feud, he becomes George Jackson but still subject to being searched and interrogated by the Grangerfords whereupon he pleads, "I'm only a boy," and then he, in characteristic form, concocts yet another story about his tragic life:

> I told them how pap and me and all the family was living on a little farm down at the bottom of Arkansaw, and my sister Mary Ann run off and got married and never was heard of no more, and Bill went to hunt them and he warn't heard of no more, and Tom and Mort died, and then there warn't nobody but just me and pap left, and he was just trimmed down to nothing, on account of his troubles; so when he died I took what there was left, because the farm didn't belong to us, and started up the river, deck passage, and fell overboard; and that was how I come to be here.[28]

The Grangerford family is so smitten by the boy, and sympathetic with regard to his tragic life history, that they offer to let him stay with them as long as he wants. Yet, for the reader, even though danger is still lurking for Huck, the language and the story as a whole are ingeniously comic as he conjures up one family member after another only to have them disappear or, as he has told it before, die off so that he can seem all the more forlorn.

Ti, by the end of *The True Account*, is also a master of deception so much so that Smoke, the chief of the Blackfoot Indians, thinks of him as a "wizard" and a "dangerous liar," and is in fact anxious to kill him, whereupon Ti, coincidentally a painter, quickly sets up his easel and paints a portrait of himself. The chief arrives to finish Ti off, thrusting his lance through the nephew's chest and then letting out a "shout of triumph" at having done the murderous deed. But by then, the real Ti is gone and the chief is "left with nothing but a torn painting" because, as it turns out, "the great Smoke had [only] killed a picture."[29]

By this time, Private Kinneson has already gone off in his balloon,

Howard Frank Mosher and the Classics

but we can feel confident that Ti will be able to survive as we find Smoke killing off one portrait after another until the boy offers him the ultimate trickster deal, all the medicine of his paintings "in exchange for the safety of the American explorers." Not only will Ti survive but he has taken up the baton of his uncle, insuring, also, the safety of the Lewis and Clark expedition. In *Huckleberry Finn*, Jim will eventually have to leave Huck's side, for in the immediate post–Civil War era, it will no longer be safe for him to remain alongside a white child. In similar fashion, Mosher's Private Kinneson must now take leave of the nephew that he taught so well, that uncle knowing, far better than anyone else, that he is still a "runaway uncle" who can never be sure what will happen to him if ever he is caught.

• VII •

William Faulkner's *Go Down, Moses* and Mosher's Mourning the Inevitable Loss of a Kingdom

Drawing a distinction between Ernest Hemingway's *The Old Man and the Sea* and William Faulkner's short story collection, entitled *Big Woods*, Matt Low stipulates that "the act of fishing is certainly not the same as the act of hunting. For better or for worse, the much less active—almost leisurely—practices of fishing are not nearly so demanding, on both the human and ecological levels, as the week-long bear hunts."[1] In referring to "human and ecological levels," Low is declaring that challenges, both man-made and nature-caused, are not as difficult for the fisherman as are the challenges for the hunter who must track down his prey, sometimes over the course of days through untamed forests, and then have the necessary skill, once the prey is found, to shoot it even though, as the narrator of *Go Down, Moses* describes it, that prey can sometimes materialize "out of nothing, magnificent with speed," such that, even in death the animal seems not to have lost anything of its essence. When questioned, by a student at the University of Virginia back in 1958, as to the meaning of the hunt in "The Bear," Faulkner replied that

> the hunt was simply a symbol of pursuit.... The protagonist could have been anything else besides that bear ... not only to pursue but to overtake and then have the compassion not to destroy, to catch, to touch, and then let go because then tomorrow you can pursue again. If you destroy it, what you caught, then it's gone, it's finished. And that to me is sometimes the greater

part of valor but always the greater part of pleasure, not to destroy what you have pursued. The pursuit is the thing, not the reward, not the gain.[2]

It might at first seem that, as pertains to the interview and the novel itself, there is a contradiction. In the interview, Faulkner advocated not destroying the prey, but a large part of *Go Down, Moses* is devoted to the process whereby hunters go through their yearly ritual of stalking prey and then killing it as the boy Isaac McCaslin himself actually does, having first killed smaller animals around home and then, out in the woods, having shot and killed his first buck at the age of 12.

What we must remember though is that, before the advent of modern civilization, man had to hunt in the wild in order to acquire his food. That activity was a vital part of the cycle of life, not only human life but the cycle of life in the animal world. As the days during the Fall season began to grow cold, men would venture out into nature, with their guns, and hunt down the food that would mean the difference as to whether or not their families would survive through the winter. It was a ritual for these men who would meet at a hunters' cabin and go out together, drinking and telling stories to fortify themselves while they tracked and waited and tracked some more, doing what their fathers had done before them, and their fathers' fathers before that. Bringing the meat back, they with great expertise, before the era of refrigerators, would salt the meat down, store it in smokehouses and ration it until the arrival of warm weather would start the whole process again.

By shooting his first deer, at the age of 12, Isaac has entered fullblown into the ritual. We are told, in "The Old People" section of the novel, that when he killed the deer, "something happened to him: in less than a second he had ceased forever to be the child he was yesterday."[3] Even at that tender age, he has entered into manhood, and a particularly insightful manhood because he has the "compassion" to which Faulkner referred, in the University of Virginia interview, a capacity, even as he takes the buck's life, for "loving the life he spills." This is why, when another splendid buck comes along, later in the day, he does not shoot it. This is why, in all of his decades of hunting, he will marvel at Old Ben, the majestic bear that is at the heart of *Go Down, Moses*, but he will not shoot it either, preferring instead to simply watch as it "faded back into the wilderness without motion as he had watched a fish, a

• VII •

William Faulkner's *Go Down, Moses* and Mosher's Mourning the Inevitable Loss of a Kingdom

Drawing a distinction between Ernest Hemingway's *The Old Man and the Sea* and William Faulkner's short story collection, entitled *Big Woods*, Matt Low stipulates that "the act of fishing is certainly not the same as the act of hunting. For better or for worse, the much less active—almost leisurely—practices of fishing are not nearly so demanding, on both the human and ecological levels, as the week-long bear hunts."[1] In referring to "human and ecological levels," Low is declaring that challenges, both man-made and nature-caused, are not as difficult for the fisherman as are the challenges for the hunter who must track down his prey, sometimes over the course of days through untamed forests, and then have the necessary skill, once the prey is found, to shoot it even though, as the narrator of *Go Down, Moses* describes it, that prey can sometimes materialize "out of nothing, magnificent with speed," such that, even in death the animal seems not to have lost anything of its essence. When questioned, by a student at the University of Virginia back in 1958, as to the meaning of the hunt in "The Bear," Faulkner replied that

> the hunt was simply a symbol of pursuit.... The protagonist could have been anything else besides that bear ... not only to pursue but to overtake and then have the compassion not to destroy, to catch, to touch, and then let go because then tomorrow you can pursue again. If you destroy it, what you caught, then it's gone, it's finished. And that to me is sometimes the greater

part of valor but always the greater part of pleasure, not to destroy what you have pursued. The pursuit is the thing, not the reward, not the gain.²

It might at first seem that, as pertains to the interview and the novel itself, there is a contradiction. In the interview, Faulkner advocated not destroying the prey, but a large part of *Go Down, Moses* is devoted to the process whereby hunters go through their yearly ritual of stalking prey and then killing it as the boy Isaac McCaslin himself actually does, having first killed smaller animals around home and then, out in the woods, having shot and killed his first buck at the age of 12.

What we must remember though is that, before the advent of modern civilization, man had to hunt in the wild in order to acquire his food. That activity was a vital part of the cycle of life, not only human life but the cycle of life in the animal world. As the days during the Fall season began to grow cold, men would venture out into nature, with their guns, and hunt down the food that would mean the difference as to whether or not their families would survive through the winter. It was a ritual for these men who would meet at a hunters' cabin and go out together, drinking and telling stories to fortify themselves while they tracked and waited and tracked some more, doing what their fathers had done before them, and their fathers' fathers before that. Bringing the meat back, they with great expertise, before the era of refrigerators, would salt the meat down, store it in smokehouses and ration it until the arrival of warm weather would start the whole process again.

By shooting his first deer, at the age of 12, Isaac has entered full-blown into the ritual. We are told, in "The Old People" section of the novel, that when he killed the deer, "something happened to him: in less than a second he had ceased forever to be the child he was yesterday."³ Even at that tender age, he has entered into manhood, and a particularly insightful manhood because he has the "compassion" to which Faulkner referred, in the University of Virginia interview, a capacity, even as he takes the buck's life, for "loving the life he spills." This is why, when another splendid buck comes along, later in the day, he does not shoot it. This is why, in all of his decades of hunting, he will marvel at Old Ben, the majestic bear that is at the heart of *Go Down, Moses*, but he will not shoot it either, preferring instead to simply watch as it "faded back into the wilderness without motion as he had watched a fish, a

VII. Mourning the Inevitable Loss

huge old bass, sink back into the dark depths of its pool and vanish without even any movement of its fins."[4]

There, Faulkner draws a connection, not a distinction, between bear and fish, leaving us with no choice but to accept what he had said in the interview, that the animal being pursued "could have been anything else besides that bear." And it is likewise not so important whether or not the pursuit is a difficult one—such as what a bear hunting expedition might present—or the "leisurely" waiting for a fish to arrive and nibble at the bait as one sits on the bank of a river holding the fishing pole. Mosher, calling himself in *North Country* an "inveterate fisherman," recounts how he began fishing when he was five years old and then, by age 12, he was going on fishing expeditions, leaving his Catskills home and venturing off, with his father and uncle, into Canada and Maine. By the time he was 50, he had decided to drive the whole distance along the Canadian border and, during that journey, found time to stop at the Flathead River in Montana and hook his line in hopes of catching a "big fish" that he had seen some previous time before. Referring to it as "my fish," Mosher says that, in contending with that trout, he "felt connected" to both the river and the countryside through which it flowed. And when he catches it, he simply marvels at it—just as Isaac McCaslin might have done—marveling at the "big male upward of two feet long and weighing perhaps five pounds, with lemon-yellow belly and vermilion spots the size of dimes on his sides."[5] Some might think that a magnificent specimen, such as that, would be the perfect trophy to hang on somebody's wall, but Mosher, after admiring it for a bit, let the fish go free. There have been many fishermen who have released fish after they had been caught, so Mosher's act of compassion, toward his fish, need not be considered all that unusual. However, just as the boy Ike McCaslin is somehow different from the other men in the hunting party, so too might Mosher be something of a different sort than even the typically humane fisherman who is inclined, for one reason or another, to toss a caught fish back into the water to swim "unhurriedly" away.

Barely a man himself when he first settled down in the Northeast Kingdom region of Vermont in 1964, Mosher would work alongside his wife, teaching at the Orleans High School. But he also wanted to write short stories and so he applied to the writing program at the University of California-Irvine. In what might well have been the shortest enrollment in the history of that institution, he appeared, in 1969 on campus, and three days later was on his way back home to the Northeast Kingdom with its breathtaking vistas that include, as I noted in my introduction, "35,575 acres of public lakes and ponds and nearly 4,000 miles of public rivers and streams."[6] Upon being asked why he returned so quickly, Mosher has a ready answer. He came back to Vermont because in California he had "felt disconnected."[7] A problem arose, though, because when he and Phillis went out west, they had had to relinquish their jobs in Vermont. Then, upon their return, a job was available for her, but the position that Mosher had given up was no longer available as it had been filled by somebody else.

So, the would-be writer appealed to a local woodsman, Jake Blodgett, for employment; and while working alongside old Jake out there in the woods, he listened to the tales of bygone times, Jake's own recapitulations about the rough-hewn era of Prohibition and the other old days when people were exactly how Mosher himself yearned to be, as connected to the mountainous woods and sparkling waterways as he could possibly get. Mosher acknowledges that Blodgett served as the model for the character Noël Lord, that fiercely independent logger, in *Where the Rivers Flow North*, who lives a short distance from Kingdom Common and is so much attached to the rural landscape that he can go months without setting foot in the village itself.

But Blodgett served as a model for more than just Lord. We find the essence of Blodgett in *Disappearances*' Quebec Bill Bonhomme. And in *Northern Borders*' Austen Kittredge who lives 15 miles outside of the Common, in a place called Lost Nation Hollow that has, as its creative source, a winding river that not only provided sustenance for the Hollow but also for places above and below the Hollow as it links up with other waterways, creates falls and "passed through a flat where willow trees grew thick on both sides. Then, having already transformed from a lacy network of hidden rills into a swift brook and from a brook into a small river, it metamorphosed in character once again. It broadened out, deepened, slowed to a crawl, and entered a marshy wetlands full of ducks and snapping turtles, muskrats and minks and otters and moose."[8] Mosher's language here is so powerful that one can almost feel, within

• *VII. Mourning the Inevitable Loss* •

his bones, the river surging and ebbing. And one can certainly see, with just a minimal amount of imagination, the different species that live within it or meander along its banks.

Actually, it is Austen Kittredge III, Kittredge's grandson, who is telling the story of the river just as it had been told to him by that grandfather who, as we listen, takes on the appurtenances of not only Jake Blodgett but also Sam Fathers—the part-Indian, part-black mentor of Ike's in *Go Down, Moses*—who initiates the boy, smearing his face with the blood of his first buck which "marked him forever one with the wilderness." Just as Fathers had done with Ike, Grandfather Kittredge takes his grandson out to a deer stand to wait and learn, among other things, patience and humility until the day comes when this boy also will shoot his first buck and thereby enter into the realm of a special kind of manhood that, much more than just the indicator of a level of skilled marksmanship, is an indicator of his understanding and appreciation of how humans are bound to the world of nature, not so much different from how the ducks and turtles and other animals are linked, for their survival, to the life-giving river of the grandfather's Lost Nation origin story.

In his essay on "The Bear," John Lydenberg argues that, for the hunters in that story, "the bear is more than a bear" but it is instead "the preternatural animal that symbolizes for them their relation to Nature and thus to life.... [B]eneath the conventional ritual lies the religious rite: the hunting of the tribal god, whom they dare not, and cannot, touch."[9] This is something that Grandfather Kittredge understands completely as he "refused to shoot a bear." Something that Ike understood as well, even before he was old enough to go on the hunt which, in those early days, had not been so much a hunt as it was the fulfilling of a commitment "to keep yearly rendezvous with the bear which they did not even intend to kill,"[10] for killing it would be tantamount to killing, in Lydenberg's words, "the tribal god" who is not just a physical link but, more importantly, the spiritual connector that affords the hunters the very lives they are blessed to have. When hunters do catch up to Old Ben, and Boon Hogganbeck ultimately kills him, it is not so much that they did so by their own devices as it is a case of the giant bear being tired of the centuries-long struggle within which he had been embroiled. Riddled with dozens of bullets in his hide, disfigured by the traps that had been set to catch him, it is almost as if he had been lying in wait, not that he had been tracked down, but that he wanted to finally be caught, like Vermont's last panther that Noël Lord thought he had killed by virtue of his own skill and courage but, upon further contemplation, realizes it was the panther who was giving himself up as he came "down to the camp and killed the deer and scared the horse in order to be chased and shot and killed."[11] We might assume at this point, that both the panther and the bear are gone and thus the woods will be a much safer place. But nothing could be further from the truth, because the physical deaths of those animals serves as but an omen of something else that is about to come, something so devastating that it, in all its various guises, forms the tragic underlying thread that runs through the bulk of both Faulkner's and Mosher's works.

It was the mysterious Aunt Cordelia who, in *Disappearances*, warned Wild Bill Bonhomme, "You can't possess land, any more than you can possess another person. We dispossess ourselves through possessions."[12] This is the same message that Faulkner conveys, in *Go Down, Moses*, when he says that there was never any land and slave heritage for Ike to repudiate because the land had never belonged to the Chickasaw chief Ikkemotubbe to be able to sell to Ike's grandfather, old Carothers, because God had not provided the earth for one man "to hold for himself and his descendants inviolable title forever, generation after generation, to the oblongs and squares of the earth, but to hold the earth mutual and intact in the communal anonymity of brotherhood."[13] Ike wants to relinquish any claim to his grandfather's estate, particularly since the ownership of land, in old Carothers's case, is inextricably tied to the ownership of human beings, an ownership so unimaginably horrible that we find the elderly Ike, in the "Was" section of the novel, owning little else besides the cot that he uses to sleep on when he is camping in the woods. However, as the woods recede further and further into nothingness, we find the old Uncle Ike not charting a new path, based on the promise of his youthful connectedness to nature, but instead following down a path similar to that of old Carothers himself, Ike now unable to express any real affection for either his young cousin Roth's black mistress or their recently born child.

When Faulkner has Ike saying or thinking or feeling "*maybe in a*

• **VII. Mourning the Inevitable Loss** •

thousand or two thousand years," he has reference to the miscegenation that a union between Roth and the mistress would represent. A thousand years is almost like saying never, and one thus wonders how the author himself felt about the issue. When I took my "Faulkner" seminar from Joseph Blotner at the University of Michigan, during the Fall of 1983, I made it a point to go to that professor's office to discuss the Mississippi writer, from the perspective of a young black man who had himself grown up in the rural South and was now contemplating how I should feel about this white male author who seemed to have been so dedicated to exploring the complexities of race in terms of analyzing the remnants of the land upon which blacks were at one time held in legal bondage. Well aware that Faulkner had been a writer-in-residence in the late 1950s at the University of Virginia, where both Blotner and I had spent significant periods of time during different academic eras, I took advantage of that Faulkner biographer's general largesse, to students, and asked, "If I had come into his office at the University of Virginia and told him that I admired his work greatly, how would he have felt about me?" Blotner, who was not only Faulkner's biographer but also his dear friend, answered me by saying that the writer was not above believing that blacks, such as Ralph Bunche (the Nobel Peace Prize winner) and Joe Louis (the heavyweight boxing champion), were able to achieve, what they did, only in direct proportion to the amount of white blood they had running through their veins.

That may sound like a racist statement; but if it is, then there are many people, both black and white, who feel the exact same way. As inept as Ike is in resolving the race problem, he does have a keen understanding of not only the social circumstance of race but also the profound psychological underpinnings as he advises Roth's mistress, "Marry a black man. You are young, handsome, almost white; you could find a black man who would see in you what it was you saw in [Roth], who would ask nothing of you and expect less and get even still less than that, if it's revenge you want."[14] Ike, and likewise Faulkner, does understand what slavery has wrought. That past still guides so much of our current interaction, even down to whom we can and cannot marry, where we should avoid sending our children to school, and what to do about the socioeconomic class disparity situation.

Howard Frank Mosher and the Classics

Though he was asked often enough about it, Faulkner could not come up with a solution to the race issue. Nor could he offer a solution for the vanishing wilderness. When asked about the meaning of the "possession and destruction" of the woods, the author lamented, "I think that man progresses mechanically and technically much faster than he does spiritually, that there may be something he could substitute for the ruined wilderness, but he hasn't found that."[15] Sam Fathers is the "priest" of the woods, who oversees Ike's apprenticeship for that same position, and yet neither of them has the power to stop Major de Spain from selling timber-rights to a Memphis lumber company that will strip the land of not only its majesty but also its potential for immortality and the immortality of those who believed that in communing with nature, they were drawing closer to God. Had there been something available to substitute for the ruined wilderness, Sam Fathers would have known what that other thing was. But there is no adequate substitute for nature, which is why when Old Ben, the very epitome of nature, goes down, Fathers collapses on the spot and it will be only a matter of days before he is gone as well.

In *Rivers Flow North*, Mosher's version of the Memphis lumber company is the Northern Vermont Power Company that is building a dam and wants Lord to close a gate on the property that he is leasing even though doing so will flood out his cedar still. The power company is concerned that if the gate is not closed, then too much water will come down the flume. In this conflict, the question becomes one of who will get their way—the mega-company with its unlimited resources or the independent-minded logger trying to hold on to his livelihood. When the company official, who comes out to see Lord, asks him what he wants, Lord answers cagily, "I might consider them old pine trees." Thinking that he now has Lord exactly where he wants him, the official then lays out what the company has in mind.

> Now you can retire under your trees. We've been talking about moving your cabin up the ridge and arranging for you to be caretaker for the park. Visitors could come up by motor launch and you could show them how folks lived back in the olden days. You could give tours of the trees, explain how they go back in your family.[16]

However, Lord has something else in mind that he keeps so much a secret to himself that, for a while, he will not even tell his companion,

VII. Mourning the Inevitable Loss

the part-Indian woman, Bangor, who is fond of saying, in response to Lord's eccentric ways, that he is the kind of person who would cut off his own nose just to spite his face. Her characterization of him is, in some ways, an accurate assessment of his obstinacy. But his eccentricity is the same eccentricity that had allowed generations of his ancestors to make their living off the land; and the obstinacy of Lord is one and the same as the obstinacy of the pine trees themselves that had weathered the elements for a thousand years, so intent were they on their own survival.

Lord has no intention of being a tour guide to the trees "for city people to gaze at." In doing so, he would have been as out of place as old Uncle Ike was out of place traveling with the new generation of hunters, one of them—Will Legate—actually saying, about Ike, that "he aint got any business" here. We, as readers, gain some perspective on the connection between the old woodsmen as we reflect back on how Lord was only 14 years old when he shot the panther that had appeared as a threat to all the nearby farms. The age is important because—not unlike Ike McCaslin and Austen Kittredge III—the young Noël Lord, in killing the panther, had partaken in a rite of initiation into the forest, a process that even he could not completely understand although it was he who was doing the killing.

In comparing Moby Dick to Faulkner's bear and other iconic literary animals, Bart Welling argues that such animals "dwell in and corporealize a zone of possibility between natural referent and material signifier ... hovering or swimming or pacing visibly on the brink of a perpetually deferred transcendence."[17] One imagines the swimming fish, the pacing panther, or the hovering owl of Mosher's *Northern Borders* where Austen III "had the feeling that my grandfather and I and the owl were somehow linked together, though I could not say how."[18] That owl will come to the Kittredge farm to prey on the grandmother's chickens. But the grandfather will not shoot it. Nor will Austen III. It will be the grandmother who shoots it, but even as she does so, shooting it dead, it clings to a tree branch and hangs upside down, "defiant and fierce, even in death." The owl is just like Faulkner's bear that dies and yet, in refusing to "crumple," instead "seemed to bounce" from the ground, *signifying*—to use Welling's word—that there is something more profound going on than simply the death of an animal.

Howard Frank Mosher and the Classics

This "zone of possibility" where such animals "dwell" is an elusive place not available to most human beings. But the prospect conjures up thoughts of what Faulkner might have meant when he talked about the spiritual thing that "could substitute for the ruined wilderness" if only mankind could fathom what the missing thing was. As he engages in his project against the power company, it strikes Lord that "he had been wrong about the cat." Instead of the animal being referred to as a panther, it is now "the cat" which, as it turns out, was of a yellowish color, meaning that it might have been a jaguar or a bobcat or even a bear, that last option being what Bangor chooses to call it since it does not matter which particular animal it was, anyway, so much as it matters what was the animal's meaning.

Welling comments further on the mystery that he associates with the various animals, pointing out that "paradoxically, their energies are liberated only when they are killed, threatened, or pursued" and they "continually frustrate human characters' attempts at interpretation—of the animals themselves and, through them, the physical universe whose emissaries they might be."[19] The cat was delivering a message to Lord, one that it took the old logger practically his whole life to decipher, just as Grandfather Kittredge has been trying to uncover what it means for a majestic white owl of the wilderness to venture down out of the woods and onto the farm to hunt in the yard for chickens. The cat and the owl, in the two respective novels by Mosher, are just what Welling says, emissaries sent from an unfathomable universe meant to deliver a warning. What the owl had been warning Grandfather Kittredge of becomes all too clear as that patriarch and his grandson are listening to the radio and learn that a "gigantic hydroelectric dam" is about to be built that will cause water to flood millions of square acres of the wilderness. Much of that wilderness is so untamed that it does not even exist on the map, though, as it turns out, the elder Kittredge has been to the untamed region before and will return now for two reasons: first, to map out the "doomed" area and then, second, to recover the remains of a former "wife" whom he did not want to leave buried where the tons of water would soon be coming to cover the land.

The building of the dam will spell the end of Lost Nation Hollow as well. As Grandfather Kittredge tells Austen III, "Lost Nation Hollow

• **VII. *Mourning the Inevitable Loss*** •

is a bygone place. I watched it pass into history.... The farms are all gone. The big woods are gone. The best of the hunting and fishing is gone.... What is there for any of us to come back to?"[20] In an *Atlantic* online interview, appropriately entitled "Disappearing Eden," Mosher was asked what he thought the future held for the section of Vermont that he has affectionately labeled, in his fiction, as simply the Kingdom. In answering the question, he echoed Faulkner's concern with regard to what in the world could possibly replace that which was being ravaged in the name of human progress. Speaking quite frankly on the subject, and with a startling degree of specificity, Mosher said, "I think the future, if we're not very careful to protect the land, is going to be bleak.... When I first came to northern Vermont there were between 600 and 700 family farms just in the county where I lived. Today there are fewer than 200."[21] Witnessing such overwhelming change must have been, for Mosher, the same thing experienced by many of his awestricken fictional characters who could only stand by and watch the ending of one era, not knowing what the new era was going to bring.

Lord, on the other hand, seems to have come up with a plan. He will no longer be able to draw oil from the cedar trees but he has the pine trees that mean so much to him even though the company representative cannot envision what that could possibly be, beyond them comprising the prospective environs for a tourist park. But just as Lord won't be a tour guide, the pine trees will not be a tourist park either. Lord's ancestors "would have approved of" him "cutting them, sound or hollow" before turning them over to the power company for whatever usage they might conceive of. So, that is what Lord has planned, to cut down the pine trees which he believes will bring him at least eight thousand dollars so that he can buy a sawmill in Oregon that was advertised in a logging magazine.

He and Bangor feverishly saw down the trees in anticipation of several truckers coming to transport the hundreds of logs into town. They are all cut down but then something suddenly happens; the panther reappears. He is the reincarnation of Faulkner's bear that had never really been killed since a gun cannot kill a spirit. Nor could even the mightiest dog, in and of itself alone, have performed the feat. We recall that, in "The Bear" section of *Go Down, Moses*, even the massive "indomitable and unbroken spirit" dog, Lion, could not alone bring down Old Ben. And when Boon Hogganbeck's blade does finally draw the mortal life out of the bear, that is when, as Bart Welling would say, the animal's "energies are liberated" more so than ever before.

With a name like Lord, Noël can only be the "priest," a Sam Fathers–like figure; and though he has shot at the panther before, he must know, at some point, that the mechanized instrument of gun and bullets will not be enough, just as "he knew that even a big and experienced Walker hound was no match for a panther."[22] Much like Old Ben had allowed himself, over the course of time, to be seen in the woods only by people like Fathers and Ike, the panther pauses just long enough so that it and Lord can stare at one another, straight in the eye, an act of mutual recognition that they, while not completely trusting of each other, can at least acknowledge that their predicaments are similar as they struggle for survival against the oncoming forces of commercial enterprise. Like Grandfather Kittredge, who in *Northern Borders* refuses to kill the owl that had been swooping down, making off with his wife's chickens, Lord winds up hoping that the wounded panther can escape even though that animal had been plundering the countryside, gutting heifers and sheep, as he went along his way.

Regarded by local farmers as variously a "renegade" or a "marauding" bear, this last panther of the Vermont wilderness becomes a sign of just how powerful nature still can be. It had not rained in the county for five straight months, but just as the truckers are coming for the logs, the most devastating natural disaster, ever to hit the state, arrives in the rain-driven torrents that will become the historic flood of 1927. It will rain for three straight days, wiping out bridges and roads, sparing not even the state's lieutenant governor who becomes a drowning victim. Needless to say, the trucks will not be able to transport the logs. Yet, Lord is determined to get the logs where they need to be. Where that is, exactly, becomes anyone's guess as he rides the logs down the flume which now, with all the rain, is a river. Five hundred logs blast through the gate that this logger had promised the company representative he would close, and one wonders, now, what of the disaster might the old woodsman have been able to surmise when he made that promise in the first place.

• VII. Mourning the Inevitable Loss •

The logs themselves become one big powerful "phalanx" that rams right into the newly constructed dam. In a manner of speaking, this is how Lord has taken his revenge. Yet, the power company has the resources to rebuild. Meanwhile Lord is dead, ultimately unable, at his advanced age, to overcome the very machination that he, at least in part, had been responsible for putting into place. Bangor recovers the body and is preparing to bury it when she discovers that the magazine—within which was the advertisement for the Oregon sawmill—is exactly 10 years old. The great likelihood is that the property has long ago been sold, maybe two or three times, even, since when the ad had first been placed. In Lord's heart, he had never really wanted to go to that northwestern state but, like the Chickasaw Indian Jobaker in "Was" whose "hut" Sam Fathers set afire when Jobaker was nearing the end of his life, Lord finally decides that if he dies it will be at his home and at the hands of the natural elements. For Jobaker, it was fire; for Lord, the raging flood.

Sounding somewhat reconciled, in 1957, with the changes that he saw being brought on by modernization, Faulkner expressed that "it's foolish to be against progress because everyone is a part of progress and he'll have no other chance except this one so he—it's silly not to cope with it, to compromise with it, cope with it."[23] One cannot help but notice the hesitation in that statement. Faulkner certainly does not *want* to compromise with the forces that have been operating against nature. And he certainly does not want to resign himself to the prospect that the battle against those forces has been lost. At some point, perhaps 10 years or a little less, before he died, Lord might have actually thought about moving out to Oregon, contemplating such a relocation as the means whereby he might hold on to some vestige of the past he once knew. But then again, such a move would have been filled with uncertainty. Oregon might not have been what it seemed from a 3,000-mile distance. The magazine advertisement had indicated that the property "needs some repair." When Bangor looks closely at the accompanying picture of the sawmill, she is just as shocked at the building's condition as she will later be shocked that the magazine itself is so old. Half talking to herself, half talking to a horse that is standing nearby munching on some food, she utters, "They ain't fooling when they say this place needs some repair."[24] By the time Lord is dead, the "place" might not even be standing and, if it is still standing, it could be in much worse shape than when the years-old photograph was taken. It is the uncertainty of it all that Mosher wants us to ponder in trying to figure out exactly how to cope with the changes. Standing quietly, on a ridge just above Lord's grave, is the panther that has reappeared one last time before it "headed north toward Canada," searching for his own version of "Oregon." He is "limping"—like Faulkner's bullet-riddled Old Ben—hobbling off, hoping against hope, that the past he once knew is out there somewhere even as he also knows his time has all but run out.

If we thought that the woods between Kingdom County and Canada would provide a safe haven to some degree, we would have to think again as, in *On Kingdom Mountain*, the Kingdom Common town fathers have determined it would be a good idea to construct a highway extending from the Common all the way to Montreal. It will be a bit over 100 miles long and serve to connect the northernmost part of Vermont to the eastern townships of Quebec, leading on into Montreal which, at the time, was the commercial capital of Canada, even more so than Toronto. The only thing standing in the way of the project is the retired schoolteacher, Jane Hubbell Kinneson, whom her cousin Eben Kinneson regards as the "last great individualist in Kingdom County." Not needing very much money, she "burned her own wood, ate her own venison, moose, and trout, cultivated a large kitchen garden, cut her ice on the river, compounded her own medicines, walked all over her mountain for exercise, and had no taxes or electric or phone bills to pay."[25] She is the last resident of Kingdom Mountain, born 15 years after the Civil War ended, and is now prepared to protect her home "by whatever means are necessary." Fortunately, when she takes her case to district court to stop the Town of Kingdom Common and the Great North Woods Pulp and Paper Company from further destroying the countryside, the judge will be her dear old friend, Ira Allen, with whom she shares, among other things, a decided admiration for "a young southern writer ... named Faulkner." As one might imagine, Judge Allen rules in favor of his old friend, in the amount of five hundred dollars for the timber that was cut; and, in addition, he issues an order for the company to restore what it destroyed of the Kingdom Mountain Burn and the Upper East Branch of the Kingdom River. When the defendants object,

VII. Mourning the Inevitable Loss

the judge responds brusquely, telling them that if they don't like it, they can take the whole matter up later, on appeal.

That is exactly what the paper company and the Kingdom Common authorities intend to do, and much of Mosher's novel is an exploration of Miss Jane's life as she prepares for what will have to be her own defense before the Supreme Court of Vermont. In *Marie Blythe*, Abie Benedict planned on building a resort hotel on the mountain. Now, in *On Kingdom Mountain*, Jane has felt, for some time, it was not just a highway that her opposition wanted to build, but a highway first and then, afterward, a ski resort that would be the first one ever built in the northern New England region. Such commercial development would have been entirely against the wishes of, among others, her father who was Morgan Kinneson, the 17-year-old boy who, one day, took off walking through those very woods in search of his brother Pilgrim. Those woods were "where Pilgrim had taught him to wait for a buck to slip down to a stream to drink" and where the two brothers "caught the vividly colored little trout" and then sometimes, at Lake Memphremagog, "they'd watched the snow geese alight, thousands of them, sailing out of the dense clouds."[26]

As I mentioned earlier, Mosher is quite adept at portraying these nature scenes to the point where a reader can easily envision, in his mind, what the author is describing in words. After breakfast one morning, Jane and her companion set out to walk the pike road until they cross a plank bridge where "the quick highland brook slowed to a creeping flow, winding darkly under cedars and hemlocks and losing itself a dozen times over in slangs and beaver backwaters before entering the river at the spawning pool. The bog water was tea-colored and icy cold. The backs and sides of the blue-backed char that lived here were dark as well."[27] "Char" is the term that she uses for trout just as she uses other "antique phrases" such as "glen" instead of valley and "burn" instead of brook. But whatever they are called, they are all in danger and Judge Allen held the Common as well as the pulp and paper company liable for "significant damage" to not only the Kingdom Mountain Burn but also the spawning bed of what he rightfully acknowledged as "Miss Jane's char." *Rightfully* acknowledged because Jane had not, to use Faulkner's phraseology, meant to hold the land for herself and her descendants "inviolable title forever" but indeed "intact in the communal anonymity of brotherhood." That is her goal and Judge Allen understands how the fulfillment of that goal is in danger.

But if Mosher is so good at his novelistic portrayals of the wilderness, then perhaps those portrayals could serve as a substitute for that wilderness in the event that, upon appeal, the Common and the pulp and paper company win. Even if Jane lost, we would still have the benefit of Mosher's vivid ecological descriptions. In examining this particular issue, it is useful to consider what the Renaissance-era critic Philip Sidney had to say about the matter. In his *Defense of Poesy*, that writer went to great lengths to describe how people, who work in other fields besides poetry, are severely limited. For example, the historian is limited to the point where he can only recapitulate "what men have done." The lawyer can only present what "men have determined." Even the metaphysic, while being a "supernatural" force of sorts, is limited in his powers of creation. "Only the poet," said Sidney,

> disdaining to be tied to any such subjection, lifted up with the vigor of his own invention, does grow in effect into another nature in making things either better than nature brings forth or, quite anew, forms such as never were in nature.... So as he goes hand in hand with nature, not enclosed within the narrow warrant of her gifts but freely ranging within the zodiac of his own wit.
>
> Nature never set forth the earth in so rich tapestry as diverse poets have done, neither with so pleasant rivers, fruitful trees, sweet-smelling flowers, nor whatsoever else may make the too-much-loved earth more lovely.[28]

At the 2011 Renaissance Comparative Prose Conference, Renaissance scholar Charles Ross gave a talk on Sidney and, afterward, I was able to ask him, "Do you agree with Sidney that the poet does a better job, of recreating nature, than nature does itself?" In answering me, Ross explained that the Renaissance-era audience believed strongly in the presentation of stories. "The universe is just there," said Ross, commenting further on those times, "but it is the poet who tells the story."[29] That was those times, but one wonders how applicable Sidney's perspective is to the work of Mosher even though, within Mosher's fiction, we find so many of a poet's devices such as metaphor, lyricism and vivid imagery. For that matter, one wonders if Sidney's theory can be applied to Faulkner who, early on in his career, was committed to the poetic art

• *VII. Mourning the Inevitable Loss* •

form as is evidenced by *A Green Bough*, *The Marble Faun*, and *This Earth*, all works of his that were devoted to using words to portray what we might have thought could only have been accomplished by viewing or feeling, for oneself, the world of nature.

It would be nearly two centuries later, during the Age of Enlightenment, that Gotthold Ephraim Lessing would offer a view—on the issue of whether language can adequately portray nature—that would be entirely at odds with what Sidney had said. In *Laocoon: An Essay upon the Limits of Painting and Poetry*, Lessing gives us several lines from a poem that describe flowers and then he goes on to say that, however acceptable the poem might be in some ways, it still fails in its effort to recreate those flowers' essence. He further explains:

> It might be very pleasant to hear the lines read if we had the flowers in our hand; but, taken by themselves, they say little or nothing. I hear in every word the laborious poet, but the thing itself I am unable to see.... I do not deny that language has the power of describing a corporeal whole according to its parts. It certainly has, because its signs, although consecutive, are nevertheless arbitrary. But I deny that this power exists in language as the instrument of poetry. For illusion, which is the special aim of poetry, is not produced by these verbal descriptions of objects, nor can it ever be so produced. The coexistence of the body comes into collision with the sequence of the words, and although while the former is getting resolved into the latter, the dismemberment of the whole into its parts is a help to us, yet the reunion of these parts into a whole is made extremely difficult, and not infrequently impossible.[30]

For Lessing, language does not have the power to describe a "corporeal whole," except possibly by examining that whole in terms of its various parts. And even then, the language is effective if it is being used to describe something, for example, that is mechanical or akin to a large box with smaller boxes enclosed in it. Language, in Lessing's view, is accordingly useful for the limited purpose of describing such things as colors, sizes, and shapes.

When it comes to nature, however, dividing something into its parts becomes more difficult because the "arbitrariness," though a vital part of nature, becomes so much more difficult to verbalize. The writer is, in essence, a magician—specifically, according to Lessing, an "illusionist"—who necessarily fails because he cannot recreate what he is describing. Trying to describe a flower or a tree or a stream is hard enough. But one grasps Lessing's point all the more upon considering, for example, how difficult it was for even Faulkner to portray the dead buck, that Ike shot, still possessed, even in death, of the same "magnificent speed" that he had held when still alive. Most of the *hunters* would not have been able to understand all of that, even if they had been there watching the deer fall when Ike shot his gun. It took a very special hunter, such as Ike McCaslin or Sam Fathers, to be able to see *that* part of the buck, and then combine it with other parts to be able to adequately envision the whole. For a writer to be able to perform that task for a general audience—that is, formulate with his words "the reunion of these parts into a whole"—would be, as Lessing put it, "not infrequently impossible."

We are thus brought back to our consideration of whether Mosher's novel, *On Kingdom Mountain* with all its vivid description of the forest, would be an adequate substitute for the mountain itself if Jane should ultimately lose the legal case. In an interview he gave the same year that novel came out, Mosher talked about visiting the Oxford, Mississippi area to see, in person, what the Yoknapatawpha County of Faulkner's novels really looked like. As it turned out, said Mosher, "when I looked for Faulkner's town and countryside, and didn't really find them, I realized that the only place they really exist is in his books."[31] It sounds, in that interview, like Mosher might have had some ambivalence with regard to just how fortunate we are, exactly, to at least have Faulkner's verbal representations of the evaporating wilderness. Having traveled all the way to the Oxford area—and saw nothing there that resembled the fictional town of Jefferson or the de Spain hunting camp—must have left the Vermont author somewhat discombobulated. But then again we do have the books, written by Faulkner, to remind us how things were.

Yet, one is drawn to wonder even about the effectiveness of books being able to convey what once was since, more and more, we are becoming a society that not only reads less but talks to one another, about literature, even less than that. While we were discussing Faulkner, Mosher made it a point to say that, upon visiting Oxford, the only time he saw anything that did resemble, what Faulkner wrote about, was when he went to a bookstore and there, on the wall, were photographs of what

• VII. *Mourning the Inevitable Loss* •

the Mississippi writer had described in his novels and short stories.[32] At one time, the de Spain hunting party had had to travel just 30 miles to get to the wilderness. By the time Uncle Ike is taking his last trip out, the distance has become 200 miles; that was in 1941. Now that we are well into the twenty-first century, there is only a bit of that wilderness left, and any ambivalence that Mosher might have felt—at being only able to witness it in literature or on a bookstore wall—must have been intertwined with a certain degree of sadness in terms of how severely limited his own words are in the effort to describe the awesomeness of a landscape that could only have been made by the Creator of the entire world.

It stands to reason, then, that Jane's defense of the mountain is as critical as anything she has ever attempted in her life. She had argued in district court and now, as she argues her case before the five black-robed justices of Vermont's Supreme Court, she talks about how her grandfather led hundreds of escaped slaves over the mountain and into Canada for their freedom. She tells them about how her great-grandfather was instrumental in arriving at an agreement wherein the land was to be held in trust for the Memphremagog branch of Abenaki Indian Nation. The mountain, during that ancestor's time, was so "remote and forbidding" that neither the United States nor Great Britain had any desire to own it, but now Kingdom Common, says Jane, wants to "steal it" through the process of eminent domain.

The Kingdom Common lawyer, who also happens to be her cousin, declares to the court that the Common's purpose in acquiring the land is certainly not to build a "winter resort." They, so he says, only want to build the highway. But then he adds, as a corollary to that statement, that it is not the Common's *intention*, "at this time," to build a resort. What Jane is well aware of is that once they get control, they can do whatever they want, including turn it into a tourist park like what the Northern Vermont Power Company had planned for the land that Noël Lord lived on, a plan that included converting him from a logger to a resident tour guide. In fact, the Kingdom Common Township wants to purchase not only Miss Jane's farm but also her wood-carving building and put them both on display as a "slice of living history," with her presumably on display too as a piece of living history to be gawked at by outsiders who have no appreciation for the meaning of the mountain and no appreciation for Jane herself whose "ancestors had lived their hard, worthwhile lives" there, "preserving the wild country intact."[33]

Miss Jane argues valiantly on behalf of not only those ancestors but also on behalf of "future generations" and on behalf of the mountain itself because, as she says, "mountains are silent" as are "rivers, ponds, and forests." But counsel for the Common is shrewd, arguing that the highway will bring revenue for the schools and jobs for local residents while hardly changing the mountain at all since it will follow along the path of a road that had already been in existence for some time. Those arguments are convincing enough for the court to rule in the Common's favor but, by now, Jane has realized that she will have to be shrewd as well. The daughter of a full-blooded Abenaki Indian, she has drawn up a will, leaving her home and other possessions to her lawyer cousin and black half-sister, to be held in trust for the Memphremagog Abenaki nation, in perpetuity. As for all the other land that comprised Kingdom Mountain, Jane has been diligently working on transferring it to the Appalachian Land Trust, an organization that has pledged to carry on her fight, against the building of the highway, all the way to the United States Supreme Court.

It is left for readers to conjecture as to whether or not that organization will succeed. In arriving at a conclusion about what will become of Kingdom Mountain, I am inclined to draw upon my personal experience in researching and writing about a black neighborhood that once existed in the heart of what is now downtown Charlottesville, Virginia. At one time, there were dozens of black businesses, of all sorts, thriving in the dead center of the town that otherwise had substantially denied blacks socioeconomic opportunity. For black youth, growing up in such a world, those businesses were essential for—as Miss Jane argued so eloquently in defense of her mountain—"future generations so that they may know where they came from and who their ancestors were and, knowing that, have a clearer idea of who they are and who they may yet become."[34] Unfortunately, a multitude of black youth, now trapped in brutal poverty in Charlottesville, were denied the best possible idea, of what they might have become, because the community of black businesses—that might have served as a striking example of success in the

• *VII. Mourning the Inevitable Loss* •

midst of oppression—was no longer there, having been razed by the town leaders through the process of eminent domain.

Similarly, in *On Kingdom Mountain*, the Kingdom Common town fathers seek, as I said earlier, to employ eminent domain to achieve what, in their minds, will be "progress." And they intend to financially compensate Jane. But arguing her case more vigorously than ever, she responds with a vital question: "How, pray, do you compensate someone for taking away her history and traditions? How do you propose to compensate me for taking away and defiling the place that binds me to my family?"[35] The Kingdom Common town fathers, and certainly the pulp and paper company, are not concerned about that. They have no interest in understanding, let alone preserving, the complexity of relationships between blacks and whites and Native Americans that nevertheless forms the basis of this nation's heritage. What Renae Shackelford (my co-investigator) and I discovered—I should say, what *I* discovered, since she was born and raised in Charlottesville and already knew—is that the powers-that-be would just as soon cover up a bothersome past. On what was once Vinegar Hill—the name of the black community that was demolished in Charlottesville—one is now hard-pressed to find a single black business and, even more troubling, the state of affairs is such as it is now because of an intentional design that was decades in the making, strategically planned out, and with rationales along the lines of what Mosher's Kingdom Common lawyer had offered as the benefits, for society, of providing a convenient highway through an otherwise forlorn wilderness.

As Mosher was driving Renae and me through various places in the Kingdom, I asked him which of the mountains was the one that he used as a model for *On Kingdom Mountain*. I can recall quite vividly that we were riding down a road where there seemed to be a plethora of such mountains and he answered smilingly, "It could have been any one of these."[36] Then he took us on into the town of Westmore so that we could take a look at Lake Willoughby with its unbelievably beautiful vista that, from the north end, reminds one of a Norwegian fjord with high peaked mountains framing a narrow inlet. Lake Willoughby is broader than such an inlet which, depending on one's tastes, makes the fjord pale by comparison. Mosher had us watch a loon bobbing up and down in the middle of the lake. Renae had us stop and watch a nature-made spigot funneling water in a steady stream out of a rock. Mosher estimated that—10,000 years ago—a massive glacier moved down through the mountains and created the lake. Standing there marveling, with us, as if he was going through the process of transforming himself into a character from the pages of one of his own books, the writer intoned words I had heard before: "Some people call it God's country."[37]

But then there was another side to this trip that Mosher was taking us on through the mountains, a side that he spoke of very little even as he slowed the car down so that we could see better. Right by the lake, there was a building where one could rent boats. A little further along, there was a commercial camping ground that had obviously sprung up only recently. At some distance, even further but still in view of the lake, there stood what looked like a hotel or the beginnings of what would later become a resort. There were so few cars, going back and forth on the road, that it did not dawn on me, until much later, that it had not been a road, at all, that we had been traveling on, but, in hindsight, it was what appeared to be the makings of a highway. And it did not dawn on me either, until much later, what he meant when he had said, in his solemn and matter-of-fact tone, "I can't see them not developing it more."[38]

· VIII ·

Mosher and Shakespeare
On the Immortality of Romantic Love

Nearly 80 years old in "Delta Autumn," Uncle Ike sits in the midst of what was once the vast and unfathomable wilderness and, meditating out loud to a whole new generation of hunters, he renders an opinion on what the apex of a relationship between man and woman might be. Couching his language in terms of earthly matrimony, he at first reduces that matrimony to a role that bears no resemblance to the ultimate that can occur within a relationship between two people but then, upon further consideration, comes to the conclusion, "I think that every man and woman, at the instant when it don't even matter whether they marry or not, I think that whether they marry then or afterward or don't never, at that instant the two of them together were God."[1] Prior to that statement, the old man had been talking about how he "reckon[ed]" God made the world as the sort of place that He himself "would have wanted to live in," but then Ike has to reconcile himself to the reality that since man, over the course of his millennia-long sojourn, has gone about the process of slowly decimating that world, what is left to hold onto is a spiritual connection that finds its source in that one and same God. Physical attraction between two people is quite normal as is the formal ceremony that, for many purposes, unites those two individuals. However, the depths of true love, between a man and woman, go far beyond the limits of sex and ceremony and into a realm where, as Ike had suggested, they are one with the God who created them.

Upon examining three of Shakespeare's plays—*Romeo and Juliet*, *Antony and Cleopatra*, and *Othello*—we can see how even death cannot destroy a love relationship that, while in some parts physical, is more steeped in the elements of another world which even the parties to the love themselves cannot completely comprehend. In an essay exploring the manner in which Shakespeare "purified and idealized" an earlier version[2] of the Romeo and Juliet story, the critic David Lanphier notes that "the role of the universe as an element of influence in the love of Romeo and Juliet is an extremely important one ... allusions throughout to the role of 'the stars' and 'the heavens' suggest an outside force, a universal force, larger than both of the lovers, which seems to control what happens to them."[3] Down in the garden of the Capulet home, Romeo first listens to a soliloquy delivered by his newfound love and then responds:

> O, speak again, bright angel, for thou art
> As glorious to this night, being o'er my head,
> As is a wingèd messenger of heaven
> Unto the white-upturnèd wond'ring eyes
> Of mortals that fall back to gaze on him
> When he bestrides the lazy puffing clouds
> And sails upon the bosom of the air.[4]

Those words are consistent with how Juliet will later speak out to a vast region beyond this earth as she beseeches:

> Give me my Romeo, and when I shall die,
> Take him and cut him out in little stars,
> And he will make the face of heaven so fine
> That all the world will be in love with night [3.2.23–26].

It is far beyond the capacity of human beings to comprehend what the limits of the universe are, but one thing that both Romeo and Juliet do understand is that the love they have for one another is—to use Juliet's words—"infinite" and "boundless," somehow attached to the infinity of the universe itself. Lanphier pointed to a "universal force" that seemed to "control" the two lovers; and indeed the chain of events that to a large extent governs their lives is not a fortuitous chain but one that has linked such lovers down through the ages as they have sought, as best they could, to keep a faithful vigil against the forces that would just as soon have them forever wrenched apart.

Mosher's most striking version of Shakespeare's young couple is Pilgrim Kinneson and Manon Thibeau. Pilgrim was the Protestant

• **VIII. *The Immortality of Romantic Love*** •

young man and Manon was the French Canadian Catholic who, in *On Kingdom Mountain*, fell in love with one another but "both sets of parents honestly believed that if Pilgrim and Manon married outside their faith, they and their children and all their descendants to come would burn in Hell forever."[5] The parents of those lovers forbade them from marrying someone of a different religious denomination, a dictate prompting Manon to run away from home. Then when she disappeared, Pilgrim signed up to join the Union Army and himself disappeared, making it so that, as we saw in my Chapter III, his younger brother Morgan would have to take off in search of him.

I also noted, in that earlier chapter, that by the time Mosher got to writing *Walking to Gatlinburg*, it is Pilgrim who disappears first, enlisting in the Army, and then Manon disappears, believed by her family to have been so distraught that she wandered off and died in a nearby bog. Mosher offers us yet another version of what happened in an extended short story that he calls "Second Sight," so titled in reference to Jane Hubbell's gift of being able to ascertain things beyond what the ordinary human being is capable of perceiving. True to the order of disappearances in *On Kingdom Mountain*, it is Manon who disappears first, in the short story, and then her lover who, as Miss Jane tells it, "ran away out west and didn't write home for six years. All that time he was dead to us. Even after he finally contacted us, he never came home."[6] In the short story, it is not Jane's uncle, Pilgrim, who runs away but instead it is her younger brother, Robert Burns Hubbell. And instead of the Civil War as a backdrop, it is the final year of World War I, a difference of time frame that lends itself to the notion that the era, in which these events take place, is not as important as the timeless emotion of love itself.

As was the case with Romeo, the Scottish poet Robert Burns—after whom Robert Burns Hubbell is named—faced stern resistance from the father of his beloved. The object of the poet's love was a woman named Jean Armour with whom he would eventually have nine children. But early on in their relationship, her father went so far as to destroy the young couple's marriage certificate and then send her away to live with an uncle who was given the charge of making sure that the two lovers had no opportunity to be together, a task at which that uncle failed miserably, but a task undertaken nonetheless with just enough resolve to make the lovers' moments of privacy difficult to achieve and the periods of absence, from each other, a source of agony for Jean and Robert, the latter of whom was, in response, compelled to pen the words:

> Oppressed with grief, oppressed with
>   care,
> A burden more than I can bear,
> I sit me down and sigh:
> O life! thou art a galling load,
> Along a rough, a weary road ....[7]

Jean's father did not approve of the relationship between his daughter and Robert because he did not feel that the young man was good enough. Burns was, at the time, in dire financial straits; moreover, he had an established reputation as a "ladies' man," unsuitable, in her father's estimation, for any sort of romantic union with his child.

The situation was remarkably similar to that of Juliet who would have liked to explain, to her father, what her feelings were for Romeo but she dared not because that guardian of hers has already arranged for her marriage to Count Paris, and in the event of her objection, that father has a rather harsh warning:

> I tell thee what: get thee to church o' Thursday,
> Or never after look me in the face.
> Speak not; reply not; do not answer me ....
> Graze where you will, you shall not house with me.
> Look to 't; think on 't. I do not use to jest.
> Thursday is near. Lay hand on heart; advise.
> An you be mine, I'll give you to my friend.
> An you be not, hang, beg, starve, die in the streets,
> For, by my soul, I'll ne'er acknowledge thee.
> Nor what is mine shall never do thee good [3.5.167–69, 200–06].

Juliet's father, Capulet, is prepared not only to disinherit her but also toss her out in the street if she does not obey, so opposed is he to her marrying anyone of the Montague clan, the family to which Romeo belongs. Yet, we are never told what exactly is the basis of the inter-family discord that so drastically separates the Capulets from the Montagues. The disharmony seems to be based on little or nothing, so meaningless and yet the cause of two people, who are in love, not being able to gain the consent, of their respective families, to so much as see one another.

• *VIII. The Immortality of Romantic Love* •

In the play *Othello*, the love that exists between Othello and Desdemona could be summarized in two lines taken from Othello's rather lengthy explanation to the duke, in the face of Brabantio's (her father) accusation against the Moor, that she was "abused, stol'n from, and corrupted / By spells and medicines bought of mountebanks."[8] Of course, Brabantio has been influenced to a large extent by Iago and Rodrigo, both of whom have ulterior motives for wanting to see Othello and Desdemona break up. However, the father is not in need of all that much coaxing in the matter, as there already exists a cultural racism that Shakespeare is exposing as all the more ridiculous considering how Othello stands head and shoulders above other men in terms of not only bravery but also virtue and the intensity with which he is capable of love. And with regard to those specific character traits, Desdemona is his equal, their union having been the meeting of two supremely compatible souls of such an order as to epitomize what Faulkner's Uncle Ike meant in his assertion that two people can have a love so strong as to be the equivalent of a supernatural force. Othello's explanation of it to the duke is "She loved me for the dangers I had passed, / And I loved her that she did pity them" (1.3.193–94). In other words, she admires his military exploits and he appreciates her sensitivity in understanding what all those wartime experiences involved. Yet, even Othello's characterization of their relationship falls short of describing its essence as it is of such an unfathomable magnitude as to be in that category of things for which even the most brilliant of words will, in the final analysis, prove to be insufficient.

The reason that the two lovers die in that play has a lot to do with the shallow way people regard relationships with which they are uncomfortable. We saw it in *To Kill a Mockingbird* and *A Stranger in the Kingdom* where even friendship between the opposite sexes, of two races, was enough to cause social upheaval. Professor Arthur Little goes so far as to draw an analogy between those situations and the event of a young child seeing, or even just imagining, his parents engaged in sexual intercourse. In response, the child has a need to "repress this moment," either eliminate it from consciousness or "distort" it, in some way or another, to maintain his equilibrium. In *Othello*, Little argues, the "presence of Othello's black, male body, especially as defined in relation to Desdemona's white, female body, emerges as the crucial scene in need of erasure in order to satisfy the fictions of a Western European cultural order."[9] The Western European cultural fictions, to which Little refers, include some version of white supremacy. That a black man could have sex with a white woman cuts against the grain of society's equilibrium; and society's response, much like that of the child who has seen more than he can handle, is to eliminate it or (as Iago and Roderigo do in their warning to Brabantio) distort it into something that is hideous.

In their edition of *Antony and Cleopatra*, Jonathan Bate and Eric Rasmussen point out one of Antony's followers, Enobarbus, as being Shakespeare's alter ego, "the nearest thing anywhere in his complete works to a considered self-portrait."[10] What this means, if those critics' assessment is correct, is that nowhere else, in all of the dramatist's works, is there a character who is more the voice of reason than Enobarbus. So, his analysis of who Cleopatra is, at her deepest essence, must hold some important truths. Enobarbus, describing the Egyptian queen, avers:

> Age cannot wither her, nor custom stale
> Her infinite variety: other women cloy
> The appetites they feed, but she makes hungry
> Where most she satisfies. For vilest things
> Become themselves in her, that the holy priests
> Bless her when she is riggish.[11]

By that description, Cleopatra was not just physically beautiful but she was also an intriguing woman with many diverse aspects to her character. Yet, there are those who, like Octavius Caesar in the play, would reduce her to the status of a common "whore." Even the historical Cleopatra is said to have had her share of romantic experiences, including an affair with Julius Caesar and marriages to two of her own brothers, Ptolemy XIII and then Ptolemy XIV when the older brother died. But, as Enobarbus says, even "vilest things / Become themselves in her," which is to say that her relationships, whomever they are with, assume a certain air of dignity as if she was not too far different from the mythical goddess of love, Venus herself, whom one might assume, to use Enobarbus's words, is still blessed by the "holy priests."

As was the case with Uncle Ike, Mosher puts little stock in what some might consider to be the significance of formal wedding vows.

• *VIII. The Immortality of Romantic Love* •

Nor, for that matter, does the author believe that the number of relationships, that a woman has had, detract from her capacity for love with all the intensity that, for example, existed between Antony and Cleopatra. At the age of 15, circumstances made it so that Marie Blythe wound up with John Trinity who disdained the life of a working man so much so that, at one point, he offered her as the bargaining chip in a poker game. But things got better for her when she and the logger-turned-trapper Jigger Johnson moved out to Pond Number Four where they lived for a period of four years that would turn out to be the "busiest and happiest" of her life. But he died in an accident on the pond which then led to that dangerous point in her life when she worked as a dancer in the barroom section of Bull Francis's Pond House.

Shortly thereafter, she became first a housekeeper and then a nurse, both positions she held at the "state tuberculosis sanatorium for indigent patients." The love interest there was Dr. Philbrook Jamieson who, in time, grew so close to her in every facet of their lives to the point where "their love had come to seem a part of their work together."[12] Then as World War I continued to escalate, he joined up, hoping to help soldiers on the front who had been inflicted with poison gas. Unfortunately, he himself wound up being gassed, dying as a consequence and leaving Marie with what one might assume was a devastating void.

Yet, if one considers what the fourteenth century Italian poet Petrarch's view on love was, then physical presence might not be what is most important. With regard to the woman that many assume to have been the love of that poet's life, he may not have ever even met her, but instead admired her from afar and then proceeded to spend 40 years writing about her in an accumulation of verse, *Rerum vulgarium fragmenta*, that marks a progression away from the physical and toward the spiritual, along the lines of how Romeo and Juliet spoke of each other in terms of "heaven" and the "stars." In poem CLX of that collection of verse, Petrarch expounded on the ecstacy of romantic love even while he stipulated that such a love, in its pure essence, is something more than human.[13] If Petrarch did actually meet this object of his affection, a woman named Laura, it is unlikely that their relationship was ever consummated in physical terms due to her being already married to another man, Count Hugues de Sade, and thus unwilling to engage with Petrarch beyond limited visual encounters. But what we do have are the 366 poems of the *Rerum vulgarium fragmenta*, poems that speak to something vastly different from ordinary romance since love, for Petrarch, becomes one and the same with miracles and immortality. If we look at love in that particular way, then the depths of Marie and Dr. Jamieson's relationship is not felt so much when they are together at the sanatorium as when he is off overseas at the front, writing her long letters that she cannot even read, but that she spends quiet evenings listening to as one of the nurses, within whom she confides, does the reading for her.

In his magnificent treatise entitled *De Vita Solitaria*, Petrarch insists that if a man were to "closely apply his inmost ear not to the tongue but to the heart.... I believe that he would admit without cavil that he had heard his naked conscience honestly confessing that happiness consisted ... in the inward possession of truth rather than in the applause of strangers or in fragile reputation."[14] What we notice in the Shakespeare plays—the ones that are my primary consideration for this chapter—is that each of the lovers is prey to the actions of onlookers who do not have the best interests of the lovers at heart. Octavius Caesar goes so far as to have, in his employ, spies who will inform him of Antony's comings and goings. Caesar proudly proclaims, "I have eyes upon him, / And his affairs come to me on the wind" (3.6.70–71). At one time a military ally, Caesar will eventually become Antony's bitter foe, and the latter man seems scarcely able to extricate himself from what Petrarch, in *De Vita Solitaria*, calls the "tricky contrivances" of others. Try as they might, Antony and Cleopatra can never get out of view of "strangers" who can render a fake applause at the same time they are intent on causing the couple's demise.

This is the reason why, in all likelihood, Mosher has Noël Lord and his housekeeper, Bangor, living on the outskirts of town. Lord had first met her, in 1886, when she was a teenage prostitute working at the Sky Blue House in Maine. Every Spring thereafter, for 17 years, he took respite, from his logging drive, to spend two to three weeks with her, a ritual that seemed more like extended romantic dates than the strictly sexual type of encounter that one usually associates with her line of business. Then two things occurred that would put an end to that relationship. As pulping began to replace the cutting and then driving of logs

• **VIII. *The Immortality of Romantic Love*** •

down the river, the Penobscot Log Driving Company sold out, which resulted in a dramatic decline in the prostitution business, and so the madam of the Sky Blue House burned her establishment to the ground and absconded with the money that Bangor had helped her save.

Still physically attractive, Bangor in short time reestablished herself in a traveling tent show until, by 1907, she had put on so much weight that she tipped the scales at 250 pounds. It was a rainy night at the Kingdom County fair when the barker sent her off to get some food and then, by the time she got back, he had packed up and left. She had no place to go but, as divine intervention would have it, Lord appears and, not recognizing who she is, engages her in conversation. In response to her request for a job, he takes her on as cook and housekeeper, but the situation evolves into much more than that as their previous relationship becomes reestablished, a relationship that Professor Unhae Langis, in describing Shakespeare's Cleopatra, refers to as "constant to the 'chief end' of integrating honor and love ... her resolution to this underlying virtuous goal throughout the play is unshakable."[15] Further on in her analysis, Langis characterizes the Egyptian queen as "virago," which is to say that Cleopatra is something of a scold, loud and ill-tempered but, perhaps even more important, she is warlike and brave when necessity calls her to action. We have the evidence of this when Antony is about to go into battle, proclaiming, "I'll fight at sea," and Cleopatra responds, "I have sixty sails," so anxious is she to join in the fight, offering him ships regardless of the fact that she and her lover will be going up against insurmountable odds.

Bangor is no more legally married to Lord than Cleopatra is to Antony, but the lovers in those two respective couples are as much connected to each other as any two people who have been joined in legal matrimony. When it comes to taking on the outside world, Bangor is just as prepared as Cleopatra, at one point bringing Lord his deer rifle to fend off the Northern Vermont Power Company official. Then when she and Lord are all but driven off their land, she takes one handle of the woodman's saw and helps him cut down the pine trees that will garner them eight thousand dollars for the trip to Oregon where Lord has indicated they can go and purchase a sawmill. But the incident that most exemplifies the Bangor-Lord love relationship is when they are in town one late afternoon, seated at the hotel restaurant and the power company's steam crane operator, "an enormous man," takes it upon himself to harass Bangor, demanding to know why she is staring at him and then when he is not satisfied with Lord's explanation that her eyesight is bad, he rips the hat off of her head and "sailed it across the room."

What happens next is reminiscent of Antony and Cleopatra when, in essence, they are standing back to back against the ever threatening might of Octavius Caesar. Lord is a powerfully built, six-foot-four-inch mountain of a man who once fought a "giant boxer from Montreal" in a chain fight at the Kingdom County Fair and was like Shakespeare's "Herculean Roman" who professed to his Egyptian queen, "If from the field I shall return once more ... / I and my sword will earn our chronicle" (3.13.204–06). Equally ready to fight, Cleopatra urges Antony on, declaring that his bravery is an integral part of his character, to which her lover responds, "I will be treble-sinewed, hearted, breathed, / And fight maliciously" (3.13.209–10). At the hotel restaurant, when Bangor's hat flew off her head, Lord picked up a liquor bottle and rammed it through the crane operator's teeth. The enormous man was held in place by the hook that Lord had driven through his hand, stapling it to the tabletop. Meanwhile, Bangor, joining in the fray, grabbed the nearby "power-company official" and slung him through the plate-glass window. Then the two of them, the logger and his "housekeeper," climbed up on their wagon and headed out onto the county road that led to their pond in the mountains, on the other side of which was the cabin where they lived.

It is a quite telling detail, in the three Shakespeare plays that I am using, that all of the male heroes are cut, so to speak, from the same warrior-figure cloth. Antony and Othello are most obviously that type of man as they are military leaders at the forefront of formidable armies. But Romeo is also possessed of a killer instinct and in instances when he is called upon to use it, he inflicts mortal wounds on first Tybalt and then Paris, both of those opponents being no match for our hero who, in the mold of the virtuous fighter, unsheathes his sword only when he is left with no other recourse.

Mosher's Pilgrim Kinneson likewise had no inclination, though he had the skill, to hurt another human being. As *Gatlinburg*'s narrator tells

VIII. The Immortality of Romantic Love

us, "He had shown Morgan how to shoot with Hunter, Pilgrim's old cap-and-ball musket, converted from their grandfather's flintlock.... Even after he had stopped hunting, stopped killing things altogether, Pilgrim was the best shot Morgan had ever known."[16] Pilgrim, though caught up in the Civil War, was actually a man of peace just as Noël Lord had, at a certain point in his life, carved out the peaceful existence that he found with Bangor as they talked and fished and harvested cedar oil on the land that they called their home.

That complex combination of peacefulness and warrior spirit was the makeup, as well, of *Northern Borders*' Grandfather Kittredge. When his grandson, Austen III, is cheated at the county fair, the grandfather tried to get the boy's money back and, at nearly six feet, two inches in height, he posed a viable threat to the barker until 15 other "carnies" showed up with "short chains, others had iron bars. One man wielded a pipe wrench. He menaced with it like a short baseball bat."[17] Like Shakespeare's Antony, at war with Caesar, the grandfather temporarily retreats but then returns with no "fewer than thirty armed neighbors" who proceed to assist the older Austen not only in getting his grandson's money back but also in getting some manner of revenge against the carnies by demanding even more money so as to be able to buy an elephant from the carnival, an animal that the grandfather had previously witnessed being mistreated.

That series of events in Grandfather Kittredge's life renders him one of Mosher's more intriguing characters; but the author, with his presentation of Kittredge at the carnival, has barely scratched the surface of who that Lost Nation resident actually was. We get to see him living out his life on the farm with his wife and then, when she passes on, him making sure that she is buried in "not a coffin" but a "sarcophagus, in the unmistakable shape of a mummified Egyptian figure ... commodious enough for a large man, and inside it, propped on the fragrant evergreen bough ... were her most treasured Egyptian artifacts."[18] Her interest in such artifacts had stemmed from the time when she was an orphan and had been shipped overseas, first to Canada and then to America on a British-owned steamship where there in the hold were thousands of Egyptian mummies. As a girl, Austen's grandmother had been consumed by awe at those mummies who had "about them an air of aloof serenity and wisdom as though, besides resins and plant fibers and desiccated bone, they contained some wholly spiritual essence rendering them invulnerable to the very worst that mortals could do to them, including wrenching them out of the ground and using them to stoke the smoldering coal in the furnaces of orphan ships."[19] Since that time, the grandmother had become an ardent collector of all things related to Egypt and, in her passing, there must have been, in the grandfather, something akin to the same "honor and love" to which Professor Langis refers in terms of how much Cleopatra respected Mark Antony.

The grandfather sees to it that his wife is buried in the manner that she had wanted, but the intrigue does not stop there, for that grandfather had once been in love with another woman. In fact, they had lived as husband and wife (though they never married) until she died and then he buried her at a place where she could rest peacefully. Austen III learns about all of this because it is he who must accompany his grandfather to this place so rugged, in terms of the terrain, that our narrator regards getting back to it as a "hellish odyssey." But they must go back because construction of the hydroelectric dam will flood the whole region and as the elder Kittredge tells his grandson, "I can't and won't leave her here to be buried under all that water."[20] It seems that his dedication to her is at least as strong as what he felt for his wife. What Austen III will later learn is that his grandfather's first "wife" died from grief, one day after her son was stillborn and, no, his grandmother did not compare to the other woman and yet old Kittredge and his second wife "abided each other for nearly fifty years" and that in itself is more special than what most people, who profess to have love for each other, experience in their lives.

One reason, and perhaps the most important reason, that Grandfather Kittredge had remained out in the wilderness with his first love was because she was a Native American and theirs was a relationship that society would not have accepted with ease. In the case of Bangor, in *Where the Rivers Flow North*, it is not just because the crane operator flung her hat, across the room, that compels Lord to smash a jagged bottle into his face. That operator had also called Bangor "squaw" in such a manner as to make the word sound derogatory. Indeed she was Native American and Lord must have known, if they lived around people, that

VIII. The Immortality of Romantic Love

the sort of thing that happened with the crane operator would happen again and again, regardless of his reputation as a cunning and dangerous fighter. Even Othello, with all his military accolades, wonders about the significance of his race, at one point meditating, "I am black / And have not those soft parts of conversation / That chamberers have" (3.3.304–06). His blackness has made him question his chivalry even though he is, far and away, the most chivalrous man in the play. Viewed a certain way, it is his blackness that contributes, more than anything else, to his ultimate undoing. After he has killed Desdemona, he laments that he "loved not wisely, but too well" (5.2.404), but in actuality there is no such thing as loving one's betrothed "too well." In fact, the more love that one has for his significant other, the better.

Nor is Othello correct in wishing that he had loved more wisely. In his essay "*Othello* as an 'Assay of Reason,'" Philip McGuire actually criticizes the character Iago for being wise. McGuire asserts that the "act by which Iago moves Othello to murder Desdemona and thus destroy himself is essentially intellectual."[21] Othello need not have been too hard on himself for not loving with any significant degree of intellectuality. If successful love was, to any significant degree, based on intellect, then our greatest academic institutions would, long ago, have been deluged with courses offering us the specifics. No, Othello's problem had nothing to do with the wisdom or depth of his love, but the problem had to do with the society at large, of which Iago is but one representative. Had it not been Iago intent on destroying the Desdemona-Othello relationship, then it most assuredly would have been someone else.

Such is the reason why *Gatlinburg*'s Morgan Kinneson parts ways, at a certain point, with the escaped slave Slidell Collateral Dinwiddie whom Mosher acknowledged, in his Aldrich Library talk, was based on his own wife, Phillis. Mosher went on to explain that Phillis had been his 17-year-old high school girlfriend and now they had been together 47 years.[22] As far as Slidell and Morgan were concerned, they were as deeply in love with each other as any other couple in all of Mosher's works. We are told in fact that when he was with her, Morgan "felt wholly alive." However, unlike Phillis, Slidell is black and therefore dangerous for Morgan to be traveling with, particularly in the Civil War-era South where he is searching for his brother.

Howard Frank Mosher and the Classics

It is the social circumstances, with which those heroic couples must contend, that garnered so much of Shakespeare's attention. In *Othello*, the issue concerned black and white. With Cleopatra and Antony, the problem was how she was Egyptian, with significant Greek heritage, while he was distinctly a Roman. And then there is *Romeo and Juliet* which, with its absurd Montague-Capulet conflict, serves as a warning to all of us that there lurk, just outside of any meaningful relationship, forces that would prefer almost anything instead of a loving union.

As fate would have it, Jane Hubbell Kinneson, in *On Kingdom Mountain*, would actually get the opportunity to meet the offspring of the romantic interlude between her father Morgan and Slidell. Sitting there in Montreal, listening to her black half-sister talk about the depths of the relationship that existed between their father and a woman who was not Jane's mother, Jane breathes out the words that are a mantra for Mosher, words that, in some form or another, must have served as a mantra for Shakespeare too. Says Jane, "All the best stories are about love," to which Jane's half-sister, Elisabeth, agrees. That mantra not only enables us to understand the nature of the relationship that existed between Slidell and Morgan but it also enables us to comprehend the meaning behind Jane's relationship with a man named Henry Satterfield.

In the midst of a winter storm, the bizarre aviator is forced to land his biplane right there on the mountain. As soon as it has landed, the storm "suddenly" dissipates, as if the elements themselves had ordained what was later to come. Over the course of the following weeks, Jane and Henry lived together as one might imagine a married couple would, though, as we recall from what Faulkner's Uncle Ike had to say about the matter, a certificate and a ceremony would have been but of little significance anyway. It does not even matter that Henry might be using Jane to locate what he believes is hidden treasure from the Confederate raid on Kingdom Common. And it certainly does not matter that he is a "man with a dark complexion," though, as Mosher tells us, "tongues wagged" and people "whispered that Miss Jane Hubbell Kinneson had taken up with a man of color."[23] Centuries after *Othello* first appeared on stage, the diabolical Iago has never left the scene.

What matters most to Jane and Henry, however, is that they fish and hike together and enjoy quiet evenings talking about life. When

VIII. The Immortality of Romantic Love

even her own cousin contrives against her in the highway dispute, it is Henry who lends support as she makes her stand during the arduous legal process. And when she dies, a woman "well into her eighties," she will have no regrets but, in fact, will leave behind, on her tombstone, crucial words of advice, words which include the mantra she had conveyed to her half-sister:

> Always declare yourself to the person you love.
> Live each day not as though it is your last, but as though
>   It is the last day of the lives of the people you meet.
> All the best stories are about love.[24]

Such declarations of love are a mainstay of Shakespearean drama. Before the advent of devious external forces, Desdemona professes to Othello that although her love for him is already boundless, "the heavens forbid / But that our loves and comforts should increase / Even as our days do grow" (2.1.210–12).

As we listen to her speak about how "the heavens" have ordained that their love should only "increase" with the passing of time, we are reminded once again of what Professor Lanphier had said, with regard to Romeo and Juliet, about "the role of the universe as an element of influence." In the case of Othello, he responds to Desdemona's declaration, of love, with a declaration of his own as he tells her, "Amen to that, sweet powers! / I cannot speak enough of this content. / It stops me here; it is too much of joy" (2.1.213–15). It is as if the human mind and body are not large enough vessels to contain what love is, even as those involved acknowledge that at least they do have some sense of what it is. The human limitation is reflected, most profoundly, as we watch Othello kissing Desdemona while he is also preparing to kill her. Yet, the limitation is about to be transformed into something greater as we hear him tell her, "I will kill thee / And love thee after" (5.2.20–21), words that would seem to be incomprehensible but for Othello's own recognition, later in the play, as pertains to the importance of the "spirit" and the "soul."

When Romeo believes Juliet is dead, he is eager to, as he puts it, "set up my everlasting rest / And shake the yoke of inauspicious stars / From this world-wearied flesh!" (5.3.110–12). He kisses Juliet on the lips and then readily drinks the poison. Of course, as it turns out, Juliet is not dead, but when she finds out that Romeo has killed himself, she is just as eager to join him among what we might now consider to be the *auspicious* stars. As Romeo had kissed her, she now kisses him and then makes her "happy" exit.

From the way Shakespeare posits the death scenes in his play, it seems as if it does not really matter which of the lovers die first because whichever one dies first, then the other will not be far behind; it would seem that whoever goes second will have little trouble in locating the other. That is why we are not too worried when Ludi Too, in *Gatlinburg*, kills Pilgrim up there in the mountains. Mortal death will find Manon as well. The point, though, is that before death came to the couple, they were able to live out their time together, here on this earth, as the precursor for a world they will enter into next.

Pilgrim's lover might as well have been Cleopatra who, upon Antony's death, is preparing herself to join him as she says:

> I have
> Immortal longings in me....
> Methinks I hear
> Antony call: I see him rouse himself
> To praise my noble act....
>   Husband, I come!
> Now to that name my courage prove my title!
> I am fire and air: my other elements
> I give to baser life [5.2.322–32].

Cleopatra was never Antony's earthly wife, yet she says, "Husband, I come!" For lack of a better word as to what their union will consist of in the future, Shakespeare uses the term "husband," but such terms, one might imagine, will not have as much bearing as the phrase "fire and air" becomes a better way of defining who both of them are now.

"Housekeeper" is the term used to describe Lord's companion, Bangor; but when Lord dies, the process, whereby she honors him, marks her place as something above what one would characterize as just a cleaning woman. Shakespeare's Antony had been defeated in battle and when he dies, what is left, as Professor Joyce MacDonald argues, is for Cleopatra "to dress herself as a queen and a goddess and thus to second him in the project of performing the existence of that mysterious 'greater thing' that would make him whole and glorious."[25] What MacDonald

• **VIII. The Immortality of Romantic Love** •

has in mind is not that Cleopatra join Antony in a world of grand mythology, though that is a place where, to some extent, one can find the two of them located today. And in that mythology, as Professor Lisa Starks reminds us, "Antony is often seen as a failure, loser, or has-been hero.... Certainly he does not meet the qualifications of a Classical hero."[26]

The ritual that Cleopatra performs for Antony marks the transition away from a world, which sees him as a failure, and into the next world where, to use MacDonald's words, he will be "whole and glorious." That is the mission of Bangor who watches as Lord goes down in his never-ending struggle against the all-consuming Northern Vermont Power Company. When he is gone and there is nothing left but his physical body, she dug a "quite shallow" hole and then "slid his body into the grave, cradling him in the crook of the horse's legs. She placed the rifle across his arms, took off the sheep coat, and covered up his head and chest and part of his legs."[27] She had had to go back to get the coat and rifle, both of which belonged to Lord and were as much a part of him as were Antony's armor and sword.

Bangor had shot the horse, in part, so that she could bury him alongside his master; but, more importantly, she could not just leave the animal to suffer after carrying out what she had planned to do next. First, she put on her best red dress, then she burned their cabin down. Making her way back to Lord's grave, she stretched herself out prone across it and with a calculating simplicity—like Cleopatra applying one asp to her breast and another to her arm—waited for a death that is, in her case at least, not really death but, as MacDonald said, a "mysterious greater thing."

Thus it is not just a mystery where Cleopatra, and the other great lovers of Shakespeare's and Mosher's works, are headed toward; but their mortal deaths are the culmination of what the fortuneteller Louvia, in Mosher's novel *The Fall of the Year*, calls "the greatest mystery," that which is—as I suspect MacDonald would likewise argue—an extension of the act of love itself. That fortuneteller regularly consults a rose-colored quartz rock that she, interestingly enough, calls her "Daughter." Even more interesting is the fact that Mosher dedicated this particular book to his wife, Phillis, whom in that dedication he called "the Fortuneteller's Daughter." It consequently becomes quite clear to us that, for Mosher, this "daughter" that he indeed married is the primary source to be consulted on *all* matters related to love, whenever and wherever these issues may present themselves.

As I indicated in Chapter III, a key part of the epitaph on Jane Kinneson's tombstone concerns the prospect of being able to live each day "as though it is the last day of the lives of the people you meet." During the question-and-answer session after Mosher's Aldrich Library talk, he informed me that it was Phillis from whom he had stolen the saying.[28] Later when I got the chance to ask Phillis herself if she really lived that way, she rendered me the succinct response, "I try."[29] It was those two simple words that spoke volumes about not only how she treats people, in general, but the words also spoke volumes about the profundity of the relationship that she has with her dear husband. As she said those brief words, in the soft tone that characterizes her style of talking, my mind raced back to a point earlier that same day when the author had escorted Renae and me to the Irasburg cemetery where the grave marker for Phillis and him has already been erected, with their names etched upon it, years in advance of when their physical remains will be laid to rest while their spiritual aspects venture on to a place where others, who experienced such magnificent love, have already gone before.

Conclusion

"Not Gently" in Steinbeck's *Travels with Charley*, Twain's *The Innocents Abroad* and Mosher's *The Great Northern Express*

In 1958, John Steinbeck wrote a rather curious essay, for *Saturday Review*, entitled "The Easiest Way to Die." The essay was published at about the same time that the author was confronted with his own failing health. The next year, 1959, he would write a letter to his literary agent, Elizabeth Otis, and inform her, "The hospital found many small things wrong with me but they couldn't find the big thing."[1] By this time, of course, the author had already given us a substantial body of work, including classics such as *Of Mice and Men* (1937), *The Grapes of Wrath* (1939), and *East of Eden* (1952). But now it was the late 1950s and, considering his illness, it became all the more important that he not only continue to write but also wage a battle against the physical deterioration that threatened to put limits on his once formidable creative skills.

Deeply concerned about her husband's failing health, his wife Elaine urged him to "take it easy," which was what other family members and friends had suggested too, but the author was intent on a different direction, a direction best described perhaps by the Dylan Thomas poem, "Do Not Go Gentle into That Good Night," where the near death situation is posited not as one of peaceful repose but instead a time when one should strive, with unabashed resolve to seize the most from life.[2] Steinbeck himself was not interested in being an invalid and so, hooking up a camper to the back of a small truck, he set out to rediscover America, this land which he had already written about extensively, but about which he still felt that there was much to learn.

Thomas's poem is, in the literal sense, addressed to his father on his deathbed; however, in a broader sense it is a poem addressed to everyone, particularly as they come closer and closer to the stark reality of their own physical mortality. At this point, it becomes all the more important—as Edward and Lillian Bloom convey in their essay "Dylan Thomas: His Intimations of Mortality"—to be "buoyed ... by an awareness of danger" and realize the importance of an "attachment to the dynamic process of death rather than in passive adherence to mere existence."[3] Certainly, at the point when one has to come to grips with the mortal limitation of his own life, then that person should, all the more, be willing to question what the meaning of life might be, and not only question but investigate the possibilities, at least philosophically but preferably by continuing to explore those possibilities in as many venues as one's physical condition will allow.

In 1867, Mark Twain boarded a ship, *The Quaker City*, and ventured out to witness the world as he had never experienced it before—certain parts of Europe, large sections of Asia, and a substantial part of the so-called Holy Land. Speaking for other passengers, as well as himself, Twain, in *The Innocents Abroad* (1869), expressed that upon arriving in France, "[W]e had no disposition to examine carefully into any thing at all—we only wanted to glance and go—to move, keep moving!"[4] Their mutual objective was to see as much as possible and thereby gain access to perspectives that they might not ever before have considered. Traveling further on into Italy, they bore witness to numerous and varied scenes such as vagabonds prodding heavy-laden donkeys to market, porters carrying boxes "as large as cottages" on their backs, and peddlers of every sort trumpeting the availability of goods for sale.

We notice, as Twain describes those street scenes, that he has a great appreciation for people who would ordinarily not receive much attention. He, furthermore, is inclined to refer to them in terms that one would not ordinarily expect. For example, handicapped individuals in Constantinople become, in Twain's terminology, "wonderful" cripples; and by just their sheer number, the "dwarfs" in Milan become absolutely "luxuriant." Not that Twain does not also find certain kings and queens

• *Conclusion. "Not Gently"* •

to be interesting, especially in terms of their rise of power. But he continuously juxtaposes those examples of royalty with beggars and the like who surround the splendid churches and magnificent palaces, those settings in themselves becoming sites of unavoidable irony.

As he nears the end of his fascinating travelogue, Twain comes to the conclusion that "broad, wholesome charitable views of men and things can not be acquired by vegetating in one little corner of the earth all one's lifetime."[5] The traveling is what allows one to meet new people, and learn new things, in the process of gaining insights into the general workings of humanity. It would be almost a century, after Twain made his trip, that Steinbeck would set out to gain a greater understanding of the American landscape than what he already had; and yet, once out on the road, he is not at all sure if he is indeed accomplishing what he had set out to do as, in *Travels with Charley*, he finds himself thinking, "I came out on this trip to try to learn something of America. Am I learning anything? If I am, I don't know what it is. So far can I go back with a bag full of conclusions, a cluster of answers to riddles? I doubt it, but maybe."[6] It is the "maybe" of that statement that is so intriguing. What has he learned? For one thing, the message has been reinforced in him that one "cannot judge a book by its cover."

Needless to say, humanity, throughout time, has been "judging books" by their covers. The lesson against doing such is conveyed by Steinbeck as he tells about the time when he was traveling through Louisiana and picked up a "nice-looking" thirty-something-year-old man who turned out to be so filled with hate that, at a point, the author had no choice but to kick him out of the truck. The good-looking man had, in the most vitriolic language, insisted that he would die first, before letting his children go to school with blacks; but before he died he would, as he put it, "kill me a whole goddamn flock of niggers before I go."[7] That was when Steinbeck ordered him out of the truck and then drove on, unable though to avoid hearing that good-looking man wailing away in one final hate-filled tirade.

Then, in Oregon, that author encountered an "evil-looking" man, so disfigured in the face that, says Steinbeck, "if he were a horse I wouldn't buy him." As fate would have it, the writer was in need of two tires for his truck, and the only establishment that was open in the "shut-up town"—where he now found himself, in the middle of the night—

was a service station that just so happened to be owned by the evil-looking man who, as the author contemplated the situation, must have been one of only a small number of people still awake in the town, and certainly was the only person manning the station. Steinbeck was not holding out much hope that he would be able to get the needed tires, especially since this station owner did not have, in stock, the particular size that was needed.

To the author's surprise, though, the station owner began placing one phone call after another, and "the process was endless because between each call there was a line of cars waiting to be filled with gas and oil, and all this had to be done."[8] Ultimately, the phone calling wound up being successful. He had placed a call to a competitor, then another call to a member of his own family. Within a matter of hours, Steinbeck had his tires and the evil-looking man had, in the author's eyes, now taken on the appearance of a saint.

This vacillating back and forth between the good and the bad was a theme in *Moby-Dick*; we will recall our investigation into what exactly the whale might represent. Twain, in *The Innocents Abroad*, was confronted with a similar dilemma. Goodness and evil, for this author as well, seem so intertwined that we are often left wondering if any proposed line, between the two characteristics, would in any case be accurate. Commenting on Twain's perspective in the travelogue, Richard Fleck observes how "of all foreign nations he had seen during the 1867 voyage of the *Quaker City* the most unholy, wretched of places were the Holy Lands themselves."[9] In physical terms, Twain found the Holy Land to be the dirtiest of all the places he had seen. He notes the "dismal scenery" of Palestine and the "howling swarm of beggars" in Egypt, sights that make him reflect on how traveling to these places has robbed him of the "grandest pictures" that were presented to him when he had been a youth listening at the feet of the elders as they rendered their versions of how the Middle East would look if he ever got the chance to visit.

So, upon seeing the Holy Land for himself, it turned out to look nothing like what he had expected. But beyond that, he also was made, upon visiting the place for himself, to think yet again about life's complexities, specifically with regard to goodness and evil's inextricable interconnectedness. Arriving at "Joseph's Pit," he stops and reflects on

• *Conclusion. "Not Gently"* •

how a band of brothers could be so jealous of a sibling that they would leave him to face a solitary death in such a pit, their action having been triggered by something so simple as a coat of many colors. Joseph's response, upon being rescued and then advancing on to the greatest heights of Egyptian society, was to forgive those brothers and offer his assistance to them in the midst of a devastating drought.

Upon visiting the "Pool of Hezekiah," Twain contemplates the David who was once a shepherd boy fighting against Goliath. But then that boy, as king, was able to partake of profound evil himself. Having seen Uriah's wife as she emerged naked from this pool, David succumbed to lust such that he could order Uriah onto the battlefield to face a certain death, the king in this way being able to have access to the object of his carnal desire.

Just as Joseph's brothers would eventually repent for their offense, David would likewise beg forgiveness from God, the same God who had enabled him to defeat Goliath, the God that David, then, had so completely disappointed. This intertwining of good and evil was a reality that could not escape Twain's contemplations any more than it could escape Mosher's thoughts when, for example, he wrote about him and Phillis arriving in the Northeast Kingdom in the mid–1960s and, not long thereafter, coming to the conclusion that

> *no place*, no matter how idyllic, is without its dark underside. While some flatlanders might refer to the Kingdom as "God's country," I could not romanticize this northern fragment of Appalachia if I intended to write about it. The abusive sex shows at the fair and the barbaric cockfights at the Leonard brothers' were as much a part of the Kingdom's traditions and culture as the colorfully dressed, comical straw harvest figures in old-fashioned overalls and sunhats that began to appear on farmhouse porches in early October.[10]

The flatlanders are those who do not live in the mountainous region and, for those particular outsiders looking up at the vast beauty of the green mountains, it might indeed seem that goodness, and even godliness, dominates the lives of those who live there. But one need only recall the Irasburg Affair or the fact that young women had to endure life as carnival strippers, and then it will be clear what Mosher means when he talks about the "underside."

Howard Frank Mosher and the Classics

It was the whole picture, the idyllic world, as well as its dark underside, that Mosher wanted to explore firsthand when, at age 65, he began an extraordinary mission. Just as Steinbeck undertook his cross-country trip after learning that he was seriously ill, Mosher, upon learning that he had cancer, planned his own extensive road trip. As I mentioned in Chapter VII, the author had made such a trip before when, to celebrate his 50th birthday, he traversed along the United States/Canadian border, by car, to "search out what remained of the rest of America's northernmost frontiers."[11] But now, after learning of the cancer, this new trip, 15 years later, would somehow be different, as if in the traveling this time, he might commune even more effectively with those whom he had been concerned about all along and who, in a sense, were responsible for shaping him as a literary artist.

Many people, as they get on in age, tend to slow down and then, when told that they have contracted a serious illness, put a halt to their productive lives. Such could have been Steinbeck's approach, and we see him mulling over just such a possibility as he comments, in his *Saturday Review* essay, on communities that have urged their elderly on into the next world "with a little food and water, and rarely do they eat or drink it all. Since society has decreed them dead, they die … simply because it is expected of them."[12] The expected, however, is not what Steinbeck did, even against the wishes of his agent, his wife, and his doctor. Instead, he undertook the journey that was a perpetuation of his lifelong vocation, a vocation that he was nowhere close to retiring from even when it was determined that he was seriously ill.

The main title of his *Saturday Review* essay—"The Easiest Way to Die"—suggested that going on ahead and giving in to expectations might have been the best way to go, especially considering his medical situation. But when one then considers the essay's subtitle—"Reflections of a Man about to Run for His Life"—it becomes clear that any thoughts of giving up his vocation are just that, mere thoughts, as he proposed to actually pick up the pace in a manner that he explained to his agent:

> I am trying to say clearly that if I don't stoke my fires and soon, they will go out from leaving the damper closed and the air cut off.
> It is so seldom that you and I disagree that I am astonished when it happens. Between us—what I am proposing is not a little trip or reporting,

Conclusion. "Not Gently"

but a frantic last attempt to save my life and the integrity of my creative pulse.[13]

There are parts of that letter that remind one of the essay's subtitle. This will not be a "little trip" but a "frantic ... attempt to save [his own] life," said the author, a message that is indeed reflected in the *Saturday Review* essay subtitle with its own strident assertion that here was a man about to "run for his life," a metaphorical statement about what Steinbeck would do in terms of becoming a long-distance traveler who, after the journey was over, would then convey his experiences in the form of a modern-day travelogue.

With his typically outlandish humor, Mosher referred to his illness as a MacArthur Fellowship. After all, that is what he tells us—at the beginning of *The Great Northern Express* (2012)—he had been waiting to receive in the mail when instead he got the letter informing him of his cancer. The cancer notification was just as effective a tool to put him on the road as if he had actually won the prestigious fellowship which regularly awards hundreds of thousands of dollars to the so-called geniuses in order that they, unencumbered, might continue with their genius work. Mosher got the call, so to speak, just as if the MacArthur Fellowship advisory board itself had said *Here are the funds that will allow you to travel as extensively as you wish if that is what it takes for you to continue your work*.

So, after his 44 radiation sessions, Mosher did just that. He, to use Steinbeck's words, was about to "run for his life." Or put another way, he had been abruptly brought around to an even more profound comprehension, than what he had known before, of what he needed to do in pursuit of his craft; and just as importantly he had come to comprehend the urgency involved in undertaking that task. Ronald Primeau, in his essay "Romancing the Road," tells us what long drives meant to Steinbeck who felt that they "free the mind for thinking, sorting, daydreaming, and creating."[14] Indeed, such was the goal of Steinbeck as he undertook his cross-country trek; but just as essential, to the undertaking, was that it be done incognito. Professor Christian Knoeller asserts that "this purposeful anonymity is essentially a strategy that positions the author as he wanders, allowing him to inhabit the margins socially—arguably a sort of Everymen—able to pass as a person having affinity with even the lowliest of folks he encounters."[15] It was this sort of blending in that allowed Twain, in Venice, to "study the gondolier's marvelous skill" without that gondolier ever changing his natural way of guiding the gondola down the "great canals." Twain's anonymity, furthermore, allowed him to observe the Constantinople goose-rancher as he guided, with his pole, a hundred geese in an effort to sell as many of them as he could. Then, in Istanbul, the writer becomes part of the throbbing street bazaar crowd with its varied assortment of "beggars, asses, yelling peddlers, porters, dervishes, high-born Turkish female shoppers, Greeks, and weird-looking and weirdly dressed Mohammedans from the mountains and the far provinces."[16] Watching, unobstructed, the writer was able to ascertain traits that are common to all humanity, that Turkish bazaar scene having taken on the appurtenances of society in general with its customs and manners reflected in how people react to their close proximity to others.

So intent was Mosher in maintaining *his* anonymity that, at a mall parking lot just outside of Boston, he allowed himself to be disrespected, in a most egregious manner, without ever even explaining who he was. The author had been scheduled to do a book signing and as he pulled up to the one space that was available, he saw in it a stand-alone sign that read: "AUTHOR'S EVENT TODAY. THIS SPACE RESERVED FOR HOWARD FRANK MOSHER." He drove up to the sign and was about to move it aside when a young man, all dressed up in black, rushed out, shouting as he came, "Hey! … That sign is there for a reason."[17] The young man demanded that Mosher move his car, whereupon the author, quite respectfully, drove off, combing back through the parking lot until he was able to find another space, albeit a spot that was far less hospitable, located, as it was, "beside a large green dumpster."

Once he, walking, had made his way up to the front of the mall, he came across the young man again, the man not even recognizing, as Mosher was preparing to give his talk, that this author, and the man who had been turned away, were one and the same person. The car Mosher drove was 20 years old and his "ancient Red Sox jacket and cap" had further reduced him in human value in the eyes of the young man who, as it turns out, happened to be the store manager as evidenced by a badge that hung visibly from his neck, proclaiming him so. Mosher

• *Conclusion. "Not Gently"* •

went on ahead with his talk but vowed afterward to stay away from the chain bookstores.

Relishing in the propensity of others to judge him as just another man—if not less—Mosher, in *Northern Express*, tells us of another instance where he is run off from a place where he was supposed to be. This time the location is a five-star oceanside resort in Miami, Florida, where a ladies' literary society had arranged for him to stay. But as he pulls up in his "rust-bucket Chevy," not one but two doormen run up to tell him that he cannot stay because he has no reservation, even though in actuality Mosher did have a reservation. Again, appearances dictated how he would be treated and, rather than argue, he simply drove away until he reached a Budget Inn where he only had to pay about twenty dollars to stay for the night, and that turned out to be more his "cup of tea."

It reminds us of Steinbeck driving from place to place, on his cross-country tour, staying over in two-dollar-a-night cabins, one-dollar-a-night trailers, and a sundry assortment of auto courts. When push came to shove, he would just go to the camper—"Rocinante"—that he had hooked up to the back of his truck, and bunk there, an approach to winding down the day that oftentimes allowed him the opportunity to meet new people such as when he was in Maine and stopped near a camp of migrant workers. "Those people might have been murderers, sadists, brutes, ugly apish subhumans for all I knew," wrote Steinbeck in *Travels with Charley*, "but I found myself thinking, 'What charming people, what flair, how beautiful they are.'"[18] To establish contact, Steinbeck had released his dog, Charley, to wander off to the camp so that the author could then come to the rescue whereupon he would learn about all manner of things such as when it was that they had first come across the border and how the way had been smoothed for them by contractors or by the farmers themselves for whom the migrants would be working.

Mosher, on his cross-country trip, was likewise inclined to visit with practically anyone whose path he crossed as he ventured from one bookstore to another, in town after town. As was the case with Twain, sometimes the encounters would be with the upper crust of society, but the most educational experiences would be with the commoners whose stories were most profound due to the processes that they had undergone, in their lives, simply to be able to survive. At the Budget Inn, Mosher had been on the phone to Phillis when something that sounded like a "pistol shot" rang out and she, having heard it over the line, demanded, "BARRICADE YOUR DOOR, HOWARD FRANK!"

However, barricading his door was the last thing that Mosher would have been inclined to do. He will eventually go out to check and see what is going on. After all, he had been told that this is where the homeless live, people who are bound to have enough stories in them to serve a writer for a lifetime. As fate would have it, though, the noise is coming from some young revelers in the next room who if not quite old enough, yet, to have gathered, within themselves, very many interesting tales, at least on that night they became part of an intriguing story of alcohol consumption, a broken-down wall, and the arrival of local police. In the aftermath of it all, Mosher returned to bed, in a sense fulfilled, having been, in the words of Edward and Lillian Bloom, "buoyed by danger" and the "attachment to a dynamic process rather than passive adherence to mere existence." Those words might well have been written by Mosher himself, for the "MacArthur Fellowship," that he had won, spurred him on to engage in just such "dynamic" varieties of life, on a journey that I believe, with all my heart, he would have gone on anyway.

Notes

Introduction

1. Frances Hyde Dearborne, "My Mountain Home," *Poets and Poetry of Vermont*, ed. Abby Maria Hemenway (Rutland, VT: George A. Tuttle, 1858), 124.
2. Helen Warner, "Farmers' Boys," *Poets and Poetry of Vermont*, 386.
3. Dorothy Canfield Fisher, *Vermont Tradition: The Biography of an Outlook on Life* (Boston: Little, Brown, 1953), 323.
4. Ethan Allen, *A Concise Refutation of the Claims of New-Hampshire and Massachusetts-Bay, to the Territory of Vermont; with Occasional Remarks on the Long Disputed Claim of New York to the Same* (Bennington, VT: Governor and Council of Vermont, 1780), 11.
5. Arthur W. Biddle and Paul A. Eschholz, introd., *The Literature of Vermont: A Sampler* (Hanover, NH: University Press of New England, 1973), 4.
6. Frances M. Frost, "Language," *Blue Harvest* (Boston: Houghton Mifflin, 1931), 39.
7. Fisher, *Vermont Tradition*, 9.
8. Rowland E. Robinson, introd. note, *Danvis Folks* (Boston: Houghton Mifflin, 1896), iii.
9. Yvonne Daley, *Vermont Writers: A State of Mind* (Hanover, NH: University Press of New England, 2005), 27.

Chapter I

1. Stephen Crane, *The Red Badge of Courage* (1895; New York: Pocket, 2005), 6.
2. Crane, *Red Badge*, 11–12.
3. Steven W. Sears, *Landscape Turned Red: The Battle of Antietam* (New Haven: Ticknor & Fields, 1983), 294–296.
4. Crane, *Red Badge*, 33.
5. Lyndon Upson Pratt, "A Possible Source of *The Red Badge of Courage*," *American Literature* 11.1 (1939): 8.
6. John W. Busey and David G. Martin, *Regimental Strengths and Losses at Gettysburg*, 4th ed. (Hightstown, NJ: Longstreet House, 2005), 125.
7. Busey and Martin, *Regimental Strengths*, 260.
8. Walt Whitman, "The Million Dead, Too, Summ'd Up," *Specimen Days and Collect* (Glasgow: Wilson & McCormick, 1883), 79–80.
9. Howard Frank Mosher, *Walking to Gatlinburg* (New York: Shaye Areheart, 2010), 73.
10. John E. Curran, Jr., "'Nobody seems to know where we go': Uncertainty, History, and Irony in *The Red Badge of Courage*," *American Literary Realism* 26.1 (1993): 4.

Notes—Chapter II

11. Walt Whitman, "The Real War Will Never Get in the Books," *Specimen Days*, 80–81.
12. Marilyn Boyer, "The Treatment of the Wound in Stephen Crane's *The Red Badge of Courage*," *Stephen Crane Studies* 12.1 (2003): 8.
13. Emily Dickinson, "Poem #3," *The Complete Poems of Emily Dickinson*, ed. Thomas H. Johnson (Boston: Little, Brown, 1960), 6.
14. Crane, *Red Badge*, 85.
15. Boyer, "The Treatment of the Wound," 7.
16. Melissa Green, "Fleming's 'Escape' in *The Red Badge of Courage*: A Jungian Analysis," *American Literary Realism* 28.1 (1995): 85.
17. Crane, *Red Badge*, 100.
18. Howard Frank Mosher, *On Kingdom Mountain* (2007; New York: Mariner, 2008), 238–239.
19. Mosher, *On Kingdom Mountain*, 239.
20. Michael Schaefer, "Stephen Crane in the Time of Shock and Awe: Teaching *The Red Badge of Courage* During the Iraq War," *Stephen Crane Studies* 13.2 (2004): 6.
21. Crane, *Red Badge*, 134.
22. Crane, *Red Badge*, 18.
23. N. E. Dunn, "The Common Man's *Iliad*," *Comparative Literature Studies* 21.3 (1984): 277.
24. Crane, *Red Badge*, 24.
25. Crane, *Red Badge*, 9.
26. Mosher, *Gatlinburg*, 92.
27. Stephen Crane, "The Veteran," *The Red Badge of Courage: A Norton Critical Edition*, 4th ed., eds. Donald Pizer and Eric Carl Link (New York: Norton, 2008), 232.

Chapter II

1. Howard Frank Mosher, personal interview, 24 July 2010.
2. Upton Sinclair, *The Jungle* (1906; New York: Penguin, 1986), 98–99.
3. Sinclair, *The Jungle*, 199.
4. Sinclair, *The Jungle*, 181.
5. Susan Meiselas, *Carnival Strippers* (1976; New York: Whitney Museum of American Art/Göttingen: Steidl, 2003), 124.
6. Meiselas, *Carnival Strippers*, 7.
7. Jim Harrison, "A Lens on History: Photographer Susan Meiselas's Quest to Understand via Images," *Harvard Magazine* (Nov.–Dec. 2010): 42.
8. Orm Overland, "*The Jungle*: From Lithuanian Peasant to American Socialist," *American Literary Realism* 37.1 (2004): 8–9.
9. Sinclair, *The Jungle*, 28.
10. Sinclair, *The Jungle*, 29.
11. Howard Frank Mosher, *Marie Blythe* (New York: Viking, 1983), 32.
12. Mosher, *Marie Blythe*, 100.
13. Mosher, *Marie Blythe*, 101.
14. Theodore Dreiser, *Sister Carrie* (1900; Mineola, NY: Dover, 2004), 27.
15. Mosher, *Marie Blythe*, 109.
16. Mosher, *Marie Blythe*, 109.
17. Meiselas, *Carnival Strippers*, 133.
18. Sinclair, *The Jungle*, 262–263.
19. Meiselas, *Carnival Strippers*, 7.
20. Meiselas, *Carnival Strippers*, 124.

Notes—Chapter III

21. Meiselas, *Carnival Strippers*, 124.
22. Sinclair, *The Jungle*, 347.
23. Stephen Crane, *Maggie: A Girl of the Streets* (1893), *Maggie: A Girl of the Streets and Other Tales of New York*, ed. Larzer Ziff (New York: Penguin, 2000), 7.
24. Crane, *Maggie*, 8.
25. David Fitelson, "*Maggie: A Girl of the Streets* Portrays a 'Survival of the Fittest' World," *Readings on Stephen Crane*, ed. Bonnie Szumski (San Diego: Greenhaven, 1998), 170.
26. Daniel Cottom, "Maggie, Not a Girl of the Streets," *Novel* 41.1 (2007): 77–78.
27. Dreiser, *Siste Carrie*, 17.
28. Charles Harmon, "Cuteness and Capitalism in *Sister Carrie*," *American Literary Realism* 32.2 (2000): 133–134.
29. Clara Morris, "A Word of Warning to Young Actresses," *Century* (May 1900): 42.
30. Mosher, *Marie Blythe*, 179.

Chapter III

1. Howard Frank Mosher, personal interview, 24 July 2010.
2. Howard Frank Mosher, *On Kingdom Mountain* (2007; New York: Mariner, 2008), 118.
3. E. Glenn Hinson, "The Progression of Grace: A Re-Reading of *The Pilgrim's Progress*," *Spiritus* 3.2 (2003): 256.
4. John Bunyan, *The Pilgrim's Progress* (1678; Mineola, NY: Dover, 2003), 10.
5. Benjamin Berger, "Calvinism and the Problem of Suspense in *The Pilgrim's Progress*," *Bunyan Studies* 8 (1998): 32.
6. Berger, "Calvinism and the Problem of Suspense in *The Pilgrim's Progress*," 32.
7. Bunyan, *The Pilgrim's Progress*, 47.
8. Howard Frank Mosher, personal interview, 24 July 2010.
9. Kathleen M. Swaim, *Pilgrim's Progress, Puritan Progress* (Urbana: University of Illinois Press, 1993), 55.
10. Howard Frank Mosher, *Walking to Gatlinburg* (New York: Shaye Areheart, 2010), 32.
11. Mosher, *Gatlinburg*, 64.
12. Mosher, *Gatlinburg*, 64.
13. Howard Frank Mosher, "Transforming History into Fiction: The Story of a Born Liar," Authors at the Aldrich, Leonard Aldrich Library, Barre, VT, 2 June 2010.
14. Mosher, *Gatlinburg*, 165.
15. Annette Gordon-Reed, *Thomas Jefferson and Sally Hemings: An American Controversy* (Charlottesville: University Press of Virginia, 1997), 168.
16. Bunyan, *The Pilgrim's Progress*, 105.
17. Bunyan, *The Pilgrim's Progress*, 105.
18. Bunyan, *ThePilgrim's Progress*, 107.
19. Bunyan, *The Pilgrim's Progress*, 102.
20. Mosher, *Gatlinburg*, 302.
21. Margaret Soenser, "Christiana's Rudeness: Spiritual Authority in *The Pilgrim's Progress*," *Bunyan Studies* 7 (1997): 108.
22. Bunyan, *The Pilgrim's Progress*, 187.
23. Bunyan, *The Pilgrim's Progress*, 234.
24. Mosher, *Gatlinburg*, 197.
25. Mosher, *On Kingdom Mountain*, 276.

Notes—Chapter IV

26. Phillis Mosher, personal interview, 24 July 2010.
27. Sylvia Brown, "The Reproductive Word: Gender and Textuality in the Writings of John Bunyan," *Bunyan Studies* 11 (2003–2004): 27–28.
28. Bunyan, *The Pilgrim's Progress*, 310.
29. Bunyan, *The Pilgrim's Progress*, 302–303.
30. Mosher, *Gatlinburg*, 227.
31. Bunyan, *The Pilgrim's Progress*, 148.

Chapter IV

1. Howard Frank Mosher, *Disappearances* (New York: Viking, 1977), 45.
2. William S. Gleim, *The Meaning of Moby Dick* (New York: Russell & Russell, 1962), 29–30.
3. Herman Melville, *Moby-Dick or, The Whale* (1851; New York: Modern Library, 2000), 777.
4. Melville, *Moby-Dick*, 747.
5. Melville, *Moby-Dick*, 115.
6. Mosher, *Disappearances*, 148.
7. Mosher, *Disappearances*, 31.
8. Mosher, *Disappearances*, 31.
9. Melville, *Moby-Dick*, 274.
10. Mosher, *Disappearances*, 51.
11. Melville, *Moby-Dick*, 778.
12. Melville, *Moby-Dick*, 778.
13. Melville, *Moby-Dick*, 803–804.
14. Robert Narveson, "The Name 'Claggart' in 'Billy Budd,'" *American Speech* 43.3 (1968): 232.
15. Narveson, "The Name 'Claggart' in 'Billy Budd,'" 229.
16. Herman Melville, *Billy Budd, Sailor* (1924), *Billy Budd, Sailor and Other Stories*, ed. Frederick Busch (New York: Penguin, 1986), 326.
17. James Fenimore Cooper, *The Cruise of the Somers: Illustrative of the Despotism of the Quarter Deck; and of the Unmanly Conduct of Commander Mackenzie*, 3d ed. (New York: Winchester, 1844), 11.
18. Cooper, *The Cruise of the Somers*, 24.
19. Melville, *Billy Budd*, 339.
20. Lyon Evans, Jr., "'Too Good to Be True': Subverting Christian Hope in *Billy Budd*," *New England Quarterly* 55.3 (1982): 342.
21. Melville, *Billy Budd*, 302.
22. Jonathan A. Yoder, "Melville's Snake on the Cross: Justice for John Claggart and *Billy Budd*," *Christianity and Literature* 43.2 (1994): 140.
23. Howard Frank Mosher, "Transforming History into Fiction: The Story of a Born Liar," Authors at the Aldrich, Leonard Aldrich Library, Barre, VT, 2 June 2010.
24. "A Conversation with Howard Frank Mosher," Shaye Areheart Books Publicity Newsletter, 2 March 2010.
25. James Weldon Johnson, *The Autobiography of an Ex-Coloured Man* (1912; New York: Vintage, 1989), 146.
26. Howard Frank Mosher, *Walking to Gatlinburg* (New York: Shaye Areheart, 2010), 328.
27. John T. Matteson, "The Little Lower Layer: Anxiety and the Courage to Be in Moby-Dick," *Harvard Theological Review* 81.1 (1988): 106.
28. Mosher, *Disappearances*, 62.

Notes—Chapter V

29. Henry Alonzo Myers, "Captain Ahab's Discovery: The Tragic Meaning of Moby Dick," *New England Quarterly* 15.1 (1942): 25.
30. Melville, *Moby-Dick*, 264.
31. Mosher, *Disappearances*, 169.
32. Geoffrey Sanborn, "The Name of the Devil: Melville's Other 'Extracts' for *Moby-Dick*," *Nineteenth-Century Literature* 47.2 (1992): 220.
33. Howard Frank Mosher, *The True Account* (New York: Houghton Mifflin, 2003), 266.
34. Wayne F. Burke, *Kingdom Come: The Fiction of Howard Frank Mosher* (Baltimore: PublishAmerica, 2005), 23.

Chapter V

1. Harper Lee, *To Kill a Mockingbird* (1960; New York: HarperCollins, 2010), 268.
2. Claudia Johnson, "The Secret Courts of Men's Hearts: Code and Law in Harper Lee's *To Kill a Mockingbird*," *Studies in American Fiction* 19.2 (1991): 132.
3. James R. McGovern, *Anatomy of a Lynching* (Baton Rouge: Louisiana State University Press, 1982), 6.
4. John Hope Franklin, *From Slavery to Freedom*, 4th ed. (1947; New York: Knopf, 1974), 363.
5. Charles S. Johnson, "Public Opinion and the Negro," 1923, *The Opportunity Reader*, ed. Sondra Kathryn Wilson (New York: Modern Library, 1999), 433.
6. Johnson, "Public Opinion and the Negro," 437–438.
7. Charles H. Martin, "Oklahoma's 'Scottsboro' Affair: The Jess Hollins Rape Case, 1931–1936," *South Atlantic Quarterly* 79.2 (1980): 183.
8. Morris Dees, with Steve Fiffer, *A Season for Justice* (1991; New York: Touchstone, 1992), 146.
9. Carl T. Rowan, *South of Freedom* (New York: Knopf, 1952), 179.
10. Mary Shelley, *Frankenstein: Or, The Modern Prometheus*, 1818, ed. Johanna M. Smith (Boston: Bedford, 1992), 121.
11. Lee, *Mockingbird*, 276.
12. Howard Frank Mosher, *A Stranger in the Kingdom* (New York: Doubleday, 1989), 54.
13. Hugh Moffett, "The Ruckus in Irasburg," *Life* (April 4, 1969): 64.
14. Moffett, "The Ruckus in Irasburg," 68.
15. Howard Frank Mosher, personal interview, 24 July 2010.
16. Lee, *Mockingbird*, 233.
17. Moffett, "The Ruckus in Irasburg," 68.
18. Moffett, "The Ruckus in Irasburg," 68–69.
19. Moffett, "The Ruckus in Irasburg," 68.
20. Mosher, *A Stranger*, 154.
21. Mosher, *A Stranger*, 285.
22. Mosher, *A Stranger*, 250.
23. John Carlos Rowe, "Racism, Fetishism, and the Gift Economy in *To Kill a Mockingbird*," *On Harper Lee: Essays and Reflections*, ed. Alice Hall Petry (Knoxville: University of Tennessee Press, 2007), 3.
24. Mosher, personal interview, 24 July 2010.
25. Mosher, *A Stranger*, 192.
26. Mosher, *A Stranger*, 387.
27. Mosher, personal interview, 24 July 2010.

Notes—Chapters VI, VII

Chapter VI

1. Sacvan Bercovitch, "What's Funny About Huckleberry Finn," *New England Review* 20.1 (1999): 11.
2. Dianne Stewart, trans., "Spider and the Crows," *Favorite African Folktales*, ed. Nelson Mandela (2002; New York: Norton, 2004), 82.
3. Howard Frank Mosher, *The Great Northern Express* (New York: Crown, 2012) 70.
4. Mark Twain, "How to Tell a Story," 1897, *How to Tell a Story and Other Essays* (New York: Harper, 1898), 3–4.
5. Mark Twain, *The Autobiography of Mark Twain*, 1924, ed. Charles Neider (1966; New York: Harper, 1975), 64.
6. Karen Sotiropoulos, *Staging Race: Black Performers in Turn of the Century America* (Cambridge: Harvard University Press, 2006), 3.
7. Howard Frank Mosher, personal interview, 24 July 2010.
8. Howard Frank Mosher, *The True Account* (New York: Houghton Mifflin, 2003), 29.
9. Twain, *The Autobiography*, 64.
10. Ralph Ellison, *Invisible Man* (1952; New York: Vintage, 1995), 102.
11. Howard Frank Mosher, personal interview, 31 May 2013.
12. Stephen Railton, "Jim and Mark Twain: What Do Dey Stan' For?" *Virginia Quarterly Review* 63.3 (1987): 403.
13. Percy G. Adams, "Humor as Structure and Theme in Faulkner's Trilogy," *Wisconsin Studies in Contemporary Literature* 5.3 (1964): 212.
14. Robert Paul Lamb, personal interview, 27 August 2013.
15. Mark Twain, *The Adventures of Huckleberry Finn* (1884; New York: Vintage, 2010), 28.
16. Mosher, *The True Account*, 324.
17. Mosher, *The True Account*, 54.
18. Twain, *Huckleberry Finn*, 141–142.
19. Mosher, *The True Account*, 45.
20. Robert Paul Lamb, personal interview, 27 August 2013.
21. Ellison, *Invisible Man*, 58.
22. Houston A. Baker, Jr., "To Move Without Moving: An Analysis of Creativity and Commerce in Ralph Ellison's Trueblood Episode," *PMLA: Publications of the Modern Language Association of America* 98.5 (1983): 829.
23. Mosher, *The True Account*, 128.
24. Mosher, *The True Account*, 125.
25. Mosher, *The True Account*, 125.
26. Twain, *Huckleberry Finn*, 100.
27. Robert Paul Lamb, personal interview, 27 August 2013.
28. Twain, *Huckleberry Finn*, 111.
29. Mosher, *The True Account*, 335.

Chapter VII

1. Matt Low, "'The Bear' in *Go Down, Moses* and *Big Woods*: Faulkner's (Re)visions for a Deeper Ecology," *Mississippi Quarterly* 62.1–2 (2009): 63.
2. Frederick L. Gwynn and Joseph L. Blotner, eds., *Faulkner in the University: Class Conferences at the University of Virginia, 1957–1958* (Charlottesville: University of Virginia Press, 1959), 271–272.
3. William Faulkner, *Go Down, Moses* (1942; New York: Vintage, 1990), 175.

Notes—Chapter VII

4. Faulkner, *Go Down, Moses*, 200–201.
5. Howard Frank Mosher, *North Country: A Personal Journey through the Borderland* (Boston: Houghton Mifflin, 1997), 212.
6. Yvonne Daley, *Vermont Writers: A State of Mind* (Hanover, New Hampshire: University Press of New England, 2005), 27.
7. Howard Frank Mosher, personal interview, 24 July 2010.
8. Howard Frank Mosher, *Northern Borders* (New York: Doubleday, 1994), 95–96.
9. John Lydenberg, "Nature Myth in Faulkner's 'The Bear,'" *American Literature* 24.1 (1952): 65.
10. Faulkner, *Go Down, Moses*, 186.
11. Howard Frank Mosher, *Where the Rivers Flow North* (New York: Viking, 1978), 180.
12. Howard Frank Mosher, *Disappearances* (New York: Viking, 1977), 244–245.
13. Faulkner, *Go Down, Moses*, 246.
14. Faulkner, *Go Down, Moses*, 346.
15. Gwynn and Blotner, *Faulkner in the University*, 68.
16. Mosher, *Rivers Flow North*, 124.
17. Bart H. Welling, "A Meeting with Old Ben: Seeing and Writing Nature in Faulkner's *Go Down, Moses*," *Mississippi Quarterly* 55.4 (2002): 482.
18. Mosher, *Northern Borders*, 91.
19. Welling, "A Meeting with Old Ben," 482.
20. Mosher, *Northern Borders*, 288.
21. Howard Frank Mosher, "A Disappearing Eden" [Interview with Katie Bacon], *The Atlantic Online*, 2 October 1997, retrieved 12 November 2009, from http://www.theatlantic.com/unbound/bookauth/hfmint.htm.
22. Mosher, *Rivers Flow North*, 182.
23. Gwynn and Blotner, *Faulkner in the University*, 98.
24. Mosher, *Rivers Flow North*, 199.
25. Howard Frank Mosher, *On Kingdom Mountain* (2007; New York: Mariner, 2008), 44–45.
26. Howard Frank Mosher, *Walking to Gatlinburg* (New York: Shaye Areheart, 2010), 4.
27. Mosher, *On Kingdom Mountain*, 107.
28. Lewis Soens, ed., *Sir Philip Sidney's Defense of Poesy*, by Philip Sidney (1595; Lincoln: University of Nebraska Press, 1970), 9.
29. Charles Ross, "Sidney's *Arcadia*: A Global Edition?" Sidney and Shakespeare Panel, Renaissance Comparative Prose Conference, Stewart Center, Purdue University, West Lafayette, IN, 22 September 2011.
30. Gotthold Ephraim Lessing, *Laocoon: An Essay Upon the Limits of Painting and Poetry*, trans. Ellen Frothingham (1766; Boston: Roberts Brothers, 1887), 105–106.
31. Howard Frank Mosher, interview with Nick Zaino, "Howard Frank Mosher—An American Writer," *The Optimistic Curmudgeon*, 26 October 2007, retrieved 12 November 2009, from http://optimisticcurmudgeon.blogspot.com/2007/10/howard-frank-mosher-american-writer.
32. Mosher, personal interview, 24 July 2010.
33. Mosher, *On Kingdom Mountain*, 204–205.
34. Mosher, *On Kingdom Mountain*, 198.
35. Mosher, *On Kingdom Mountain*, 193.
36. Mosher, personal interview, 24 July 2010.
37. Mosher, personal interview, 24 July 2010.
38. Mosher, personal interview, 24 July 2010.

Chapter VIII

1. William Faulkner, *Go Down, Moses* (1942; New York: Vintage, 1990), 332.
2. Arthur Brooke, *The Tragicall Hystory of Romeus and Juliet; Contayning in it a Rare Example of true Constancie; With The Subtill Counsels and Practises of an old Fryer, and their ill Event* (1562; London, 1780).
3. David N. Lanphier, "How Shakespeare Purified and Idealized the Love Story of Romeo and Juliet," *Publications of the Arkansas Philological Association* 23.2 (1997): 32.
4. William Shakespeare, *The Tragedy of Romeo and Juliet*, eds. Barbara A. Mowat and Paul Werstine (1597; New York: Washington Square, 2004), 71 (2.2.29–35). Subsequent references to this play are in parentheses following quotes in the regular text of my writing.
5. Howard Frank Mosher, *On Kingdom Mountain* (2007; New York: Mariner, 2008), 117–18.
6. Howard Frank Mosher, "Second Sight," *Granite & Cedar: The People and the Land of Vermont's Northeast Kingdom*, illus. John M. Miller (North Pomfret, VT: Thistle Hill, 2001), 70.
7. Robert Burns, "Despondency," *The Poetical Works of Robert Burns*, ed. Charles Kent (London: George Routledge, 1885), 102.
8. William Shakespeare, *The Tragedy of Othello, the Moor of Venice*, eds. Barbara A. Mowat and Paul Werstine (1603; New York: Simon & Schuster, 2009), 33 (1.3.73–74). Subsequent references to this play are in parentheses following quotes in the regular text of my writing.
9. Arthur L. Little, Jr., "'An essence that's not seen': The Primal Scene of Racism in *Othello*," *Shakespeare Quarterly* 44.3 (1993): 310.
10. Jonathan Bate, introd., *The Tragedy of Antony and Cleopatra*, by William Shakespeare (1603; New York: Modern Library, 2009), xxi.
11. Shakespeare, *The Tragedy of Antony and Cleopatra*, 38 (2.2.275–80). Subsequent references to this play are in parentheses following quotes in the regular text of my writing.
12. Howard Frank Mosher, *Marie Blythe* (New York: Viking, 1983), 195.
13. Francesco Petrarcha [Francis Petrarch], *For Love of Laura*, trans. Marion Shore (Fayetteville: University of Arkansas Press, 1987), 63.
14. Francis Petrarch, *The Life of Solitude*, trans. Jacob Zeitlin (Champaign: University of Illinois Press, 1924), 128.
15. Unhae Langis, "Shakespeare's Cleopatra as Virtuous Virago," *Genre* 28 (2008): 221.
16. Howard Frank Mosher, *Walking to Gatlinburg* (New York: Shaye Areheart, 2010), 3.
17. Howard Frank Mosher, *Northern Borders* (New York: Doubleday, 1994), 60.
18. Mosher, *Northern Borders*, 256.
19. Mosher, *Northern Borders*, 241.
20. Mosher, *Northern Borders*, 275.
21. Philip C. McGuire, "*Othello* as an 'Assay of Reason,'" *Shakespeare Quarterly* 24.2 (1973): 198.
22. Howard Frank Mosher, "Transforming History Into Fiction: The Story of a Born Liar," Authors at the Aldrich, Leonard Aldrich Library, Barre, VT, 2 June 2010.
23. Mosher, *On Kingdom Mountain*, 31.
24. Mosher, *On Kingdom Mountain*, 276.
25. Joyce Green MacDonald, "Antony's Body," *Early Modern Literary Studies*, Special Issue 19 (2009), retrieved 30 August 2011, from http://extra.shu.ac.uk/emls/si-19/macdanto.html.

26. Lisa S. Starks, "'Immortal Longings': The Erotics of Death in *Antony and Cleopatra*," *Antony and Cleopatra: New Critical Essays*, ed. Sara Munson Deats (New York: Routledge, 2005), 244.
27. Howard Frank Mosher, *Where the Rivers Flow North* (New York: Viking, 1978), 201.
28. Mosher, "Transforming History into Fiction."
29. Phillis Mosher, personal interview, 24 July 2010.

Conclusion

John Steinbeck, "To Elizabeth Otis," 30 December 1959, *Steinbeck: A Life in Letters*, eds. Elaine Steinbeck and Robert Wallsten (London: Heinemann, 1975), 656.
2. Dylan Thomas, "Do Not Go Gentle into That Good Night," *The Collected Poems of Dylan Thomas: 1934–1952* (1953; New York: New Directions, 1971), 128.
3. Edward A. Bloom and Lillian D. Bloom, "Dylan Thomas: His Intimations of Mortality," *Boston University Studies in English* 4 (1960): 144.
4. Mark Twain, *The Innocents Abroad* (1869; New York: Penguin, 2002), 65.
5. Twain, *The Innocents Abroad*, 498.
6. John Steinbeck, *Travels with Charley in Search of America* (1862; New York: Penguin, 2002), 107.
7. Steinbeck, *Travels with Charley*, 204.
8. Steinbeck, *Travels with Charley*, 142.
9. Richard F. Fleck, "Mark Twain's Social Criticism in *The Innocents Abroad*," *Bulletin of the Rocky Mountain Modern Language Association* 25.2 (1971): 46.
10. Howard Frank Mosher, *The Great Northern Express* (New York: Crown, 2012), 87.
11. Howard Frank Mosher, *North Country: A Personal Journey through the Borderland* (Boston: Houghton Mifflin, 1997), 2.
12. John Steinbeck, "The Easiest Way to Die: Reflections of a Man about to Run for His Life," *Saturday Review* (August 23, 1958): 12.
13. John Steinbeck, letter to Elizabeth Otis, quoted in Barbara B. Reitt, "'I Never Returned as I Went In': Steinbeck's *Travels with Charley*," *Southwest Review* 66.2 (1981): 191.
14. Ronald Primeau, "Romancing the Road: John Steinbeck's *Travels with Charley*," *Steinbeck Newsletter* 12.2 (2000): 23.
15. Christian Knoeller, "'A Profession Older Than Writing': Echoes of *Huckleberry Finn* in Steinbeck's *Travels with Charley: In Search of America*," *Midwestern Miscellany* 33 (2005): 26.
16. Twain, *The Innocents Abroad*, 268.
17. Mosher, *Northern Express*, 32.
18. Steinbeck, *Travels with Charley*, 51.

Bibliography

Adams, Percy G. "Humor as Structure and Theme in Faulkner's Trilogy." *Wisconsin Studies in Contemporary Literature* 5.3 (1964): 205–212.
Allen, Ethan. *A Concise Refutation of the Claims of New-Hampshire and Massachusetts-Bay, to The Territory of Vermont, with Occasional Remarks on the Long Disputed Claim of New York to the Same.* Bennington, VT: Governor and Council of Vermont, 1780.
Austen, Jane. *Northanger Abbey.* 1818. Eds. Barbara M. Benedict and Deirdre Le Faye. New York: Cambridge University Press, 2006.
Baker, Houston A., Jr. "To Move Without Moving: An Analysis of Creativity and Commerce in Ralph Ellison's Trueblood Episode." *PMLA: Publications of the Modern Language Association of America* 98.5 (1983): 828–845.
Bercovitch, Sacvan. "What's Funny about Huckleberry Finn." *New England Review* 20.1 (1999): 8–28.
Berger, Benjamin. "Calvinism and the Problem of Suspense in *The Pilgrim's Progress.*" *Bunyan Studies* 8 (1998): 28–35.
Biddle, Arthur W., and Paul A. Eschholz, eds. *The Literature of Vermont: A Sampler.* Hanover, NH: University Press of New England, 1973.
The Birth of a Nation. Dir. D. W. Griffith. Prod. D. W. Griffith. Perf. Lillian Gish, Mae Marsh, and Henry B. Walthall. Epoch, 1915.
Bloom, Edward A., and Lillian D. Bloom. "Dylan Thomas: His Intimations of Mortality." *Boston University Studies in English* 4 (1960), 138–151.
Boyer, Marilyn. "The Treatment of the Wound in Stephen Crane's *The Red Badge of Courage.*" *Stephen Crane Studies* 12.1 (2003): 4–17.
Brooke, Arthur. *The Tragicall Hystory of Romeus and Juliet; Contayning in it a Rare Example of True Constancie; with the Subtill Counsels and Practises of an old Fryer, and their ill Event.* 1562. London, 1780.
Brown, Sylvia. "The Reproductive Word: Gender and Textuality in the Writings of John Bunyan." *Bunyan Studies* 11 (2003–2004): 23–45.
Bunyan, John. *The Pilgrim's Progress.* 1678. Mineola, NY: Dover, 2003.
Burke, Wayne F. *Kingdom Come: The Fiction of Howard Frank Mosher.* Baltimore: PublishAmerica, 2005.
Burns, Robert. "Despondency." *The Poetical Works of Robert Burns.* Ed. Charles Kent. London: George Routledge, 1885.
Busey, John W., and David G. Martin. *Regimental Strengths and Losses at Gettysburg,* 4th ed. Hightstown, NJ: Longstreet House, 2005.
Cooper, James Fenimore. *The Cruise of the Somers: Illustrative of the Despotism of*

Bibliography

the Quarter Deck; and of the Unmanly Conduct of Commander Mackenzie, 3d ed. New York: Winchester, 1844.
Cottom, Daniel. "Maggie, Not a Girl of the Streets." *Novel* 41.1 (2007): 73–98.
Crane, Stephen. *Maggie: A Girl of the Streets*. 1893. *Maggie: A Girl of the Streets and Other Tales of New York*. Ed. Larzer Ziff. New York: Penguin, 2000.
_____. *The Red Badge of Courage*, 1895. New York: Pocket, 2005.
_____. *The Red Badge of Courage: A Norton Critical Edition*, 4th ed. Ed. Donald Pizer. New York: Norton, 2008.
Curran, John E., Jr. "'Nobody seems to know where we go': Uncertainty, History, and Irony in *The Red Badge of Courage*." *American Literary Realism* 26.1 (1993): 1–12.
Daley, Yvonne. *Vermont Writers: A State of Mind*. Hanover, NH: University Press of New England, 2005.
Dees, Morris with Steve Fiffer. *A Season for Justice*. 1991. New York: Touchstone, 1992.
Dickinson, Emily. *The Complete Poems of Emily Dickinson*. Ed. Thomas H. Johnson. Boston: Little, Brown, 1960.
Dixon, Thomas. *The Clansman: An Historical Romance of the Ku Klux Klan*. New York: Grosset, 1905.
Dreiser, Theodore. *Sister Carrie*. 1900. Mineola, NY: Dover, 2004.
Dunn, N. E. "The Common Man's *Iliad*." *Comparative Literature Studies* 21.3 (1984): 270-281.
Ellison, Ralph. *Invisible Man*. 1952. New York: Vintage, 1995.
Evans, Lyon, Jr. "'Too Good to Be True': Subverting Christian Hope in *Billy Budd*." *New England Quarterly* 55.3 (1982): 323–353.
Faulkner, William. *Big Woods: The Hunting Stories*. New York: Vintage, 1994.
_____. *Go Down, Moses*. 1942. New York: Vintage, 1990.
_____. *A Green Bough*. New York: Harrison Smith, 1933.
_____. *The Hamlet*. 1940. New York: Vintage, 1991.
_____. *The Mansion*. New York: Random, 1959.
_____. *The Marble Faun*. Boston: Four Seas, 1924.
_____. *This Earth, a Poem*. Illus. Albert Heckman. New York: Equinox, 1932.
_____. *The Town*. New York: Random, 1957.
Fisher, Dorothy Canfield. *Vermont Tradition: The Biography of an Outlook on Life*. Boston: Little, Brown, 1953.
Fitelson, David. "*Maggie: A Girl of the Streets* Portrays a 'Survival of the Fittest' World." *Readings on Stephen Crane*. Ed. Bonnie Szumski. San Diego: Greenhaven, 1998. 168–179.
Fleck, Richard F. "Mark Twain's Social Criticism in *The Innocents Abroad*." *Bulletin of the Rocky Mountain Modern Language Association* 25.2 (1971): 39–48.
Franklin, John Hope. *From Slavery to Freedom*, 4th ed. 1947. New York: Knopf, 1974.
Frost, Frances M. *Blue Harvest*. Boston: Houghton Mifflin, 1931.
Gleim, William S. *The Meaning of Moby Dick*. New York: Russell, 1962.
Goldsmith, Oliver. *An History of the Earth and Animated Nature*. London: J. Nourse, 1774.
Gordon-Reed, Annette. *Thomas Jefferson and Sally Hemings: An American Controversy*. Charlottesville: University Press of Virginia, 1997.

Bibliography

Green, Melissa. "Fleming's 'Escape' in *The Red Badge of Courage*: A Jungian Analysis." *American Literary Realism* 28.1 (1995): 80–91.

Gwynn, Frederick L., and Joseph L. Blotner, eds. *Faulkner in the University: Class Conferences at the University of Virginia, 1957–1958*. Charlottesville: University of Virginia Press, 1959.

Harmon, Charles. "Cuteness and Capitalism in *Sister Carrie*." *American Literary Realism* 32.2 (2000): 125–139.

Harrison, Jim. "A Lens on History: Photographer Susan Meiselas's Quest to Understand via Images." *Harvard Magazine* (Nov.–Dec. 2010): 41–45.

Hawthorne, Nathaniel. "The Birthmark." 1843. *Nathaniel Hawthorne: Selected Tales and Sketches*, 3d ed. Ed. Hyatt H. Waggoner. New York: Holt, 1970. 264–281.

_____. "Young Goodman Brown." 1835. *Nathaniel Hawthorne: Selected Tales and Sketches*. 149–163.

Hemenway, Abby Maria, ed. *Poets and Poetry of Vermont*. Rutland, VT: George A. Tuttle, 1858.

Hemingway, Ernest. *The Old Man and the Sea*. 1952. New York: Scribner's, 1980.

Hinson, E. Glenn. "The Progression of Grace: A Re-Reading of *The Pilgrim's Progress*." *Spiritus* 3.2 (2003): 251–262.

Johnson, Charles S. "Public Opinion and the Negro." 1923. *The Opportunity Reader*. Ed. Sondra Kathryn Wilson. New York: Modern Library, 1999. 430–443.

Johnson, Claudia. "The Secret Courts of Men's Hearts: Code and Law in Harper Lee's *To Kill a Mockingbird*." *Studies in American Fiction* 19.2 (1991): 129–139.

Johnson, James Weldon. *The Autobiography of an Ex-Coloured Man*. 1912. New York: Vintage, 1989.

Knoeller, Christian. "'A Profession Older Than Writing': Echoes of *Huckleberry Finn* in Steinbeck's *Travels with Charley: In Search of America*." *Midwestern Miscellany* 33 (2005): 22–35.

Lamb, Robert Paul. Personal interview. 27 August 2013.

Langis, Unhae. "Shakespeare's Cleopatra as Virtuous Virago." *Genre* 28 (2008): 215–229.

Lanphier, David N. "How Shakespeare Purified and Idealized the Love Story of Romeo and Juliet." *Publications of the Arkansas Philological Association* 23.2 (1997): 29–39.

Lee, Harper. *To Kill a Mockingbird*. 1960. New York: HarperCollins, 2010.

Lessing, Gotthold Ephraim. *Laocoon: An Essay upon the Limits of Painting and Poetry*. 1766. Trans. Ellen Frothingham. Boston: Roberts Brothers, 1887.

Little, Arthur L. "'An essence that's not seen': The Primal Scene of Racism in *Othello*." *Shakespeare Quarterly* 44.3 (1993): 304–324.

Lott, Eric. *Love and Theft: Blackface Minstrelsy and the American Working Class*. New York: Oxford University Press, 1993.

Low, Matt. "'The Bear' in *Go Down, Moses* and *Big Woods*: Faulkner's (Re)visions for a Deeper Ecology." *Mississippi Quarterly* 62.1–2 (2009): 53–70.

Lydenberg, John. "Nature Myth in Faulkner's 'The Bear.'" *American Literature* 24.1 (1952): 62–72.

MacDonald, Joyce Green. "Antony's Body." *Early Modern Literary Studies* Special Issue 19 (2009). Retrieved 30 August 2011 from http://extra.shu.ac.uk/emls/si19/macdanto.html.

Bibliography

Martin, Charles H. "Oklahoma's 'Scottsboro' Affair: The Jess Hollins Rape Case, 1931–1936." *South Atlantic Quarterly* 79.2 (1980): 175–188.

Matteson, John T. "The Little Lower Layer: Anxiety and the Courage to Be in Moby-Dick." *Harvard Theological Review* 81.1 (1988): 97–116.

McGovern, James R. *Anatomy of a Lynching*. Baton Rouge: Louisiana State University Press, 1982.

McGuire, Philip C. "*Othello* as an 'Assay of Reason.'" *Shakespeare Quarterly* 24.2 (1973): 198–209.

Meiselas, Susan. *Carnival Strippers*. 1976. New York: Whitney Museum of American Art/Göttingen: Steidl, 2003.

Melville, Herman. "Bartleby." 1853. *Billy Budd, Sailor and Other Stories*. Ed. Frederick Busch. New York: Penguin, 1986. 1–46.

———. *Benito Cereno*. 1855. *Billy Budd, Sailor and Other Stories*. Ed. Frederick Busch. New York: Penguin, 1986. 159–258.

———. *Billy Budd, Sailor*. 1924. *Billy Budd, Sailor and Other Stories*. Ed. Frederick Busch. New York: Penguin, 1986. 287–385.

———. *Moby-Dick or, The Whale*. 1851. New York: Modern Library, 2000.

Moffett, Hugh. "The Ruckus in Irasburg." *Life* (April 4, 1969): 62–64, 67–72, 74.

Morris, Clara. "A Word of Warning to Young Actresses." *Century* (May 1900): 40–46.

Morris, Daniel. "Pedagogical Personae: On Two Approaches to Literature and Criticism." Illuminations Lecture Series. Purdue University Philosophy and Literature Program. Beering Hall. Purdue University. West Lafayette, IN. 26 September 2013.

Mosher, Howard Frank. "A Conversation with Howard Frank Mosher." Shaye Areheart Books Publicity Newsletter. 2 March 2010.

———. *Disappearances*. New York: Viking, 1977.

———. "A Disappearing Eden." [Interview with Katie Bacon]. *The Atlantic Online*. Web. 2 October 1997. Retrieved 12 November 2009, from http://www.theatlantic.com/unbound/bookauth/hfmint.

———. *The Fall of the Year*. Boston: Houghton Mifflin, 1999.

———. *The Great Northern Express*. New York: Crown, 2012.

———. "Howard Frank Mosher—An American Writer." [Interview with Nick Zaino]. *The Optimistic Curmudgeon*. Web. 26 Oct. 2007. Retrieved November 12, 2009, from http://optimisticcurmudgeon.blogspot.com/2007/10/howard-frank-mosher-american-writer.

———. *Marie Blythe*. New York: Viking, 1983.

———. *North Country: A Personal Journey through the Borderland*. Boston: Houghton Mifflin, 1997.

———. *Northern Borders*. New York: Doubleday, 1994.

———. *On Kingdom Mountain*. 2007. New York: Mariner, 2008.

———. Personal interview. 24 July 2010.

———. "Second Sight." *Granite & Cedar: The People and the Land of Vermont's Northeast Kingdom*. Illus. John M. Miller. North Pomfret, VT: Thistle Hill, 2001.

———. *A Stranger in the Kingdom*. New York: Doubleday, 1989.

———. "Transforming History into Fiction: The Story of a Born Liar." Authors at the Aldrich, Leonard Aldrich Library, Barre, VT. 2 June 2010.

———. *The True Account*. New York: Houghton Mifflin, 2003.

Bibliography

_____. *Walking to Gatlinburg*. New York: Shaye Areheart, 2010.
_____. *Where the Rivers Flow North*. New York: Viking, 1978.
Mosher, Phillis. Personal interview. 24 July 2010.
Myers, Henry Alonzo. "Captain Ahab's Discovery: The Tragic Meaning of Moby Dick." *New England Quarterly* 15.1 (1942): 15–34.
Narveson, Robert. "The Name 'Claggart' in 'Billy Budd.'" *American Speech* 43.3 (1968): 229-232.
Overland, Orm. "*The Jungle*: From Lithuanian Peasant to American Socialist." *American Literary Realism* 37.1 (2004): 1–23.
Petrarch, Francis [Francesco Petrarca]. *For Love of Laura*. Trans. Marion Shore. Fayetteville: University of Arkansas Press, 1987.
_____. *The Life of Solitude*. Trans. Jacob Zeitlin. Champaign: University of Illinois Press, 1924.
_____. *Petrarch: The Canzoniere, or Rerum vulgarium fragmenta*. Trans. Mark Musa. Bloomington: Indiana University Press, 1996.
Pratt, Lyndon Upson. "A Possible Source of *The Red Badge of Courage*." *American Literature* 11.1 (1939): 1–10.
Primeau, Ronald. "Romancing the Road: John Steinbeck's *Travels with Charley*." *Steinbeck Newsletter* 12.2 (2000): 21–23.
Radcliffe, Ann Ward. *The Mysteries of Udolpho: A Romance*. 1794. Ed. Jacqueline Howard. New York: Penguin, 2001.
Railton, Stephen. "Jim and Mark Twain: What Do Dey Stan' For?" *Virginia Quarterly Review* 63.3 (1987): 393–408.
Reitt, Barbara B. "'I Never Returned as I Went In': Steinbeck's *Travels with Charley*." *Southwest Review* 66.2 (1981): 186–202.
Robinson, Rowland E. *Danvis Folks*. Boston: Houghton Mifflin, 1896.
Ross, Charles. "Sidney's *Arcadia*: A Global Edition?" Sidney and Shakespeare Panel. Renaissance Comparative Prose Conference. Stewart Center. Purdue University. West Lafayette, IN. 22 September 2011.
Rowan, Carl T. *South of Freedom*. New York: Knopf, 1952.
Rowe, John Carlos. "Racism, Fetishism, and the Gift Economy in *To Kill a Mockingbird*." *On Harper Lee: Essays and Reflections*. Ed. Alice Hall Petry. Knoxville: University of Tennessee Press, 2007. 1–17.
Sanborn, Geoffrey. "The Name of the Devil: Melville's Other 'Extracts' for *Moby-Dick*." *Nineteenth-Century Literature* 47.2 (1992): 212–235.
Schaefer, Michael. "Stephen Crane in the Time of Shock and Awe: Teaching *The Red Badge of Courage* during the Iraq War." *Stephen Crane Studies* 13.2 (2004): 2–9.
Sears, Steven W. *Landscape Turned Red: The Battle of Antietam*. New Haven: Ticknor & Fields, 1983.
Shakespeare, William. *The Tragedy of Antony and Cleopatra*. 1603. Eds. Jonathan Bate and Eric Rasmussen. New York: Modern Library, 2009.
_____. *The Tragedy of Othello, the Moor of Venice*. 1603. Eds. Barbara A. Mowat and Paul Werstine. New York: Simon & Schuster, 2009.
_____. *The Tragedy of Romeo and Juliet*. 1597. Eds. Barbara A. Mowat and Paul Werstine. New York: Washington Square, 2004.
Shelley, Mary. *Frankenstein; or, The Modern Prometheus*. 1818. Ed. Johanna M. Smith. Boston: Bedford, 1992.

Bibliography

Sinclair, Upton. *The Jungle.* 1906. New York: Penguin, 1986.
Soens, Lewis, ed. *Sir Philip Sidney's Defense of Poesy.* 1595. By Philip Sidney. Lincoln: University of Nebraska Press, 1970.
Soenser, Margaret. "Christiana's Rudeness: Spiritual Authority in *The Pilgrim's Progress.*" *Bunyan Studies* 7 (1997): 96-111.
Sotiropoulos, Karen. *Staging Race: Black Performers in Turn of the Century America.* Cambridge: Harvard University Press, 2006.
Starks, Lisa S. "'Immortal Longings': The Erotics of Death in *Antony and Cleopatra.*" *Antony and Cleopatra: New Critical Essays.* Ed. Sara Munson Deats. New York: Routledge, 2005. 243-258.
Steinbeck, John. "The Easiest Way to Die: Reflections of a Man about to Run for His Life." *Saturday Review* (August 23, 1958): 12, 37.
_____. *East of Eden.* New York: Viking, 1952.
_____. *The Grapes of Wrath.* 1939. New York: Penguin, 2002.
_____. *Of Mice and Men.* 1937. New York: Penguin, 1993.
_____. "To Elizabeth Otis." 30 December 1959. *Steinbeck: A Life in Letters.* Eds. Elaine Steinbeck and Robert Wallsten. London: Heinemann, 1975.
_____. *Travels with Charley in Search of America.* 1862. New York: Penguin, 2002.
Stewart, Dianne, trans. "Spider and the Crows." *Favorite African Folktales.* 2002. Ed. Nelson Mandela. New York: Norton, 2004. 79-85.
Swaim, Kathleen M. *Pilgrim's Progress, Puritan Progress.* Urbana: University of Illinois Press, 1993.
Talmage, T. [Thomas] De Witt. *The Abominations of Modern Society.* New York: Adams, Victor, 1872.
Thomas, Dylan. "Do Not Go Gentle into That Good Night." *The Collected Poems of Dylan Thomas: 1934-1952.* 1953. New York: New Directions, 1971.
To Kill a Mockingbird. Dir. Robert Mulligan. Prod. Robert Mulligan. Perf. Gregory Peck, Mary Badham, and Phillip Alford. Universal, 1962.
Twain, Mark. *The Adventures of Huckleberry Finn.* 1884. New York: Vintage, 2010.
_____. *The Autobiography of Mark Twain.* 1924. Ed. Charles Neider. New York: Harper, 1975.
_____. "How to Tell a Story." 1897. *How to Tell a Story and Other Essays.* New York: Harper, 1898. 3-5.
_____. *The Innocents Abroad.* 1869. New York: Penguin, 2002.
Welling, Bart H. "A Meeting with Old Ben: Seeing and Writing Nature in Faulkner's *Go Down, Moses.*" *Mississippi Quarterly* 55.4 (2002): 461-496.
Whitman, Walt. *Specimen Days and Collect.* Glasgow: Wilson & McCormick, 1883.
Yoder, Jonathan A. "Melville's Snake on the Cross: Justice for John Claggart and Billy Budd." *Christianity and Literature* 43.2 (1994): 131-149.

Index

The Abominations of Modern Society 44–45
Adventures of Huckleberry Finn ix, 13, 109–111, 113–120, 123–126
Ahab, Captain 70–74, 76–77, 84–90
Allen, Ethan 2, 6, 7, 9, 88, 120–122
Allen, Ira 7
Anansi, Kwaku (spider) 110–111, 123
Andrews, The Reverend Walter 97–98, 101–108
Antony and Cleopatra 14, 149, 154–160, 162, 164–165
Athenian Hall 106
Austen, Jane 77–78
The Autobiography of an Ex-Coloured Man 82

Bangor ("housekeeper") 134–135, 137, 139, 156–158, 164–165
Bartleby, the Scrivener ix, 83
Benito Cereno 82–83
Biddle, Arthur 7, 8, 9
Big Woods 127
Billy Budd 12, 69, 77–81
"The Birth-mark" 80–81
The Birth of a Nation 93
blackface minstrelsy 112–113, 115, 120–123
Blodgett, Jacob 130
Blue Harvest 7
Bonhomme, William ("Quebec Bill") 69–71, 73–76, 85–90, 130
Bonhomme, William ("Wild Bill") 69–70, 75, 85–89, 132
Brown, John 105
Bunyan, John 1, 11, 50–58, 60–68
Burns, Robert 151–152

Calvin, John 77
Cantor, Eddie 112
Carcajou 73–76, 81, 85–89
Carnival Strippers 34–35, 40, 42, 47–49, 102
Civil Rights Movement 95
Civil War x, 10, 11, 17–30, 50, 52–53, 55–58, 61–62, 65, 82–83, 89, 93, 97, 112–113, 126, 140, 151, 159, 161
Claggart, John 77–80
The Clansman 93
Clark, William 13, 124, 126
Claverack College 19
A Concise Refutation of the Claims of New-Hampshire and Massachusetts-Bay, to the Territory of Vermont 6, 7
Cooper, James Fenimore 78
Crane, Stephen 10, 17–31, 43–46
The Cruise of the Somers 78

Daley, Yvonne 10
Danvis Folks 9
Dickens, Charles 111
Dickinson, Emily 23
Disappearances 12, 69–71, 73–76, 81, 85–90, 130, 132
Dixon, Thomas 93
"Do Not Go Gentle into That Good Night" 167–168
Dreiser, Theodore 11, 31, 39, 45–47

East of Eden 167
Ellison, Ralph 123
Eschholz, Paul 7–9
Ewell, Mayella 91–92, 95–97, 99–100, 102–104

Index

The Fall of the Year 165–166
Fathers, Sam 14, 131, 134, 138–139, 144
Faulkner, William x, 2, 13–14, 116–117, 127–129, 131–142, 144–145, 162
Finch, Atticus 91–92, 97, 99, 104, 107
Fisher, Dorothy Canfield 6–9
Fleming, Henry 18–19, 22–24, 26–30
Frankenstein ix, 96
Frost, Frances M. 7–9
Frost, Robert 7, 9

Go Down, Moses x, 14, 127–129, 131–142, 144–145, 149, 153–154, 162
Goldsmith, Oliver 72
The Grapes of Wrath 167
Great Depression 32, 71
The Great Northern Express 15, 111, 167, 171–176
A Green Bough 143
Griffith, D. W. 93
grisettes 45

The Hamlet 116–117
Hawthorne, Nathaniel 73–74, 89
Hemenway, Abby Maria 5–6
Hemingway, Ernest 127
An History of the Earth and Animated Nature 72
The Holy Bible 45, 52–54, 57, 61, 63–66, 71–72, 74, 76–77, 79–82, 84, 87–88, 118, 170–171
Homer 27
Howard Frank Mosher Society ix
Hubbell, Robert Burns 151
Hurston, Zora Neale 2

The Iliad 27
The Innocents Abroad 15, 167–171, 174
Invisible Man 123
Iraq War 25–26
Irasburg Affair ix, 13, 98–101, 103, 108, 171
Ishmael 70, 72–73, 81

Jackson, Shirley 9
Jefferson, Thomas 13, 60–62, 65, 67, 83, 114, 119–120, 123
Johnson, The Reverend David Lee 98–101, 103, 108
Johnson, James Weldon 82
Jolson, Al 112

The Jungle 1, 11, 31, 33–36, 38–39, 41–43, 47–49
King Lear 69
Kingdom Common Academy 105–106
Kinneson, Charles (newspaper editor) 102, 106–107
Kinneson, Charlie (lawyer) 102, 104–105, 107
Kinneson, Elijah 105, 107
Kinneson, James 101–102
Kinneson, Jane 14, 24, 50–51, 65–66, 140–142, 144–147, 151, 162–163, 166
Kinneson, John 22
Kinneson, "Mad Charlie" (abolitionist) 105–107
Kinneson, Morgan 20–22, 24–26, 29–30, 51–53, 55–58, 60, 62–65, 67–68, 81, 83–85, 141, 159, 161–162
Kinneson, Pilgrim 19, 22–25, 27–30, 50–53, 56–58, 60, 62, 65, 67–68, 84, 141, 150–151, 158–159, 164
Kinneson, Rat 85, 89
Kinneson, Resolvèd 104
Kinneson, Ticonderoga 114, 117–119, 121, 125–126
Kinneson, True Teague 13, 88, 109, 114–115, 117–126
Kittredge, Austen 130–131, 135–138, 159–160
Kittredge, Austen, III 131, 135–136, 159–160
Korean Conflict 97
Ku Klux Klan 93

LaMott, Frenchy 105
LaRiviere, Claire 101–105, 107
Lee, Harper ix, 12, 91–93, 95–97, 99–104, 107
Lee, Robert E. 61–62
Lessing, Gotthold Ephraim 143–144
Lewis, Meriwether 13, 124, 126
Lincoln, Abraham 61, 83
The Literature of Vermont: A Sampler 7–9
Lord, Noël 14, 130, 132, 134–139, 145, 156–158, 160–161, 164–165
Lott, Eric 112
Love and Theft: Blackface Minstrelsy and the American Working Class 112

MacArthur Foundation Awards 34, 173, 176

Index

Maggie: A Girl of the Streets 11, 31, 43–46
The Mansion 116–117
The Marble Faun 143
Marie Blythe 11, 31–32, 36–43, 45, 47–49, 101–102, 141, 155–156
Mason-Dixon Line 59–60
McCaslin, Isaac 14, 128–129, 131–135, 144–145, 149, 153–154, 162
Meiselas, Susan 34–35, 40, 42, 47–49, 102
Melville, Herman ix, 1, 11–12, 69–90, 135, 170
Middlebury College 105
Moby-Dick ix, 1, 12, 69–81, 84–90, 135, 170
Morris, Clara 47
Mosher, Phillis J. 10, 14, 33, 41, 65–66, 117, 129–130, 161, 165–166, 171, 176
The Most Comical History of Ethan Allen 122
The Mysteries of Udolpho 77

North Country: A Personal Journey through the Borderland 129, 172
Northanger Abbey 77–78
Northern Borders 130–131, 135–138, 159–160

The Odyssey 27–28
Of Mice and Men 167
The Old Man and the Sea 127
On Kingdom Mountain 14, 24–25, 50–51, 62, 65–66, 140–142, 144–147, 150–151, 162–163, 166
Othello 14, 149, 153–154, 161–163

Perdue, Charles 112–113, 121–122
Petrarch, Francis 155–156
The Pilgrim's Progress 1, 11, 50–58, 60–68
Plato 77
Poets and Poetry of Vermont 5–6
Prohibition 70–71, 74–76, 85–86, 130

Radcliffe, Ann 77
The Red Badge of Courage 10, 17–30
Remus 60
Revolutionary War 6–7
Robinson, Rowland E. 9
Robinson, Thomas 91–92, 95–97, 99–104, 107
Romeo and Juliet 14, 120, 149–152, 155, 162–164

Romulus 60
Rowan, Carl 94
Royal Canadian Air Force 97

Scottsboro Boys 94–95
"Second Sight" 151
Shakespeare, William ix, 1, 14, 69, 111, 120, 149–165
Shelley, Mary ix, 96
Sidney, Philip ix, 142–143
Sinclair, Upton 1, 11, 31, 33–36, 38–39, 41–43, 47–49
Sister Carrie 11, 31, 39, 45–47
slavery 21, 24, 29–30, 55–57, 60–61, 63–64, 67–68, 82–84, 93, 97, 105, 109–120, 122–126, 132–133, 145, 161
Southern Poverty Law Center 94
Steinbeck, John 15, 167, 169–170, 172–175
A Stranger in the Kingdom ix, 12–13, 91, 97–98, 101–108, 153

Talmage, The Reverend T. De Witt 44–45
Templeton, The Reverend Pliny 105–107
Thibeau, Manon 20, 51–52, 150–151, 164
This Earth 143
Thomas, Dylan 167–168
To Kill a Mockingbird (movie) x, xi
To Kill a Mockingbird (novel) ix, xi, 12–13, 91–93, 95–97, 99–104, 107, 153
The Town 116–117
The Tragical History of Ethan Allen 120–122
Travels with Charley in Search of America 15, 167, 169–170, 173–175
The True Account 13, 88, 109, 114–115, 117–126
Twain, Mark ix, 13, 15, 109–120, 122–126, 167–171, 174–175
Twilight, The Reverend Alexander 106

Underground Railroad 21, 55–56, 63, 67
University of California-Irvine 129–130
University of Michigan 133
University of Virginia x, 112–113, 121–122, 127–128, 133
Urban Renewal and the End of Black Culture in Charlottesville, Virginia 146–147

Vereen, Ben 115

Index

Vermont Tradition: The Biography of an Outlook on Life 6, 8
Vermont Writers: A State of Mind 10

Walker, George 112
Walking to Gatlinburg 1, 10–11, 17, 19–30, 50–53, 55–68, 81–85, 106, 151, 158–159, 161, 164
Washington, George 83

Where the Rivers Flow North 14, 130, 132, 134–139, 145, 156–158, 160–161, 164–165
Whitman, Walt 20–21
Williams, Bert 112
World War I 151, 155
World War II 97

"Young Goodman Brown" 73–74, 89

www.ingramcontent.com/pod-product-compliance
Lightning Source LLC
Chambersburg PA
CBHW032059300426
44116CB00007B/817